TRANSACTIONS:
PROPERTY
DEVELOPMENT
PARTNERSHIPS

PROPERTY INFORMATION
UNIT
LINKLATERS AND PAINES

1126 DAR
PROP

TRANSACTIONS:
PROPERTY
DEVELOPMENT
PARTNERSHIPS

Clive Darlow
BSc, M Phil (Cantab), FRICS, FSVA
Godfrey Bruce-Radcliffe
Solicitor
Stuart Morley
BSc, MA, Dip TP, FRICS
John Boff
BA

© Longman Group Ltd 1994

ISBN 075200 0446

Published by
Longman Law, Tax and Finance
Longman Group Ltd
21–27 Lamb's Conduit Street, London WC1N 3NJ

Associated offices
Australia, Hong Kong, Malaysia, Singapore, USA

A CIP catalogue record for this book is available from the British Library.

Printed in the United Kingdom by Hobbs the Printers Ltd,
Brunel Road, Totton, Hampshire, SO40 3YS

Acknowledgments

The original research for this book was undertaken at the University of Westminster and was generously funded by the Crown Estate and the Continuing Professional Development Foundation.

Appreciation is also due to our researchers at the University who so expertly carried out most of the fundamental work and drafting: Imogen McClean MA (Oxon) BCL, Michael Lower LL B Solicitor, and Annabel Darlow BA (Cantab) Barrister.

Invaluable support, guidance and enlightenment were continually provided by fellow authors: Godfrey Bruce-Radcliffe and John Boff, of D J Freeman, Solicitors, and Stuart Morley of Grimley JR Eve, International Property Consultants.

Additionally, Jonathan Digby-Rogers of Investment Capital Limited gave freely of his specialist expertise and very considerable experience of property finance. Alan Magnus of D J Freeman provided valuable assistance on corporate and partnership law.

A detailed insight into the many practical aspects of property development partnerships and joint ventures, based on their extensive experiences, were very kindly provided, and patiently explained, by the following organisations and their executives:

Arlington Property Developments	Jeremy Gates, Iain Ferguson and Simon Leadbetter
British Rail Property Board	Pat Scut, Malcolm Vince
Carlisle Group Plc	Jonathan Harris
Chesterfield Properties Plc	Roger Wingate
Crown Estate	Peter Shearmur
D J Freeman	Paul Clark, Alan Magnus
Grosvenor Developments	Martin Aldred, Michael Galloway
Higgs and Hill	Alex Derbie, Nick Beale
Investment Capital Limited	Jonathan Digby-Rogers
Land Securities Plc	Neville Johnson, John Maynard
London and Wiltshire Developments Ltd	Brendan Murphy
Prudential Portfolio Managers	Michael Rolls
Strutt & Parker	Andrew Martin
Trafalgar House Developments Ltd	Patrick Gardner, Tim Garnham
Woolgate Property Finance	Robert Bruce

Finally, I record my admiration of the enthusiasm and professionalism displayed by all of those whose help has made this possible.

Clive Darlow
London
October 1994

About the Authors

CLIVE DARLOW is a Principal Lecturer at the University of Westminster and a council member of The Development Partnership Consultancy. He has extensive experience of the financing of a wide range of property joint ventures and development partnerships.

GODFREY BRUCE-RADCLIFFE is a solicitor and partner with D J Freeman where he specialises in commercial property and in particular with its development and finance. He is a council member of The Development Partnership Consultancy.

STUART MORLEY is National Head of Research at Grimley J R Eve and specialises in local economic and property market forecasting for investments and developments. He has wide experience of local authority partnership arrangements and is a member of The Development Partnership Consultancy.

JOHN BOFF is an Associate with D J Freeman, Solicitors, where he concentrates on taxation, with particular reference to property aspects, from both the public and private sector perspectives.

Contents

Contents

Preface

Property development joint ventures, in their various guises, have been employed for many years. Their use has steadily grown, as their popularity has increased. In the process they have become more complex and varied, both better to accommodate the needs, objectives, and strategies of the participants but also to respond to the ever-changing external environment in which they operate. In particular, a stronger regulatory climate has introduced new, complicated, property and corporate legislation, tighter taxation rules and accounting requirements. The property industry itself, especially the development sector, has also been witnessing traumatic change. All this has been taking place in an increasingly international context where investment is becoming globalised.

Changing political policies have also been an important influencing factor. Privatisation has been followed by the pursuit of value for money, as witnessed by the spread of compulsory competitive tendering for goods and services in the public sector and more recently by the government's renewed focus on 'partnership'. Under the leadership of HM Treasury and its 'Private Finance Initiative' the government's policy is to encourage a new era of partnership between the public and private sectors. Indeed, this commitment to 'partnership' is further demonstrated by the establishment in November 1993 of the Urban Regeneration Agency (known as English Partnerships) by the Government: a statutory undertaking launched with modest public funds (hence the need for partnership), but armed with very powerful statutory powers to speed up the development process.

Local authorities have long understood, and undertaken property development in partnership with, the private sector. However, tight central government controls, especially financial, have made the task much more cumbersome, and difficult.

One of the consequences of this growth, change and complexity of development joint ventures has been the need for a comprehensive guide and reference source to the many issues involved. Hence this book. It examines and compares all of the available legal vehicles, or structures, currently in use. It covers the principal issues to be considered in any development joint ventures: especially tax, legal and regulatory matters.

List of abbreviations

Statutes

CA 1985	Companies Act 1985
CA 1989	Companies Act 1989
FSA 1986	Financial Services Act 1986
LPA 1925	Law of Property Act 1925
PA 1890	Partnership Act 1890
LP(MP)A 1989	Law of Property (Miscellaneous Provisions) Act 1989
LRA 1993	Leasehold Reform, Housing and Urban Development Act 1993

Journals

AC	Appeal Cases
All ER	All England Law Reports
BCC	Brown's Chancery Cases
Ch	Chancery
EG	Estates Gazette
Hare	Hare's Reports Chancery
LT	Law Times
NZLR	New Zealand Law Reports
P & CR	Planning & Compensation Reports
QB	Queen's Bench Division
STC	Simon's Tax Cases
TC	Tax Cases

Terms

ACT	Advance Corporation Tax
JVC	Joint Venture Company
TOGC	Transfer of a Going Concern
VAT	Value Added Tax

Table of Cases

Table of Statutes

Table of Statutory Instruments

Chapter 1

The use and growth of partnerships and joint ventures

Background

Property development takes place within the context of a network of multi-party relationships and arrangements. The various resources which must be brought to, and combined in, any development project—land, expertise, construction, entrepreneurship, finance—are rarely all located in the hands of a single individual or body. Hence property development is invariably carried out in association with others, even if they are passive investors or lenders. But the relationship between those who become involved in the development of land may be structured in a number of ways. The history of property development shows how the legal vehicles through which the various parties undertake development are continually being modified, adapted and fashioned in the light of a changing economic, financial, legal and regulatory environment.

Recent years have seen the emergence of joint ventures as an important medium for property development. Furthermore, a joint venture may itself take a variety of forms. Interest in property joint ventures is growing and has been accompanied by an increasing amount of literature on the subject. However, the existing information and experience relating to joint ventures is largely dispersed. It often focuses on a specific issue which is in fact one only of a number to be considered in deciding whether to engage in a joint venture and the form which it should take.

Against this background, it is the aim of this book to provide a comprehensive guide to property joint ventures. This will involve, firstly, exploring the reasons for the emergence and adoption of joint ventures; secondly, defining and examining the various forms of joint venture vehicle; and, finally, identifying the considerations used in determining the choice of vehicle, including those used by the public and private sectors. Although the law relates to England and Wales only, many of the principles are universal.

Definition: what is a 'joint venture'?

Although the concept of a joint venture is not new, the recourse to joint ventures as a medium for property development has been growing. The nature of the association between those who participate in property development may be purely contractual, involving essentially debtor-creditor, employer-employee, landowner-contractor or contractor-subcontractor type relationships. These forms of relationship are estranged in the sense that the parties maintain their distinct roles, and the skill or resource which they bring to the development is exchanged for a fee or price.

Joint ventures can be distinguished from such relationships as a separate category or genus in that they exhibit an element of combination and/or profit share between the participants.

Thus, while there may be uncertainty as to the classification of certain borderline cases, there is consensus as to the central characteristics of a joint venture, namely 'the coming together or association of two or more legal entities for the common purpose of carrying out a specific project'. In the context of property development, it is a legal relationship formed between two or more parties which involves profit participation. Hence the essential elements are:

(1) ownership of land;
(2) development activity;
(3) legal relationships;
(4) profit participation.

Nevertheless, although one might be able to distinguish joint ventures from other multi-party relations in property development, the term 'joint venture' is one without specific legal meaning. The nebulous nature of the concept is evidenced by confusion and uncertainty in the relevant literature as to what exactly constitutes a joint venture. This uncertainty probably arises because there are really two types of relationship which any study of joint ventures usually attempts to cover. On the one hand, there are those forms of relationship which are co-operative, where the participants effect a form of merger and combine their efforts; while on the other, there are those where the parties maintain more distinct roles, one usually adopting a passive position as regards the development itself, but where the development profit is nevertheless shared.

It is therefore helpful to adopt a distinction between:

(1) Co-operative/combination (genuine) joint ventures—in which both parties are active, sharing effort and expertise or resources. The parties combine or come together, joining in a way which differs from a purely contractual relationship. Thus the venture is 'joint' in the sense of mutuality or union and shared objectives.

(2) Participatory (quasi-) joint ventures—in which there is profit-sharing, but the parties remain more estranged or separate. They maintain their distinct roles, but nevertheless the non-developer extracts part of the development profit. Quasi-joint ventures are therefore closer to a purely contractual relationship than are genuine joint ventures. They are 'joint' not in the sense of shared effort or combination, but in the sense of sharing in the development profit, and the legal structure is usually imposed or dictated by the party with the land or finance. The developer is active, taking responsibility for the actual development, while the other participant is passive, but able to insist on a share of the profit because of its control over a resource needed by the developer— frequently, land or finance. For example, rather than embark upon a straight sale or loan, a share of the development profit is made a condition of obtaining the requisite finance.

Most developers and landowners understand the term 'joint venture' to mean the co-operative joint venture. This is indeed the central case. However, participatory joint ventures, despite lacking the element of combination which seems to distinguish most joint ventures, do involve profit share and hence must be included in the definition of property joint ventures. Both co-operative and participatory joint ventures are therefore included.

Relevance of joint ventures to property development

Very large and financially powerful property companies can, in some circumstances, avoid a joint venture when embarking upon a development project. Without a commercial need to joint venture, and with the necessary expertise in-house, substantial organisations prefer total control, and therefore usually choose to act alone, except for very large, specialised or foreign-based developments. But for most participants in property development, joint ventures represent an important medium through which their very participation becomes possible. Joint ventures can thus form a significant part of the business of medium-sized property companies and developers. In the case of some small developers, joint ventures can constitute their entire business. Similarly, for a landowner without development capital and/or expertise, a joint venture may be the only way in which it is able to participate in the increased value of land consequent on the grant of planning permission, or in the profit following completion of a development project. Therefore the importance of joint ventures to the property market cannot be overemphasised. Joint ventures are no longer a novel means of engaging in property development, adopted by only a few: they are now a well established technique, with many players having had experience of one at some time or another. Furthermore, this utilisation of joint ventures is likely to continue well into the future. Most developers, providers of finance and landowners express the opinion that, given the size and risk of projects to be undertaken, joint ventures will remain an essential property development vehicle. They thus recognise the important role that joint ventures have come to play in the property market.

Emergence of joint ventures

Two principal types of reason underlie the modern use of joint ventures. One is general and relates to the economic/financial environment which generates a preference for joint ventures, thereby explaining their emergence as a medium for property development. The other explains the adoption of a joint venture in the particular case and is a functional explanation, deriving from the nature of the definition of a joint venture itself.

New financing and profit maximisation techniques are continually being developed in order to adapt to ever changing market conditions. In addition, the coincidence of a number of economic factors led to joint ventures, as a technique or structure, being considered with increasing interest in the UK. Other influences on their growth include the following:

(1) The emergence of the reverse yield gap, through some two and half decades as interest rates rose and property yields declined, ruling out financing by debt (eg the conventional mortgage). As a result new financing techniques had to be found.

(2) On becoming aware of the levels of profit which had been enjoyed by developers, providers of finance began to insist on a share of development profit. They were more willing to accept more risk by becoming directly involved in development.

(3) Landowners too began to insist on profit share, realising that a straight sale of property was often not the best way to maximise their return, or to exercise some control over what took place on their land.

(4) The increasing size and complexity of major projects, bringing with it greater costs and risks, meant that landowners and developers were both less financially able and also less willing to undertake development alone.

(5) The inability of some developers to take large borrowings onto their own balance sheet and the desire to keep gearing down, drove them to try to find new accounting techniques which would keep borrowings off their balance sheet. Joint ventures represented one method of doing so.

(6) Some joint venture vehicles, by insulating the co-venturers from the joint venture's liabilities, enabled funding to be made on a non-recourse or limited recourse basis. The wide availability of limited and non-recourse finance in the rising market in the mid-1980s therefore helped to spawn many joint ventures.

7) The Insolvency Act 1986 led to a greater need for a floating charge to be taken as security for loans. The scope of the floating charge could be restricted to the property being financed through the use of a joint venture company.

Thus the willingness to accept risk by parties hitherto averse to it, the increase in property values and size of major projects, the need for smaller developers to keep borrowings off balance sheet and factors leading to a shift from financing by debt to some form of equity sharing all coincided to encourage joint ventures. As participants were able to spread their involvement through different legal structures, an attractive medium for property development was increasingly available.

Nevertheless, this is not to say that joint ventures have been or will become an exclusive medium. Whether or not a joint venture is appropriate in the particular case is a question which can be answered by looking at the definitional elements of a joint venture or the purposes to which joint ventures are put, and the objectives of the participants.

The circumstances in which joint ventures may be utilised are varied. A landowner may combine its ownership of the site with the expertise of a developer. Two or more developers may combine in order to carry out a major project which no one developer could finance or assume the risk of the development alone. A landowner may wish to realise more than it would do from a conventional sale and therefore reserve entitlement to a share of the development profit. Funding arrangements may involve the lender and the borrower-developer each assuming a measure of risk and reward. There are many more situations in which a joint venture is chosen to structure the relationship(s). But if one attempts to identify what is common to these circumstances, the reasons for adopting a joint venture can perhaps be generalised to three:

(1) joint ventures enable their participants, by combining different resources and sharing risk, to undertake what they could not or do not wish to do alone;

(2) joint ventures are a useful method for financing development (and, in addition, may be off balance sheet structures);[1]

(3) the control of one party over a valued resource (typically, land or finance) may give it the power to be able to insist upon a share of the development profit, and thereby maximise its return.

Those who engage in property development, however, often prefer, ideally, to act alone (because of the control this gives over the process of the development and the underlying asset, and because the entire development profit is then retained) and will turn to joint ventures only in particular circumstances. As is clear from the above, the coincidence of certain economic factors is a significant feature of the circumstances which generate a need or desire to joint venture.

Another reason why joint ventures, and in particular joint venture companies, flourished in the 1980s was the wide availability of non-recourse and limited recourse loans at that time. Other economic conditions conducive to the emergence of joint ventures may also no longer be as relevant. Nevertheless, although joint ventures may have been produced by a particular economic background, it is likely that they will continue to be utilised well into the future, perhaps even more often than previously. As new financing techniques are developed, joint ventures will continue to be relevant as an appropriate vehicle, independently of the economic circumstances which helped to give rise to them. Moreover, as long as the need to spread risk and to obtain expertise and suitable sites in relation to property development remains, joint ventures will flourish. Indeed, joint ventures may well become more popular, as co-venturers become more cautious about the type of project in which they are prepared to become involved and thus seek to share the risks. Further, the more traditional forms of joint venture vehicle (the joint venture company and partnership) may well expand to include newer forms, such as convertible mortgages which are perhaps more suited to a weak market. Joint ventures will in the future become more sophisticated and new forms of vehicle will evolve and adapt as conditions change.

Table 1

Why joint venture?

The following reasons were most frequently given by those involved in joint ventures:
(1)   A landowner will not sell outright.
(2)   It is a method of sharing risk.
(3)   It provides a means of diversifying investment.
(4)   It facilitates obtaining of finance.
(5)   A local authority will assist with site assembly (in public sector partnerships).
(6)   The project is very large-scale, in time, value or physical size and complexity.
(7)   The co-venturer has local knowledge, contacts and influence.
(8)   One party has special or unique expertise.
(9)   One party has a reputation in a given field as a leading exponent, thereby enhancing the credibility of the project.
(10)   It is the only available option.
(11)   It provides fast access to emerging market(s) without the need for time-consuming and expensive R & D.

Reasons for entering into a joint venture

Private sector joint ventures are primarily driven by need—to obtain a resource necessary for development, or to combine in order to undertake and complete a development project. When all the elements which go to make up a property venture are located in the hands of a single organisation (as is the case with some large property companies), it is clear that it will usually choose to act alone, preferring not to joint venture. Joint ventures involve sharing both control and the profits of develop-ment. For a participant who is able to act alone, these are therefore negative features of joint ventures. The decision whether or not to joint venture can realistically be regarded as a genuine choice. But for most involved in the property market, an essen-tial resource necessary to development must be found elsewhere, or the project envisaged may be too big to be taken on alone. The underlying rationale of joint ven-tures is therefore 'synergy': the need to combine in order to fully form joint ventures. This aspect also influences the decision to participate. The following reasons for embarking upon a joint venture were most frequently put forward by a survey and structured interviews with a representative cross section of some 20 leading partici-pants:

Synergy   The most commonly-expressed reasons for choosing a joint venture. This may take a number of forms:
(1)   Risk-sharing in large projects. The increased size and cost of development has been a significant factor in explaining the more widespread use of joint ven-tures. Small and medium-sized developers are usually unable or unwilling to take on the entire development risk of a major project. Institutions, obliged to pursue a sound investment policy, are also interested in minimising or sharing risk. The demand for large property is unlikely to diminish in the future—nor, therefore, is this reason for joint venturing.
(2)   Obtaining the necessary finance. Joint ventures are an important means of raising finance for development. Few developers or landowners can undertake a project without either borrowing or agreeing to some form of equity participa-tion. Traditional providers of finance see joint ventures as an alternative to straight debt, which allows them to participate more directly in the develop-ment profit. Many developers are unable to bring an entire development onto their balance sheets. A joint venture may enable them to raise the finance nec-essary and to borrow beyond that which their balance sheet can support or their constitution allows. Sometimes a partner is chosen for a joint venture precisely because of its ability to supply, itself, or to obtain funding (for instance, if it is known to have a good reputation with funding bodies, or because of its covenant strength). Thus a joint venture may be chosen either because it permits its participants to borrow more; or because it brings in a partner who is able to raise the balance of the necessary finance required for the project.
(3)   The only way in which the landowner will 'part with' the site. A joint venture is often the only means available to a developer of obtaining the site for a project. Landowners have become increasingly aware of the profits to be made on the grant of planning permission and subsequent development. A joint venture provides a method by which they can share in this profit despite lacking the relevant development expertise. Even very large developers or property companies may be forced to joint venture in order to obtain access to a targeted site. Some landowners are unwilling or unable to part with the freehold title, and a joint venture is often the only way of undertaking a development. Land can perhaps be regarded as the most important contribution that a party may bring to a joint venture. Landowners therefore enjoy a position of some power and are able to make a joint venture a condition of obtaining the development site.

(4) Acquiring the relevant expertise. Institutions and landowners wishing to participate in development projects often lack the necessary development expertise. A joint venture allows them to obtain this expertise and at the same time to have an interest in the development project. Even developers themselves may need partnership in order to obtain some specialist input or skill for a particular project.

(5) Obtaining the benefit of local knowledge. This reason is of particular relevance to foreign investors. A joint venture with a UK company is a means of obtaining experience of the domestic property market. It also enables ready access to local markets. Companies also may enter into a joint venture with a developer/contractor based in the area in which the site is situated in order to obtain the benefit of local knowledge. This may also be relevant to the obtaining of planning consents and to the way in which a proposed development is received locally. For example, a joint venture may represent particular or unique local opportunities.

Quick access into a ready-made scheme   Some large developers and property companies enter into joint ventures in order to avoid the preliminary and time-consuming effort necessary for any development project—namely, finding the site, obtaining planning permission and other consents, and finding occupiers. Smaller developers who themselves carry out this work are rewarded by a share of the development profit, often via a lease arrangement.

Diversification   Joint ventures allow players to diversify across property types and regions. Institutions, particularly, are often interested in diversifying their property portfolios. By entering into a joint venture they are able to vary the nature of their investments, having an interest in a small(er) part of a large number of diverse projects, rather than a large part of a few.

Avoidance of capital constraints   Joint ventures can be a means of avoiding capital constraints, either statutory or contractual. For instance, The British Railways Board is regulated by the Transport Acts, which prevent it from borrowing except with the approval of the Department of Transport. Organisations operating under such constraints may have no choice but to bring in a partner in order to develop property. Companies may similarly enter into joint ventures in order to avoid borrowing restrictions contained in their Memorandum and Articles of Association.

Enhancing credibility and/or reputation   Sometimes the contribution a co-venturer brings to the joint venture is its reputation or the credibility it adds to a scheme. This may include an ability to obtain funding. But it also extends to contacts and tenants as well as an ability to bring in foreign investors. Furthermore, a joint venture may enable a smaller developer to be perceived in the market as a much larger concern than is in fact the case, because of its involvement in major projects. This is then helpful in securing other business.

As a means of buying work for a contracting arm   Some property companies enter into joint ventures on the condition that their contracting arm is awarded the building contract.

Structuring a property joint venture

As mentioned above, joint ventures are not new, nor are they peculiar to property development (although property joint ventures exhibit their own particular features). This is an important point, since it highlights the fact that a joint venture is a type of legal vehicle, a means to an end, and can be used as a medium for many different types of business activity. Some joint venture vehicles are thus a particular form of commercial/business relationship which can also be applied to property.

The distinctive feature of property joint ventures, however, is that the business relationship constructed must not only accommodate financial/commercial objectives, but must also provide an acceptable means of holding and/or managing land. Issues of general property law, such as priorities and security of legal interest, become most relevant. In addition there are various property exclusive legal vehicles based uniquely on property law.

The exercise of structuring a property joint venture must therefore take into account the commercial objectives of its participants. That is to say, the vehicle constructed must reflect the reasons for using a joint venture in the first place. Typically this is to provide a structure within which the commercial objectives of the parties can best (most profitably) be realised. But in addition, the vehicle adopted must provide a structure for holding, investing and developing land, and incorporate all the necessary mechanisms for managing land which are permitted by law.

This involves either (or in combination):

(1) finding entities (transparent or not) which provide a ready-made relationship or framework; or
(2) manipulating interests in land—constructing a relationship through the medium of the relative rights and obligations which proprietary rights in land bring; or
(3) contractual arrangements—self-determination of rights and obligations without using a special entity.

As has been noted, property development arrangements involving profit participation can take many different forms. As far as detail is concerned, no two joint ventures are alike. Thus a joint venture relationship is very much one which is built up or composed, within the limits of the law, so as to give effect to the participants' particular objectives, interests and contributions.

Forms of joint venture vehicle

The precise structuring of each joint venture may be different, but only certain types of legal vehicle fall within the joint venture definition. These are shown in the table:

Table 2

Co-operative (genuine) joint ventures

(1)   Joint venture company.
(2)   Partnership and limited partnership.
(3)   Other contractual arrangements.

Mixed co-operative/participatory joint ventures

(1)   Lease arrangements (profit-sharing leases).

Participatory (quasi-) joint ventures

(1)   Profit-sharing mortgages:
  ● participating;
  ● convertible.
(2)   Overage payments:
  ● options;
  ● imposition of covenants;
  ● conditional contracts;
  ● long lease;
  ● deferred consideration clause.
(3)   Other contractual arrangements within this category.

The different forms of joint venture vehicle are examined in detail in the following chapters. However, it should be noted here that lease arrangements lie somewhere between co-operative and participatory joint ventures. The participants do not join together so as to form a single entity; but they are locked together, through their ownership of concurrent interests in land, more closely than are the parties to a mere profit-sharing agreement. Characterisation will depend in each case upon the particular form of lease in question.

Criteria for determining the choice of joint venture vehicle

The criteria used for assessing the suitability of a particular joint venture vehicle are generated by the purpose of a joint venture itself. This is to maximise the profits of development within a legally permitted framework which best formalises the relationship which the parties wish to subsist between themselves over the course of the venture.

Individual factors influencing the choice of vehicle will acquire greater significance, or not, depending on the particular circumstances (such as the duration of the scheme) and the parties' peculiar interests or concerns. But the principal, general, considerations (which may combine to influence choice) are:

(1)   circumstantial factors (in particular, the nature/size/type of the development contemplated);
(2)   ease and cost of formation/dissolution;
(3)   regulatory framework (including formalities, capacity and compliance requirements);

(4) funding arrangements;
(5) liability (limited/unlimited);
(6) security/vulnerability of interest;
(7) management/control framework;
(8) tax liabilities;
(9) accounting treatment.

Each of the vehicles are subsequently examined in greater detail, applying to them the criteria identified above and referring, where appropriate, to their relative advantages and disadvantages. (In addition, the procedures for dispute resolution and the implications for joint venture structures of the Financial Services Act 1986 (FSA 1986) and the Companies Act 1989 (CA 1989) are separately examined). In the public sector, the new Urban Regeneration Agency and local authority partnerships are also separately considered as important participants, but with special and distinct characteristics.

Comparison of principal features

The following table provides a summary overview of some of the most common considerations which influence the choice of a suitable joint venture vehicle.

Table 3

Principal features					
	Significant formalities?	*Separate legal entity?*	*Limited liability?*	*Tax transparent?*	*Confidentiality preserved?*
Limited company	Yes	Yes	Yes	No	No
Partnership	No	No	No	Yes	Yes
Limited Partnership	Yes	Yes	Yes	Partly	Yes
Profit-sharing lease	No	No	No	Yes	Yes
Profit-sharing mortgage	No	No	No	Yes	Yes
Forward sale/ forward funding	No	No	No	Yes	Yes

External reasons for success or failure of joint ventures

These are external to the joint venture's legal structure, but can, indirectly create very major problems due to the effect they may have on the project and, as a consequence, on the relationships.

The underlying economy can become depressed. Market conditions in the business sector, or geographical area in which the project is located, can also turn adverse. The project itself can run into problems, even though the market and the economy may continue to be sound. Problems can arise due to material shortages, labour strikes, construction delays and cost overruns, design defects, absence of tenants/occupiers and funding difficulties.

Internal reasons for success or failure of joint ventures

These can be varied and range from the quality of the partner and the compatible (or incompatible) aims of the joint venturers. For example, there is the fundability and the complexity of the project itself which in turn causes difficulties within the vehicle. This may test the structure/constitution of the vehicle selected and the effectiveness of its dispute resolution provisions. Any change in control/ownership of one, or more, of the original participants may also create unforeseen problems. Looking at the reasons in more detail, the majority of participants in joint ventures interviewed expressed their satisfaction with their choice of vehicle, irrespective of the success, or failure, of the actual project. Joint ventures are a largely successful means of engaging in property development. However, there are a number of factors which may affect their success.

Choice of partner   This is perhaps the most significant determinant of the success of a joint venture and is often more important than the form of the joint venture vehicle. The choice of partner is thus absolutely crucial—it will involve a consideration of:
(1)   Its financial standing. The insolvency of a co-venturer during the life of a development is one of the principal causes of the failure of joint ventures. Those wishing to undertake a joint venture should therefore assure themselves of the continuing financial stability of a prospective partner.
(2)   Whether an identity of interest exists. Conflicts of interest should be recognised and eliminated at the start of any joint venture. If they cannot be accommodated, such conflicts can threaten the success of the joint venture. Ensuring that the parties have the same objectives and concerns minimises disputes and promotes negotiation, ie, if it is in all the participants' interests that a project is completed, there is little room left for argument. However, it may be that participatory joint ventures are in this sense more hazardous, since the participants' interests can diverge, and conflict may ensue.
(3)   Whether a good relationship and mutual trust exists or can be established. It is essential to the success of a joint venture that the co-venturers should have a good working relationship and trust each other. There may be more likelihood of success, therefore, if the co-venturers themselves have previously worked well together. If they have not, maintaining regular contact with each other (more, perhaps, than the effective management of the joint venture project requires) can be helpful in maintaining a successful relationship. Alternatively, if the parties are unable to do this, and there is a mutual feeling that the other party is unreliable, then this may lead to the early termination of the joint venture.

The market   Many joint ventures fail because of a downturn in the market. This is a hazard which co-venturers are unable to control, but it is probably the most common cause of failure. Little provision can be made to cushion the co-venturers from the effects of a collapse in the property market, but this prospect must be considered from the outset. If adverse market conditions do arise, consideration should be given at the very start as to whether the participants are sufficiently strong to weather such an event without turning in, and on, one another.

The project Another reason why joint ventures turn sour is because something unexpected goes wrong with the project. The parties should try to anticipate as much as possible—for instance, they should consider what is to happen in the event of cost overruns, or in the event that the project needs to be refinanced. Frequently, the choice of joint venture vehicle is not called into question until the project goes sour—but if the project is a success, the vehicle itself is perceived as having worked well.

The joint venture agreement is fair to both/all parties Some take the view that a joint venture will only work successfully if the terms of the joint venture agreement are fair to both/all parties. This is important to the establishment of trust between the parties and provides an incentive to both/all to see that the joint venture works. A joint venture is also more likely to be successful where the parties respect the spirit of the agreement, rather than standing on its literal/legal interpretation. When participants start consulting the legal documents, litigation may quickly follow and a downward spiral is inevitable as relationships deteriorate.

Clear identification of respective responsibilities The parties should be clear at the outset of the joint venture as to what their respective roles are, in order to avoid misunderstandings and/or future disagreement. It is important that no party should be allocated conflicting roles. In addition, the view is occasionally expressed that only co-active joint ventures are really successful—that is, it is better if a partner brings something to the joint venture other than merely finance and has a real role to play. This, perhaps, is why some participants tend to view only co-operative joint ventures as joint ventures proper.

Balancing commercial realities with legal requirements As will be appreciated from the above, it is important that co-venturers identify their objectives at the start of the joint venture, anticipate all eventualities as far as possible, and then reflect this in tightly drawn, ideally brief, legal documentation. They also need to ensure that they comply fully with any legal regulatory requirements. However, while legal advisers must observe and make the co-venturers aware of these requirements, the co-venturers themselves often prefer to take a more pragmatic approach. Monitoring of the joint venture vehicle (if carried out at all) therefore tends to be *ad hoc*. Participants also frequently express a wish for shorter, clearer documentation. To accommodate these interests and yet to also ensure that the documentation is watertight involves balancing the commercial realities of the property development business with the need to provide for unexpected potential dangers identified by the lawyers. The documentation often only becomes significant if the parties fall out, and therefore it can be seen—once again—how important it is that the parties' relationship is a good one. It is this which allows the parties to take a more flexible and pragmatic approach towards the joint venture. One way to achieve this is to separate the management of the project itself from that of the joint venture vehicle.

The participants' perspectives

Developer   A developer will most commonly enter into a joint venture in order to obtain the development site, to obtain development finance, or to share risk. Developers tend to be very pro joint venturing, since they are rarely able to act alone. Landowners and institutions, on the other hand, can choose not to be involved in development at all. In some ways, a joint venture may therefore be regarded as a developer's vehicle. Since developers are often traders, this may partly explain why joint ventures also seem to be perceived first and foremost as trading, rather than investment, vehicles, although both development and investment can be accommodated.

Landowner   A landowner will usually enter into a partnership in order to obtain development expertise. Its role in the development itself is largely marginal, the joint venture being a means by which it may share in the development profit and thereby realise more than it would do on a straight sale of the land. Its control of a suitable site may mean that a landowner is able to a make a joint venture a condition of obtaining the site—many developers have to accept this relationship because they cannot otherwise achieve access to the site. Landowners interested in development may in addition be forced to joint venture by the capital constraints to which they are subject. They are also able to control what happens on their land, which may be of major importance if they also own adjoining sites.

Provider of finance   Providers of finance typically have an investment objective when they participate with others. They will also engage in joint ventures in order to diversify their portfolios and to spread risk. The resource they have which is needed by developers—finance—may give them the power to insist on a share of the development profit, in return for which they must also usually share the risk.

Private sector and public sector joint ventures

A further distinction must be drawn between private sector and public sector joint ventures. Joint ventures between the private and the public sector have become well established in post war years, due partly to the capital and other constraints placed on local authorities and public bodies. Indeed, central government has been actively promoting 'partnerships' and joint ventures as a means of attracting private finance into the public sector.[2] However, these joint ventures exhibit significant differences to those undertaken by purely private partners. The reasons for entering into the joint venture, the relative importance of the project and the choice of partner, who takes the initiative, the exit routes, deadlock procedures and the vehicle chosen for the joint venture, are all likely to differ according to whether the joint venture is with a private sector partner or with a public authority. Different criteria, constraints and objectives apply, for example:

(1)   The need or desire to share risk is more likely to be a reason for entering into a private sector joint venture than it is a public sector joint venture.
(2)   In the private sector it is invariably the partner which is considered most important; in the public sector it is usually the project which is more important.

(3) A local authority, for instance, may be precluded from parting with its freehold title and a call option is not, therefore, a possible dispute resolution mechanism.

Local authority objectives

Local authorities have a wider range of objectives than developers, which encourages joint ventures or partnerships. These include recognition of the fact that development, generally, can:

(1) be a component of the urban regeneration process;
(2) help stimulate economic activity;
(3) encourage confidence in the future of their area;
(4) attract new business, both directly and indirectly;
(5) improve the general physical environment;
(6) generate an enhanced income, or value, from the development of this land;
(7) help create employment, both in undertaking the project itself and through its subsequent occupation and use;
(8) enhance appearance of the streetscape;
(9) add value to otherwise vacant land;
(10) maximise use of all available resources and clearly be seen to be 'self-help' in operation.

It should be recognised that, additionally, there are political considerations which often drive local objectives—especially as election time draws near!

Attractions of local authorities

Private sector joint ventures recognise the advantages that local authorities can bring to the partnership. Among those benefits most frequently identified are the following:

(1) a strong commitment to their area and to the project;
(2) availability of a range of statutory powers;
(3) key land ownership or control of access sites;
(4) extensive local knowledge and contacts;
(5) access to information data banks;
(6) introductions to other agencies and authorities;
(7) access to public funds, grants and subsidies;
(8) longevity as a partner;
(9) defined objectives and policies (albeit susceptible to changes in political control);
(10) conferral of general 'public approval and support' to the project;
(11) working with, rather than against, the local planning authority;

Tensions between local authorities and developers

In addition to very full and detailed consideration of the particular project under consideration, the private sector partner, especially a developer, should recognise the potential political problems of being associated with a local authority through a joint venture. These include:

(1) dependency on public sector politics, attitudes and bureaucracy;
(2) a loss of control by the developer;
(3) a possible compromise on quality and financial returns;
(4) potential conflict between community objectives and profit maximisation;
(5) a reluctance to take financial risk and/or an equity stake by the local authority partner;
(6) the risk that some unexpected central government edict may cause significant problems for the local authority.

Summary of advantages and disadvantages of joint ventures

These will vary, depending on the vehicle adopted for the development but will encompass many, if not all, of the benefits and disadvantages summarised in the tables below.

Table 4

The advantages of joint ventures

(1) Risk
  - Sharing
  - Reduction
  - Containment
  - Avoiding ultimate liability

(2) Land ownership
  - Retention
  - Control
  - Use in lieu of capital

(3) Profit participation via:
  - Income
  - Capital
  - Construction and infrastructure works

(4) Achieving objectives
  - Faster
  - At lower cost
  - More effectively/profitably

(5) Providing access to
  - Innovative financing
  - Development expertise
  - New markets (sectors and geographical)
  - Partners
  - Land
  - Information

Table 5

Disadvantages of joint ventures

(1) Control and management
- Not exclusive
- Increased administration and communication
- No independent timing of investment decisions
- Often involves an additional tier of management and thus expense

(2) Tax
- Timing is restricted
- Is often more complex
- Can be higher than solo ventures

(3) Sharing information and knowledge
- Disclosing 'trade' secrets
- Putting at risk a competitive advantage

(4) Sale or transfer of interests
- Requires more consultation and possible delays
- Susceptible to dispute as to the method and timing
- Can be restricted by the joint venture agreement
- Increased procedural requirements

(5) Statutory and regulatory requirements
- Need to comply with additional legal and regulatory controls
- Greater cost and longer time consequences

---

[1] This is now determined by the provisions relating to 'subsidiary undertakings' in the Companies Act 1989, and by the ASC's ED49 and ED50.
[2] See, for example, HM Treasury 'Private Finance; Joint Ventures—Guidance for Departments' (March 1993 and December 1992).

Chapter 2

Joint Venture Companies (JVCs)

General

Participants in property development may choose a private, limited company as the form which their collaborative relationship should take. They may also choose a public limited company, although this is more rare and should not be adopted without good reason as there are disadvantages as a result of certain technical rules under the Companies Acts without corresponding advantages. A new company is a joint venture in the truest sense, in that the parties combine within an entirely new legal entity which is clearly distinct from them individually.

As a separate legal entity, a joint venture company (JVC) can hold title to development land and enter into contracts in its own name. This has the advantage of simplicity in terms of the transfer of title and enables participants both to deal more easily with their interest (ie shares) in the joint venture[1] and to enlarge the JVC by issuing further shares. It also means that the co-venturers can more readily isolate the activities of the JVC from their other business activities. The JVC therefore represents a buffer between the co-venturers themselves and the development project—it is a means of hiving off, for financing and accounting[2] purposes and for the purpose of limiting liability, the obligations associated with the project.

Against this, however, it is also an incident of the separation that the participants have no direct interest in the land itself. This may be more significant following the changes made by CA 1989 to the doctrine of *ultra vires* as it affects a company: shareholders may be prejudiced by unauthorised dealings with title. In addition, in theory at least, the JVC has a measure of independence from the co-venturers themselves since requirements of both company and trust law concerning the duties of directors are such that decisions and actions taken by the JVC's directors must be in its best interests.[3] Such independence could, it may be argued be even greater after CA 1989, since JVCs will often employ their own staff (rather than be staffed by employees seconded from the parents) in order to ensure non-consolidation.[4] In practice, conflict is unlikely to be commonplace as the JVC will often be, to all intents and purposes, the creature of the co-venturers. Nonetheless, the effect of the CA 1989 definition of 'subsidiary undertaking' and accounting standards issued by the Accounting Standards Committee will usually mean that no one co-venturer exercises greater control than others (at least where off balance sheet accounting is desired).

In its simplest and most common form, the JVC will consist of only two shareholders and although it is not necessary that it be deadlocked (ie each member would retain a 50 per cent shareholding or special voting rights would be adopted), following the introduction of CA 1989 and guidelines issued by the Accounting

Standards Committee, it will usually be deadlocked where off balance sheet accounting is important to one or both of the co-venturers.

Furthermore, if the JVC is a trading vehicle (where the co-venturers intend to sell the land following completion of the development),[5] as most will be, rather than an investment vehicle, (where the co-venturers intend to retain the property as an investment), then non-corporate co-venturers may choose not themselves to hold shares directly in the JVC but instead to set up intermediary companies as the shareholders. This may be both tax efficient and capable of providing flexibility on disposal. One possible JVC structure, then, is a 50/50 company with its shares being held by wholly-owned companies held by the parent co-venturers.

However, while this is a possible holding structure for shares in the JVC itself, it should be noted that a JVC may be one part only of a wider network of more complex relations between all those involved in the project. For instance, one of the co-venturers may act as project manager for the venture and extract its fee through some additional form of profit share arrangement. Hybrid structures, perhaps including both a JVC and partnership, are also possible. Nevertheless, it is the JVC as a self-contained joint venture vehicle which is most common.

The observation is often made that, of all the forms of joint venture vehicle available, the JVC is the most popular. The explanations, however, vary. One possible reason is that the company is a trusted vehicle which business readily understands and with which it is familiar. It also benefits from the large body of existing law concerning companies so that there are few areas of uncertainty as to its legal implications, as is perhaps otherwise the case with newer forms of structure. (For example, the legal enforceability of the convertible mortgage may need to be tested in the courts if the Law Commission's proposed reform of the rule against collateral benefits is not implemented.) Another possible reason is that, until recently, many joint ventures pursued a trading, rather than investment, objective and the JVC has been perceived as a primary trading vehicle. Further, a JVC enables a floating charge (made all the more necessary after the Insolvency Act 1986) to be confined to the property which is being financed. Finally, there are a number of advantages to the utilisation of a JVC, examined below, which may lead to its adoption in a particular case. Nevertheless, it should be remembered that the selection of the particular joint venture vehicle for each specific project is dependent on a number of considerations, and it cannot be assumed that the JVC will always be appropriate. Rather, the joint venture vehicle must in each case be structured to accommodate the particular set of circumstances which exist or objectives which it is desired to attain.

Circumstantial factors

As emphasised previously, the choice of vehicle for a joint venture is dictated not merely by legal, financial, accounting and tax matters but also by the circumstances of the project itself, the nature of the property and the duration of the development or investment.

A JVC is often regarded as a trading vehicle and as such may be more appropriate if the land is to be sold rather than if it is to be retained. It is also sometimes suggested that a JVC is more attractive, as opposed to a partnership, where the parties are of unequal financial strength—limited liability will here be more important, and the JVC is in this sense an 'equaliser' because it is an entirely new entity in which shares and decision-making may be evenly balanced.[6] A JVC may, further, be suitable where multi-project joint ventures or large, complex, longer-term projects are contemplated. In these circumstances the inconvenience of the initial administrative requirements are outweighed by the long-term advantages of providing a co-ordinating centre with formal management and accounting procedures.

In the case of multi-project joint ventures, however, the danger that a JVC would be exposed to the obligations associated with other projects, or be required to subsidise them, is an additional consideration.

Joint venture structures

The structure of a basic joint venture is shown in Diagram 1. The 'A' company and the 'B' company will incorporate, and own the share capital of, the JVC which will typically hold title to the property to be developed. This JVC must prepare and file annual accounts and is subject to ACT on any dividends it pays to its shareholders. (However, in a purely UK context, if either the 'A' or 'B' company has a shareholding of more than 50 per cent in the JVC, then it will normally be possible to elect to pay dividends to that company without accounting for ACT. If the JVC is a trading vehicle and the 'A' and 'B' companies each have a shareholding of at least 5 per cent, then it will normally be possible to elect to pay dividends to both companies without accounting for ACT.)

Diagram 1

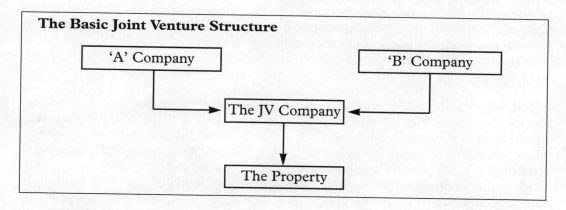

The Basic Joint Venture Structure

'A' Company → The JV Company ← 'B' Company

The JV Company → The Property

A variation of a basic joint venture structure is shown in Diagram 2. An optional refinement is the inter-position of the 'A' and 'B' Subsidiary Ltd respectively between the parent of each, and C Ltd (The JVC) to provide additional flexibility in the overall structure. It also facilitates the disposal of one of the joint venturer's interest in the transaction.

Diagram 2

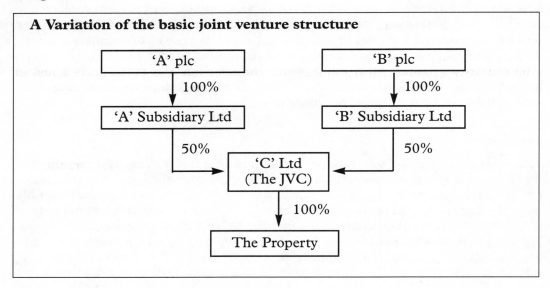

A Variation of the basic joint venture structure

Formalities and regulatory requirements

One of the most important disadvantages of a JVC is that it is subject to the regulatory framework imposed on companies by the Companies Acts. This can mean additional time and expense in relation to formation, administration and compliance and, more significantly, a loss of confidentiality.

Formation

A JVC must be created by registration under company legislation and is governed by the Companies Act 1985 (CA 1985) (as amended) and the relevant case law. Application for registration is made by filing certain documents, such as the Memorandum and Articles of Association, the address of the registered office and a statement of directors and secretaries, with the Registrar of Companies.

However, companies can be purchased or formed quickly and with minimum formality and then adapted as appropriate to the circumstances (but see page 21 below). Co-venturers will often purchase an 'off-the-shelf' company, or since the Companies Registry now offers a 24-hour service, have one formed by the solicitors involved. If it is purchased, the co-venturers will be concerned to ensure that the company purchased has no outstanding obligations which they might in the future be required to perform. (The service offered by company formation agents includes assurances on this point.)

On-going compliance requirements

These are significant and include the notification of changes,[7] procedures to be followed in relation to certain decisions (such as alteration of the Articles or objects clause), restrictions on alteration, provisions relating to reduction and withdrawal of capital and declarations of dividends, the lodgement of annual returns, the holding of meetings of shareholders, disclosure of directors' remuneration and dealings with directors, the keeping and filing of accounts, the appointment of auditors, and winding-up procedures. These requirements mean that the JVC is the most formal of the joint venture vehicles, is somewhat more cumbersome and involves extra administrative expense. Most significantly, the selection of a JVC entails a loss of confidentiality in that it must publicly disclose certain information relating to its affairs—in particular, accounting information.[8]

Capacity

A company can only operate within its objects, as laid down by its Memorandum of Association, and the conduct of its affairs is regulated by the Companies Acts. Despite the new s 3A of CA 1985 (as inserted by CA 1989),[9] certain powers should probably still be included in the JVC's objects clause, eg the power of the JVC to guarantee or to give security for any loan. Moreover, it is essential for tax purposes that the co-venturers consider at the outset whether the JVC is to have a trading or investment objective.

Documentation

The documentation relating to a JVC usually consists of the Memorandum of Association, the Articles of Association and the Shareholders' Agreement.

The Memorandum of Association

The Memorandum and the Articles of Association together represent the constitution of the JVC. The Memorandum is the primary document. Under s 2 of CA 1985, the Memorandum must state the name of the JVC, the place of its registered office, its objects, that the liability of its members is limited, the amount of share capital invested and its division into shares of a fixed amount. The Memorandum may also contain other provisions. It must be filed with the Registrar of Companies on application for registration and is, therefore, a public document.

Once registered, the Memorandum cannot be altered, except as provided by s 2(7) of CA 1985. It is also possible to entrench a clause in the Memorandum by providing that it shall be unalterable.

Thus the Memorandum of Association contains certain fundamental details of the JVC. The details of the arrangements between its shareholders will be found in the Articles of Association together, generally, with an agreement between them: the Shareholders' or Joint Venture Agreement.

The Articles of Association

The Articles of Association contain details concerning the internal management structure of the JVC. For instance, they will include provisions relating to the appointment and powers of directors, the voting rights of members, general meetings of the members, the transfer of shares and also the rights attaching to different classes of share. Since directors owe duties of confidentiality to the JVC it is also useful if the Articles expressly give them the power to give full information on the JVC to the shareholders who appointed them, if the directors are appointed (as is usual in a JVC) partly by one shareholder and partly by another.

The Articles may be altered by a special resolution (ie one requiring a 75 per cent vote in favour). It is possible to entrench a provision in the Articles, for example, by having separate classes of shares and giving extra voting rights in certain circumstances to one class. There are also certain restrictions on alteration—for instance, in some circumstances, the courts may regard an alteration as invalid if it is not for the benefit of the JVC as a whole.[10]

All the terms of the joint venture could be included in the Articles, but the co-venturers' desire for confidentiality usually leads them to enter into a Shareholders' Agreement instead, since the Articles constitute a public document. However, in deciding which provisions should be included in the Articles and which in the Shareholders' Agreement, it should also be borne in mind that a potential breach of a provision contained in the Articles may often be restrained by injunction, whereas breach of the Agreement may give rise to a right to damages only. The Articles will also bind all those into whose ownership shares may pass, whereas Agreements may not always be binding on successors in title. To avoid conflicts in interpretation it is important that the co-venturers specify whether the Articles of Association or the Shareholders' Agreement shall prevail.

The Shareholders' Agreement

The Shareholders' Agreement contains the terms of the joint venture and sets out the respective rights and obligations of the co-venturers. Thus, while the Articles are relevant to all those who happen to be the shareholders of the JVC from time to time, the Shareholders' Agreement is more in the nature of a contract personal to the initial parties (although it may provide for the assignment or novation of rights and duties in the event of a transfer of shares). The Shareholders' Agreement is commonly therefore the principal document as far as the joint venture is concerned.

It may be desirable to make the JVC itself a party to the Agreement so that it is both bound by, and able to enforce, its provisions. The Agreement will usually contain matters concerning the distribution and calculation of profit, taxation (eg the manner in which losses or reliefs are to be surrendered and any group tax election), funding and expenditure, restrictions on dealings with shares, the types of decision for which majority/unanimous consent is required and those specifically within the power of the Board, the administration and staffing of the JVC, the manner in which the property is to be disposed of and the procedures to be followed in the event of deadlock, default or dispute.

As the Memorandum and Articles of Association are concerned with the constitution and internal management of the JVC itself, and the Shareholders' Agreement sets out the terms of the joint venture, all three should be considered together for consistency.

Limited liability

The limited liability which a company provides is one of the principal reasons for selecting a JVC as the joint venture vehicle. It enables the co-venturers to isolate the joint venture project from their and each other's business activities, and to limit their personal liability vis-à-vis third parties who deal with the JVC. Each co-venturer's liability is limited to the amount of its respective shareholding. Thus, where the parties are of unequal financial strength or where it is particularly important to a co-venturer that it should not be exposed any further than the amount it has invested in the joint venture, and/or that other assets unrelated to the project should not be vulnerable to the possibility of having to subsidise the JVC, then a JVC may be the best option.

However, it is often observed that in practice the liability of shareholders in a JVC may be little different to that of participants in other joint venture structures, including partnerships. This may be so in one or more of the following situations:

(1) Insistence on parent company guarantees. The provision of finance, by third parties, to the JVC will often be conditional upon guarantees being given by the parent company co-venturers.

(2) Commercial constraints. A co-venturer may be reluctant to stand by and allow the JVC to fail since this could have an adverse effect on its own standing and reputation within the business community. It may result, in certain circumstances, in the personal liability of the JVC's directors.

(3) Personal liability of directors. Directors of the JVC will be personally liable in some circumstances of insolvency, eg where the JVC goes into liquidation having incurred indebtedness at a time when the directors knew or ought to have known that there was no reasonable possibility of avoiding liquidation.[11]

(4) Shadow directors. A co-venturer may be regarded as a shadow director of the JVC, with the same duties as a director, where the directors of the JVC customarily act in accordance with the directions or instructions of the co-venturer(s).[12]

(5) Cross default liabilities. These may arise in relation to other borrowings, depending on how widely those provisions are drawn. The JVC may be deemed to be a subsidiary of one of the co-venturers, or the provisions may catch associated companies.

(6) Obligations to ensure solvency. A co-venturer may insist upon a clause in the Shareholders' Agreement to the effect that each will keep the JVC funded to the extent that is necessary in order to ensure solvency. Moreover, if the JVC is itself a party to the Shareholders' Agreement, this obligation may be enforceable by a receiver or liquidator.

(7) Lifting the veil of incorporation. Where the 'corporate veil' is lifted, liability may extend beyond the assets of the JVC. This may occur where:
    (a) there is fraudulent trading, under statute;[13]
    (b) there has been fraud or improper conduct, under case law;
    (c) there is wrongful trading;[14]
    (d) the co-venturer is deemed to be carrying on its business through the subsidiary or JVC;
    (e) directors have an involvement with property;[15]
    (f) there have been loans and quasi loans to directors.[16]

(8) Proposed EC Directive. Under a proposed EC Directive there may be unlimited liability in respect of subsidiaries where the parent intervenes.

Nevertheless, although in practice the liability of shareholders in a JVC may in some circumstances be extended and although partnerships may be structured so as to insulate the co-venturers from the effects of joint and several liability, the participants in a JVC can usually control the circumstances of extension of liability.[17] This still makes the JVC advantageous as far as liability is concerned.

Funding

A JVC can be beneficial to co-venturers because of the flexibility it offers in relation to funding. A company is unique in being able to offer a floating charge over its assets as security for borrowings,[18] and banks often allow companies more freedom with their assets than they do other types of creditor. A JVC also facilitates refinancing since its separateness makes it easier to demonstrate that its only liabilities are those related to the joint venture project.

The specific funding arrangements may, however, often be an area of some contention in the negotiation of the joint venture agreement. The participants must agree at the outset as to whether the joint venture is to be funded by equity or debt, or both; and if it is to be financed by debt, whether the JVC is to borrow from one or more of the co-venturers, from a third party or from both. The financing structure will often be tax-driven, and will be subject to numerous conditions and (probably) guarantees.

The share structure of a company provides flexibility if the joint venture project is to be equity-funded. The different classes of equity capital also enable the co-venturers to make a choice as to the way in which the profits of development should be extracted.

However, if the joint venture is to be funded only by the co-venturers themselves, they will often inject funds by way of loan stock rather than solely by subscription for shares. This is because it is easier to extract debt than equity capital from a JVC if the project is successful. If the project is unsuccessful, a capital loss for tax purposes can be established whether or not the JVC is a trading venture on the grounds that the loan to the JVC constitutes a 'debt on a security'.

Furthermore, interest payable by the JVC on a loan should be deductible for corporation tax purposes, whereas payments by dividend are not.

Third party providers of funds will normally require the company's property to be charged to them as security and will also usually insist upon a debenture, and probably at least some guarantees[19] from the co-venturers themselves. (With the willingness of the banks in the 1980s to provide limited or non-recourse loans, the JVC represented the ideal vehicle.)

Distribution policy

The Shareholders' Agreement may set out in detail the basis on which profits are to be calculated and distributed, if special arrangements differing from the normal accounting treatments are required. Distribution may be dictated principally by tax considerations, but the nature of the joint venture and the commercial objectives of its participants will also be relevant. Moreover, accounting policies should be agreed at the outset since this will determine when profit is to be recognised.

Extraction of profit

In the case of a JVC with an investment objective, the profits of the joint venture will be extracted by dividends paid to the shareholders as profits accrue. Dividends may only be distributed to shareholders in accordance with CA 1985, eg profit must be 'realised' profit, and a 'dividend' covers benefits other than the payment of a cash distribution.

In the case of a JVC with a trading objective, profits will usually be distributed following a sale of either the development or the company itself, following completion. Distribution at the end of the project is the usual course adopted in relation to a single project joint venture, although this can result in cash-flow problems during the development period and large sums of money arising at the end of the joint venture. In some circumstances the co-venturers may therefore prefer to specify an alternative date after which distribution is to be made, eg on practical completion, or when the joint venture becomes cash positive. As far as multi-project joint ventures are concerned, profits may be realised on an annual or project-by-project basis and the profit-sharing arrangements will need to be more sophisticated.

Co-venturers also have a choice as to whether to use loans to the JVC, and in such circumstances will extract some or all of their profit by way of payment of interest.

The proportions in which the profits are to be shared by the co-venturers must be agreed at the outset. Often this will be identical to the share ratio in the JVC, but occasionally it will not (especially where the co-venturers are of unequal financial strength).[20] Moreover, the Shareholders' Agreement may provide for the profit-share ratio to vary over the course of the joint venture, particularly if either or both participants envisage the possibility of having to take on additional responsibilities (if the need arises) once the joint venture has commenced. Variation may be tied, for instance, to the amount of financial obligations accepted by the co-venturers—although this approach ignores significant non-financial contributions to the project. Nevertheless, it is usually prudent to include a profit-share variation mechanism as this avoids the problem of future disagreement.

Calculation

The Shareholders' Agreement should also contain the formula under which profits are to be calculated and the order in which they are to be distributed. The method of valuation will also need to be agreed upon. However, similar calculation provisions will be found in all forms of joint venture agreements and no peculiarities arise out of the vehicle being a JVC.

Losses

The question of how any losses are to be apportioned is similar to the question of profit distribution. Again, this will need to have regard to the impact of tax law, and losses are usually shared in the same proportions as profits. However, an important point in relation to JVCs is the impact of insolvency legislation. Where a shareholder is deemed to be a shadow director, the effect of the Insolvency Act 1986 may be that the shareholder will have to contribute to the JVC's losses even though it believed itself to be protected by the corporate veil from third party creditors. Similar results arise if directors it nominated incur personal liability and look for an indemnity to the shareholders who nominated them.

Management structure

Management of the JVC should be distinguished from that of the project itself, although clearly the two are related. The effect of CA 1989, and accounting standards which have followed it, is such that the management of a JVC must be far more carefully structured than in the past if it is important to the co-venturers that the JVC's borrowings remain off their respective balance sheets. This is because the Act concentrates on the substantive control of a company rather than on technical ownership. Management of the JVC must not be conducted in such a way that it and one co-venturer might be regarded as being 'managed on a unified basis' or that one shareholder seems to exercise a 'dominant influence' over the JVC. In addition, the JVC will be deemed a subsidiary undertaking (and thus need to be consolidated) where one shareholder has the ability to exercise voting control. Hence not only must voting rights be carefully structured but the entire management framework of the JVC must be reviewed in the context of the CA 1989 provisions. The Act therefore has significant implications on matters relating to the allocation of voting rights, the secondment of staff and the location of decision-making, etc.

Directors

The management of the JVC will be undertaken by its directors, who are appointed by the JVC's shareholders and who, together, constitute the Board. Their powers are regulated by company law, along with the Articles of Association and the Shareholders' Agreement. Where the JVC is deadlocked there will usually be an equal number of directors with equal voting rights. If it is not deadlocked, the major participant will either have the right to appoint more directors, or voting rights will be weighted. However, if the avoidance of consolidation is an objective, then the JVC must be deadlocked and care should be taken to ensure that this is in fact so—for example, the chairperson should not have a casting vote.

The directors are under a duty to manage the JVC in accordance with the general law and the Memorandum and the Articles of Association. In addition, they owe fiduciary duties to the JVC as its agents. Most significantly, the directors are under a duty to exercise their powers for the benefit of the JVC, to avoid conflicts of interest and to exercise skill and care in management. In contrast, they do not owe fiduciary duties to the JVC's shareholders (ie the co-venturers). Thus the JVC may be the ideal vehicle for separating the joint venture project from the co-venturers' other business activities, but at the expense perhaps of having to surrender a measure of control over the venture. While this theoretical loss of control was probably relatively unimportant in practice in the past, it may become more significant in the future as CA 1989 effectively requires companies to be more independent if they are to escape consolidation.

Secondment

This need to exhibit independence, at least if its financing is to be off balance sheet, also means that directors are more likely to be employed and remunerated by the JVC itself rather than be seconded from the co-venturers. Prior to 1989 this was considered inappropriate where the joint venture involved only a single project, but it will probably now become more common despite the extra administration and expense which it involves.

Decision-making

The Board of Directors and the JVC's shareholders together have control over the JVC. But the way in which control is distributed between them is, subject to the companies legislation, a matter to be agreed upon and then set out in the Articles of Association.

Most decisions will be taken by the Board but the shareholders may wish to reserve certain major decisions to themselves, especially over matters of policy. Alternatively, limits may be placed on the directors' decision-making power by formulating a detailed objects clause, or by reaching express agreement on key decisions in advance. Again, this decision-making structure must steer clear of giving effective control to one of the co-venturers if consolidation is undesirable.

If the JVC is not a deadlocked one, the minority shareholder(s) will want some protection to be built into the Shareholders' Agreement in addition to that provided by the Companies Acts and the general law, for instance, that certain fundamental decisions require unanimity.

As already emphasised, the provisions of CA 1989 concerning off balance sheet accounting—in particular, the 'dominant influence' provisions—may mean that in the future JVCs will be more autonomous and independent from the co-venturers than they have been in the past. The desire for control must therefore be weighed against the desirability of off balance sheet accounting.

Dealings with shares

Participants in a JVC have no direct interest in the land itself. Instead, their interest in the joint venture project is represented by the shares which they hold in the JVC. Shares in a joint venture company will rarely be easily marketable in any event and the Shareholders' Agreement, or the Articles, will usually contain restrictions and limitations on dealings with shares. This is because each co-venturer has an interest in and will want to exercise at least some control over the identity of the other participant(s) in the joint venture, a factor clearly of importance to its success. The original co-venturers must therefore decide at the outset the form which restrictions should take and the method for valuing their interests.

For example, the transfer of shares may simply be prohibited. This in effect gives to the remaining shareholder(s) the power to consent to, or to impose conditions upon, a sale. Alternatively, a sale may be made expressly subject to the other's consent. In addition, provision will be made for any new shareholder to undertake the vendor shareholder's obligations, in order to ensure that the project is completed. Obligations cannot be assigned but only novated.

The Shareholders' Agreement, or the Articles, may instead confer pre-emption rights on each of the shareholders. Thus if a shareholder wishes to dispose of its shares to a third party purchaser it must first give notice of the sale to the other shareholder(s) who then has the right of first refusal, for example, at the price offered by the third party.[21] The disadvantage of this form of restriction is that the remaining shareholder cannot actually prevent the introduction of a new joint venture partner, if it cannot afford the price offered.

The Shareholders' Agreement may also include put or call options, enabling a shareholder (after serving notice on the other) to sell its shares to the other (a put) or to buy the other's shares (a call). However, put and call options may only be able to be invoked in limited situations, for example, where the other shareholder has come under the control of a company which was not a party to the original joint venture agreement and which is not a member of the same group as that shareholder, or under specific default/deadlock provisions.

Whatever the form of the restriction on dealings with shares in the JVC, regard must be had to the dominant influence provisions of CA 1989 if the co-venturers want to avoid consolidation. A 'participating interest' includes an interest which is convertible into an interest in shares and an option to acquire shares. Thus the very presence of, for example, put and call options may run the risk of enforced consolidation.

Winding up

Exit routes prior to completion

The ways in which a co-venturer may leave the joint venture prior to completion of the project should be agreed by the participants at the outset. Thus a JVC may be unwound prior to completion due to the default (including insolvency) of one party or following deadlock. It is more usual, however, for a disposal of shares to take place on the exercise of rights of pre-emption, or put and call options. In a recent, perhaps exceptional, case[22] a speculative joint venture project failed and the court held that, in the absence of express agreement, assets transferred to the co-venturer were held on a resulting trust for the transferor. The possibility of failure in the purpose of the joint venture should always be covered therefore by express wording in the Shareholders' Agreement, and the possibility of the courts' equitable jurisdiction being invoked should not be overlooked.

Apart from insolvency, however, it is more common for the JVC to be wound up following completion of the joint venture project.

Winding up following completion

Due to regulation by the Companies Acts, the winding up of the JVC is a formal and cumbersome procedure. If the joint venture is successfully completed as intended, the development will either be retained by one or more of the co-venturers or sold. Where it is to be retained, the Shareholders' Agreement should provide for this by giving the party who intends to retain it the option to purchase the development or the other party's shares in the JVC. In the former case, the JVC will be wound up following sale. Where the development is sold, the JVC will similarly be wound up, following a sale of the property. Alternatively, the JVC itself—in which the property is vested—may be sold.

Formalities of winding up   The voluntary winding up of a company may be either a members' or a creditors' winding up. Since it is the directors and members who control the process in a members' winding up, the co-venturers will prefer this to a creditors' winding up. This is only possible, however, if the directors are able to make a statutory declaration of the solvency of the JVC. The declaration, embodying a financial statement of the JVC's assets and liabilities, must be delivered to the Registrar of Companies, for registration.

The JVC must also appoint a liquidator at a general meeting. After the liquidator has wound up the affairs of the JVC, an account of the winding up must be prepared, showing how it was conducted, and then must be explained at a general meeting. Following the meeting, the account is sent to the Registrar of Companies and three months after registration the JVC is deemed to be dissolved.

(This fairly complex procedure is in contrast to the termination of a partnership, which may be dissolved unilaterally (unless the Partnership Agreement provides otherwise) and with little formality.)

Corporate or property disposal   The JVC will in the majority of cases be wound up following a sale of the property which has been the subject of the joint venture. However, in some circumstances sale of the JVC itself may be more advantageous.

By selling the JVC the co-venturers avoid the two tiers of tax (ie on disposal of the property and then on disposal of the shares in the JVC) to which all companies are inherently vulnerable, although this can be mitigated by paying dividends before winding up. In addition, the co-venturers may be able to extract a higher price for the property if the JVC itself has tax losses which a purchaser can take over (although this potential benefit is often illusory). The co-venturers may also be able to extract a higher price because of the advantages to the purchaser in adopting the corporate rather than the property route (such as savings on stamp duty, Land Registry fees and VAT).

The advantages and disadvantages from each party's perspective must be balanced in each case. But the JVC, unlike the other joint venture vehicles, does at least give the co-venturers this extra option.

Tax treatment

Introduction

The tax treatment of a JVC follows a combination of the very substantial volume of tax legislation specifically related to companies (and similar entities) and the more general tax legislation as it affects separate legal entities. Other joint venture vehicles do not generally have the benefit/disadvantage of such a heavily codified tax regime.

It is therefore necessary, when considering a JVC as the potential vehicle for a joint venture, to consider very carefully the possible outcome to the venture and precisely what is required in terms of the injection of finance, extraction of cash and utilisation/sale of the property in both general commercial and specifically tax terms.

Financing: two important aspects to consider

Structuring the ownership of the JVC   This is particularly important from a tax point of view if trading losses generated by the JVC are to be available to the joint venturers. The joint venturers may, for example, wish to ensure that share capital is established and maintained in a certain proportion to ensure that trading losses of the JVC can be surrendered to them (and in that proportion). They will also need to ensure that the Articles of Association of the JVC (and other formal agreements entered into regarding the JVC) do not upset the availability of such tax losses through, for example, inappropriate distribution provisions upon a winding up, option arrangements that upset the balance between shareholders for these purposes, loans with profit participation etc. A very detailed review is therefore required in this area.

Structuring ownership is also important in order to ensure that dividends can be paid up by the JVC without Advance Corporation Tax (ACT), although this is frequently only a cash flow, rather than an absolute, cost advantage. The ownership structure should also be consistent with the joint venturers' own tax planning. Losses will only be available for surrender in a joint venture context between a trading JVC and its corporate joint venturers. Suitable vehicles for holding the shareholdings in the JVC must therefore be selected or formed, also taking into account each joint venturer's proposed disposal route upon completion of the venture.

In some circumstances, one or more joint venturer may itself have losses available for set-off against the profits of the JVC. Any such arrangement should be carefully provided for in the ownership structure (and Joint Venture Agreement).

Tax relief on the financing costs   It will usually be possible to arrange that the JVC obtains tax relief in respect of interest costs. A more particular concern is likely to be the timing of that relief and whether it is preferable to ensure that the loss generated in early year(s) (usually only in part by interest) is available to the joint venturers on surrender by the JVC.

Operation of the JVC: various issues arise

(1) It needs to be decided from the outset whether the JVC is to be a trading or investment vehicle. From a corporation tax point of view, there is no viable third alternative and a single vehicle involving a mixture of both activities is not recommended because of the uncertainty of tax treatment that results.

Once the decision is made, it is advisable to ensure that everything related to the JVC (particularly its accounting treatment) is consistent with that decision. In practice, it is possible to move from an investment to a trading structure at a later stage (on a change of decision with regard to the property) but the reverse process (movement from a trading to an investment status) risks crystallising a tax charge based on the then current market value of the property less its stock cost.

(2) The timing and amount of any distributions by way of dividend should be carefully arranged so that the payments are as tax efficient as possible from the points of view of the JVC itself and the joint venturers. In this respect, it is desirable to ensure that dividend arrangements are left as flexible as possible so that up-to-date tax planning is possible.

(3) A JVC will normally require separate registration for VAT purposes (its shareholding structure will normally prevent registration as part of a VAT group of companies).

The provision of services between the joint venturers and the JVC (and indeed between themselves) will need to be carefully reviewed from a VAT point of view. Because at least three separate legal entities are involved, there is potential for supplies to be regarded as made for VAT purposes even where there is no express consideration for those supplies. It may therefore be necessary to account for VAT and arrange for recovery of that VAT by the recipient of the 'supplies'.

The end of the venture

It may be possible to find a buyer for the JVC as opposed to the property—but such a buyer will take into account the tax charge inherent in such a company when agreeing the price. It is also usual to find that the shares in the JVC have a very low base cost. Sale of the shares in the JVC is therefore not usually a viable option (unless the JVC is held via an offshore vehicle not liable to UK tax on capital gains).

Most disposals will therefore be of the venture property, potentially generating a taxable profit within the JVC.

It should be noted that it is not possible to avoid a trading profit by use of an offshore JVC (UK trading profits are taxable in the UK whatever the residence of the person making those profits). However, an offshore JVC will not be liable for the investment profit made on a UK property sale (although there are other potential UK tax charges generated through use by a UK resident person of an offshore vehicle).

Once the profit is generated within the JVC, there is a need to consider extraction of the funds. It is usually beneficial to pay the maximum amount of dividend with ACT that can be set against the JVC's corporation tax liability, if the joint venturers are individuals. However, if corporate joint venturers are involved, it will usually be more beneficial to pay the maximum dividend under cover of a consortium election without ACT. A dividend received by one UK company from another is not subject to corporation tax in the hands of the recipient company (whether or not ACT is paid on the dividend). Once dividends are extracted, the balance will normally be extracted by winding up the JVC. The proceeds on winding up will be compared with the (indexed) cost of the share capital and the profit taxed as a capital gain.

Greater opportunities for tax planning relate more to the way in which the JVC is set up. If the profits generated by the JVC are effectively reduced by extraction of profit by charges for finance and other services rendered by the joint venturers (or associated parties), the problems inherent in a large profit generated within the JVC itself at the end of its life are avoided.

Summary of advantages and disadvantages of a JVC

Advantages

(1) Separate legal identity—this has the advantage of simplicity as far as the transfer of title is concerned and also facilitates dealings with shares. Since it is the JVC and not the co-venturers which holds title to the land, options, rights of pre-emption and any transfer of the co-venturers' interests (eg shares) need not be registered with the Land Registry, because they do not as such recognise dealings with land. The separateness of the JVC further enables the co-venturers to isolate the joint venture project from their other business activities.

(2) Certainty in relation to legal effect and implications—because of the large body of law which surrounds the operation of companies, whereas newer forms of joint venture vehicle (such as convertible mortgages) may raise doubts about their legal enforceability.

(3) Provides a co-ordinating management centre—which is advantageous in relation to long-term or multi-project joint ventures.

(4) Limited liability—this is one of the principal reasons for selecting a JVC and contributes to its separateness. It is of particular benefit where the co-venturers are of unequal financial strength. Although the benefits of limited liability may not be so extensive in practice, the JVC still enables liability beyond a co-venturer's shareholding to be controlled through the giving of guarantees.

(5) Flexibility in raising finance—arises because of the JVC's ability to offer a floating charge over its assets, the financing opportunities provided by the share structure of a company and the willingness of banks to allow companies more freedom in the management of their assets. Refinancing is also facilitated by the adoption of a JVC since it is easier to show that the JVC's liabilities are confined to the joint venture project, and a JVC capital may be expanded, if necessary, through the issue of more shares and in some cases by flotation on the market.

(6) Marketability of shares (ie liquidity)—there is a more ready market in shares, whereas it is more difficult to dispose of fragments of ownership in land. Less formalities are required on a disposal of shares, making it easier and less expensive to transfer them.

(7) Off balance sheet accounting—where the JVC is carefully structured to achieve this objective, without contravening the much more stringent legislation now in force.

Disadvantages

(1) No direct interest in the land—an interest in the land itself provides greater security. This may be particularly important to minority shareholders as the JVC itself holds the land.

(2) A measure of loss of control—at least in theory, because of the separateness of the JVC and the duties of its directors. This loss of control will be more marked following CA 1989, especially if off balance sheet accounting is an overriding objective, or a highly desirable incident of the joint venture project.

(3) Need for compliance with formalities and regulatory requirements—the need to comply with statutory requirements means that the JVC may be a relatively expensive vehicle to use for transactions of limited size.

(4) Loss of confidentiality—the requirements of company law that certain documents relating to the affairs of the company be made public entails a loss of privacy for the co-venturers.

(5) Restrictions on the withdrawal of capital—as provided in the relevant formal documents.

(6) No ready exit routes—are available to co-venturers who combine in a JVC. (Although this may also be considered an advantage as it strengthens commitment to the project.)

(7) Cumbersome winding-up procedure—which must be followed in accordance with the Companies Acts.

(8) Tax treatment—of a JVC is disadvantageous for co-venturers who wish to be taxed separately. (This is often the reason for adopting a partnership, which is transparent for tax purposes, instead.)

(9) Additional layer of management and reporting—between the project managers/co-ordinators and the owners of the JVC itself.

(10) Guilt by association—the JVC can become 'tainted' if a co-venturer's primary, separate business activities, encounter financial difficulties and/or attract unfavourable publicity.

---

[1] Subject to any restrictions contained in the Shareholders' (ie the joint venture) Agreement.

[2] The accounts of the JVC and those of a co-venturer may need to be consolidated into group accounts.

[3] Whilst directors must act in the interests of the company, individual shareholders can of course act in their own interests (within limits). But see also Mahon J in *Berlei Hestia (NZ) v Fernyhough* (1980) 2 NZLR 150 at p 165. 'When articles are agreed upon whereby a specified shareholder or group of shareholders is empowered to nominate its own director, then there may be grounds for saying that in addition to the responsibility which such directors have to all shareholders as represented by the corporate entity, they may have a special responsibility towards those who nominated them.'

[4] The new CA 1989 definition of 'subsidiary undertaking' and accounting standards issued by the ASC will usually mean, however, that no one co-venturer exercises greater control than the others (at least where off balance sheet accounting is desired).

[5] ie it is not intended by the co-venturers that the land should be retained by either of them following completion of the development—rather, the land (or the company) is to be sold at a profit.

[6] This is not necessarily the case however, particularly where the contributions and/or bargaining strengths of the participants are unequal. Moreover, a system of checks and balances can be built into a partnership, eg through voting rights or options.

[7] Eg changes in the JVC's name, in the address of its registered office and any change made to its objects clause.

[8] Accounts must be filed with the Registrar of Companies and an annual return to the Registrar is required.

[9] Which provides that a company has the power to 'do all such things as are incidental or conducive to the carrying on of any trade or business by it'.

[10] See, eg, Lindley MR in *Allen v Gold Reefs of West Africa Ltd* [1900] 1 Ch 656 at 671.

[11] Insolvency Act 1986, s 214.

[12] This would have implications also for off balance sheet accounting.

[13] Insolvency Act 1986, s 213.

[14] Insolvency Act 1986, s 214.

[15] Companies Act 1985, s 320.

[16] Companies Act 1985, s 330 *et seq*.

[17] Through the way in which they structure covenants and guarantees.

[18] In addition to making it easier to raise capital, a floating charge allows the lender to appoint an administrative receiver in the event of insolvency and thereby pre-empt the appointment of an administrator under the Insolvency Act 1986.

[19] Eg as to repayment of the loan or as to performance.

[20] If its greater entitlement to profits leads a co-venturer to insist on greater control over the JVC, this will have accounting implications.

[21] Or, perhaps, at a price based on a valuation of the net worth of the company.

[22] *Rowan v Dann* [1991] NPC 19.

Chapter 3

Partnership and limited partnership in England and Wales

Partnership

General

A joint venture may take the form of a partnership or limited partnership. In England and Wales[1] neither is recognised as a separate legal entity and hence co-venturers who are partners are able to preserve their own tax status in relation to the profits of the joint venture. The major difference between the two is that in a limited partnership some of the partners (ie the limited partners) enjoy limited liability. Such partners, however, may take no part in the management of the partnership business. Co-venturers who wish both to be taxed separately and to be active in the management of the joint venture may therefore choose to use a partnership as the joint venture vehicle. But if one or more wishes to forego management control and responsibility, and to adopt a more passive role, they may instead prefer to enter into a limited partnership.

Definition: Partnership Act 1890   The joint venture company and the partnership are the principal legal vehicles through which joint ventures may be undertaken, and the choice as to what form the joint venture should take in the particular case is commonly assumed to amount to a choice between the two. Both are combinative joint venture vehicles in the sense described above, although there are significant differences between them.

A partnership is regulated by the Partnership Act 1890 (PA 1890), relevant case law and any Partnership Agreement between the parties. The Act defines partnership as,

> '... the relation which subsists between persons carrying on a business in common with a view of profit.'[2]

In determining whether a partnership exists, regard must be had not only to any written contract between the parties but also to the way in which they have conducted themselves and to the surrounding circumstances. Co-ownership of land to be developed will not of itself create a partnership (PA 1890, s 2(1)) and neither will the sharing of gross returns (PA 1890, s 2(2)). However, the sharing of net profits is *prima facie* evidence that the relationship in question is a partnership (PA 1890, s 2(3)) and 'an agreement to share profits and losses may be said to be the characteristic—if not to be the essence—of a partnership contract.'[3]

Hence, all contractual profit-sharing arrangements between co-venturers are vulnerable to the possibility of being regarded by the courts as constituting partnerships. The fact that the co-venturers include in their agreement a clause negativing a partnership will not preclude the courts from holding that a partnership has in fact been created.[4] The generality of the definition in s 1(1) and the informal way in which a partnership may therefore arise means that co-venturers should consider at the outset whether their relationship is likely to be viewed as a partnership. If this is likely to be the case, they should anticipate such a finding by expressly recognising the partnership and ensuring that their agreement then displaces, in so far as it is possible to do so, those parts of PA 1890 which they believe would be an inappropriate feature of their relationship.

A joint venture may take the form of a partnership despite the fact that it is confined to a single project and thus lacks the continuity which the requirement of 'carrying on a business' would seem to denote. Although some of the early decisions on the meaning of 'business' did suggest that an element of continuity was necessary in order for an association to constitute a partnership,[5] it is now clear that single transactions—such as joint ventures—may produce one.[6]

Some minor doubts have also been expressed as to whether a partnership can arise where the objective of the joint venture is to hold the property as an investment (rather than to trade it on completion) since this is less easily regarded as a 'business'. However, such an interpretation of PA 1890 is probably an unduly restrictive one and investment joint ventures should be able to take the form of a partnership. Indeed, where the joint venture involves an investment, rather than a trading, activity, the vehicle adopted is more likely to be a partnership than a joint venture company. This is due to the fact that an investment company cannot be a consortium company, with the concomitant ability to surrender losses by way of consortium relief.

Although there may be no more than twenty partners, this restriction is unlikely to be important in practice and can in any event be circumvented by the use of a parallel partnership.

Characteristics   A partnership is characterised by informality, unlimited liability, agency and its lack of legal personality.

A partnership may be found to exist although the partners did not, nor wanted to, regard themselves as such. There are no particular formalities, such as writing, which must be complied with before a partnership can arise. Nor are there formalities to be observed during its continuance (save in respect of accounts if every member is a limited company). This provides flexiblity and, in contrast to a joint venture company, means that the affairs of the joint venture remain confidential. The desire for flexibility and privacy may therefore lead to the selection of a partnership in preference to a JVC.

A second, and far more significant, characteristic of a partnership is the unlimited liability which it involves on the part of its members. This is often the principal reason for declining to adopt a partnership as the joint venture vehicle.

Linked to the unlimited liability of partners in respect of the partnership obligations is the power of each partner, as an agent of the partnership, to unilaterally enter into transactions which bind the others. For this and other reasons the partnership should only be used as a joint venture vehicle where the co-venturers already trust and interact well with each other.

A partnership is not recognised in English law as a separate legal entity. A consequence of its lack of legal personality is that the partnership itself cannot hold title to the development property which is the subject matter of the joint venture. Not less than two nor more than four of the partners, or their nominee (being a trust corporation unless the nominee wishes to assume the mantle of a beneficial owner), must instead hold title to the land. General property law requirements in relation to, for instance, the transfer and registration of interests in land therefore become relevant. This can make the transfer of a co-venturer's interest more inconvenient and problematic. It also illustrates that the freedom from legal formalities of the partnership itself may not be matched by an absence of formalities in relation to the co-venturers' legal title to the land. Furthermore, although a partnership exhibits an element of combination and co-operation (in common with a JVC) its lack of legal personality prevents it from being as separate and discrete a vehicle as is the JVC. However, it does operate in practice very much as an 'entity' rather than as an 'aggregate' and its legal transparency can be advantageous in other ways, eg in terms of taxation. Moreover, the co-venturers are able to have a direct interest in the land providing them with security and protection from dealings in respect of it.

A partnership is thus a profit-sharing arrangement in which co-venturers combine more effectively than they do, for example, in a pure overage agreement. The co-venturers may be either individuals or companies. Typically, subsidiary companies will be formed to act as the partners, for tax efficiency and as a means of mitigating the effects of unlimited liability. It is this last feature, together with a lack of familiarity with the structure on the part of business and the administrative problems caused by lack of personality, which perhaps accounts for the partnership's unpopularity (in the past at least) in comparison with the JVC. However, as will be seen below, it is primarily for reasons associated with its tax treatment that a partnership structure may be favoured instead of a JVC.

Circumstantial factors

As far as the nature of the project is concerned, partnerships tend to be more appropriate in respect of single projects (because of their flexibility) or large projects which are to be developed over a long period of time. They are also suitable in the case of large projects where it is intended that parts should be sold off as they are completed, because of the ability of partners to agree to access the partnership funds, by repayment of capital or drawings.

A partnership may be used for either an investment or a trading joint venture, but if the objective is an investment one it may well be preferable to a JVC for tax reasons.

The legal and business character of the co-venturers is a further factor influencing the adoption of a partnership. It is sometimes said that a partnership is only appropriate where the parties are of equal financial strength, because the risk of insolvency/default (and therefore of being liable beyond the capital invested in the partnership) is greater. Furthermore, if one partner is very large and one small, the large partner may believe that indebtedness is secured primarily on the larger partner's covenant and may seek to extract a price for this. Banks will look to the stronger covenant but may price any loan on the basis of the weaker covenant leading to less efficient funding arrangements.

Some partnerships are characterised by fairly substantial co-venturers who are each able themselves to bring to the joint venture the necessary funding. Partnerships tend to be equity funded because of the difficulties associated with them raising finance.[7]

Finally, where one of the co-venturers is a pension fund, charity or trust, it may not have the capacity under its constitution to become a partner, or even to form a limited company which would then enter into the partnership. Similarly, co-venturers with exempt tax status will be taxable on trading profits and so may well be unwilling to enter into a partnership directly. Here special purpose companies would have to be used as the partners unless this too was prohibited, in which case either a JVC or limited partnership would have to be invoked instead.

Partnership structures The structure of a corporate partnership is shown in Diagram 3. Here the objective is to establish a partnership between two companies who wish to insulate themselves from liability arising in respect of, and directly attributable to, the partnership. This is achieved through establishing a partnership owned by two limited companies, each of which is a subsidiary of the respective parties. It should be noted that partnerships between companies are now required to prepare and file annual accounts although this requirement can be avoided by making one partner an individual.

Diagram 3

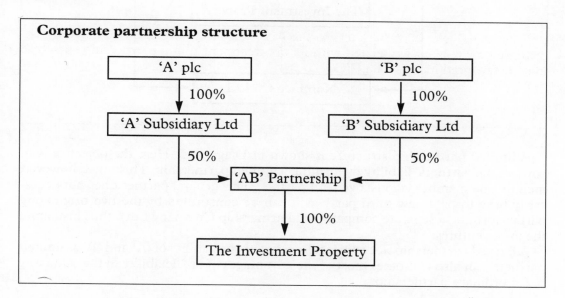

An extended corporate partnership structure is shown in Diagram 4. The addition of a nominee company, owned by the parties, results in that company being the sole legal owner of the property. This assists bankers and other lenders as they then deal with one entity on matters of taking security for their loans.

This nominee company will normally be owned 50/50 because the value to be realised through the development will be governed by the terms of the partnership itself (which is a parallel, but separate entity).

This particular structure is well suited to investment property and it provides much greater flexibility; for example, the shares in the subsidiary can be sold as opposed to a share in an 'AB' partnership. This flexibility also extends to the funding strategy and the role of the subsidiary facilitates the raising of finance.

Diagram 4

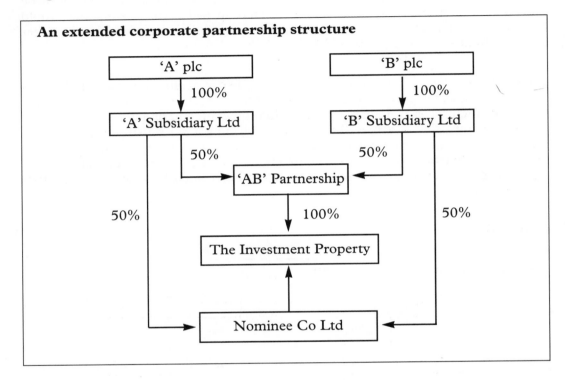

An extended corporate partnership structure

A limited partnership structure is shown in Diagram 5. Here the objective is to contain the partners' liability by forming a limited partnership. This must, however, include one member who is a general partner. This general partner does not necessarily have to be a new third party as it can be constituted by the two originating parties forming a separate company ('C Partnership Company Ltd), thus insulating the joint ventures.

A limited partnership not only legally restricts the liability of 'A' and 'B' as limited partners, but also combines most of the advantages of tax flexibility in the same way as for ordinary partnerships.

Diagram 5

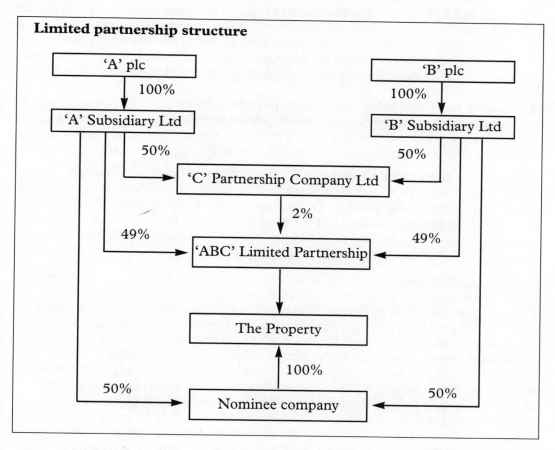

Limited partnership structure

Co-ownership partnerships and the relevance of property law

Partnership property A property development partnership may exist although the co-venturers do not co-own the land. For instance, the partnership may refer merely to the development profit, with one partner only owning the land.[8] Conversely, co-ownership of the land does not automatically entail a partnership.[9] Moreover, even where the participants in the joint venture co-own the land and share the net profits of the development, there is not necessarily a partnership in relation to the land itself, as opposed to a partnership of the profits produced by it. These distinctions are important since they identify the partnership property as either the land or the profit (or both) and what actually constitutes partnership property has significant legal implications, despite the fact that each partner is personally liable for the debts and liabilities of the partnership.

(1) Partnership property 'must be held and applied by the partners exclusively for the purposes of the partnership and in accordance with the partnership agreement'.[10]

(2) On dissolution of the partnership, every partner is entitled 'to have the property

of the partnership applied in payment of the debts and liabilities of the partnership, and to have the surplus assets applied in payment of what may be due to the partners'.[11]

(3) On the insolvency of a partner, partnership property and separate property are applied to satisfy the claims of the partnership creditors and creditors of the partners in their individual as opposed to partnership capacity, according to certain priorities.[12]

(4) Unless the Partnership Agreement provides otherwise,[13] partnership land is subject to the doctrine of conversion (which regards the interests of the beneficiaries behind the trust for sale as being all merely interests in personalty, ie in the prospective proceeds of sale rather than an interest in land).

Therefore, given these different legal effects, the Partnership Agreement should clearly state what is to constitute the partnership property. Usually, a joint venture partnership involves the partners co-owning the land, the land itself constituting partnership property in addition to the profits produced by it. This has the consequence, *inter alia*, that general property law provisions become more relevant.

Transfer of title and disposal of beneficial interest   In the case of co-ownership partnerships, the co-venturers hold the legal title to the property as joint tenants on trust for themselves as tenants in common. Where there are more than four co-owners, four of them only may hold the legal title on trust for themselves and the others. In these circumstances, it is not unusual for the legal title to be vested in a nominee company (trust corporation), which holds the site on trust for the partnership

Since the partners must hold the legal title as joint tenants, a transfer of title is less simple than in the case of a JVC. This is because all the joint tenants must participate in any conveyance of the land to a third party, each putting their signature to the transfer document. In addition, the legal title will usually be transferred when a co-venturer disposes of its equitable interest, although this is not required by property law. If the legal title to the site is held by a nominee company, it will not be transferred when one of the partners leaves the partnership. In contrast, because a JVC itself holds title to the development land and the co-venturers instead hold shares in the company, any transfer of those shares does not also necessitate a transfer of the title.

However, although a partnership may therefore give rise to complications as far as the transfer of title and the disposal of a partner's interest are concerned, the requirement that all the partners (or at least those who are legal owners) participate in any such transfer also gives partners more control over transfers. Nevertheless, special provisions relating to dealings by a partner with its own equitable interest are likely to be included in the Partnership Agreement as additional protection.

Holding device: the trust for sale   The development land co-owned by the partners is held on trust for sale. This is so even where the conveyance of the land to them did not expressly so provide,[14] although most partnerships which have been deliberately created by co-venturers will incorporate an express trust for sale. The declaration of trust is conclusive of the nature and quantum of the beneficial interests which represent the proportions in which the co-venturers will enjoy the development profit. The trust for sale may have advantages for conveyancing purposes, but it also creates some problems (in theory at least) for co-owners who are co-venturers.

A trust for sale incorporates a duty to sell the subject matter of the trust (ie the development land) coupled with a power of discretion to postpone sale.[15] The duty to sell is paramount. Thus, if there is disagreement between the co-venturer trustees as to when to sell the land or as to the exercise of the power to postpone sale, the duty to sell should prevail.[16] If the dissenting co-venturer refuses to join in the sale, the other may apply to the court under s 30 of the Law of Property Act 1925 (LPA 1925) for an order to sell the property and the court 'may make such order as it thinks fit'. In theory, therefore, one disadvantage of the adoption of a partnership as the joint venture vehicle is the vulnerability of the partners to a sale of the development property against their wishes.

However, the courts have developed a doctrine of 'secondary or collateral objects' underlying the trust for sale which in some circumstances may displace the primacy of the trustees' duty to sell. One such circumstance is where the trustees for sale (ie the co-venturers) have contractually displaced the duty to sell by providing in their Partnership Agreement that a sale of the joint venture property shall not take place without the unanimous consent of them all. Here the courts will not facilitate a breach of the Partnership Agreement by exercising their discretion under s 30 in favour of sale.[17] They will not order a sale while the underlying contractual purpose subsists. Hence all well-drafted Partnership Agreements tend to include such a provision. It should be noted that the trust for sale may itself be made subject to the consent of a named person(s) under the Partnership Agreement. This would seem to achieve the same result although the courts still have the power under s 30 to set aside a requisite consent, and may indeed do so if it is incompatible with the trustees' duty to sell. Nevertheless, the possibility that the courts may order sale under s 30 tends to cause concern.

Powers and duties of trustees under the trust for sale   While the possibility of an order for sale of the site being obtained pursuant to LPA 1925, s 30 is perhaps the most significant disadvantage, there may be yet further disadvantages arising out of the fact that a co-ownership partnership may subsist behind a trust for sale.

The land may be held by the partners as trustees on trust for themselves beneficially. This is satisfactory where there are no more than four partners, but it will be inappropriate where they exceed that number. In such circumstances, not all the partners can be trustees, since the maximum number of persons who may hold a legal estate is four; LPA 1925, s 34(2), (3) and Trustee Act 1925, s 34(2). The first four partners whose names appear on the conveyance would normally hold the site on trust for themselves and the other partners. Those partners whose names do not appear on the legal title have no general right under property law to be involved in the management and decision-making connected with the trust, and would not be necessarily involved in any transfer of title to the land, unless their consent was necessary to the execution of the trust. They should therefore insist that the terms of the trust confer on them the desired rights to participate in management decisions. In larger joint venture partnerships (and often, also, in those numbering less than four participants) the legal title will instead be held by a nominee company on trust for all the partners.

Co-venturers who are not also trustees of the legal title to the trust property are protected to some extent by the duties which trust law imposes on trustees generally in relation to trust property and beneficiaries. For instance, a trustee is under a duty to safeguard the trust assets and to manage the trust property as would a prudent person of business. A trustee is also under a duty to maintain equality between the beneficiaries.

Formalities

It has already been noted that a partnership is characterised by informality. There are no requirements of form either in relation to its creation or its continuance. The expenses of establishment and administration are also likely to be less than those of a JVC, even where the Partnership Agreement and management structure parallel the Shareholders' Agreement and management structure of a JVC.

A further advantage is that no requirement is imposed on partnerships to disclose accounts or make annual returns. However, the Partnership and Unlimited Companies (Accounts) Regulations 1993 (SI No 1820) ('the Partnership Regulations') will require a partnership where each of the members is a limited company, to lodge accounts for financial years with effect from 22 December 1994. Subject thereto, partnerships enjoy the benefits of confidentiality, which may be of importance to co-venturers.

Although the partnership itself may be free from formalities, it must be remembered that the way in which the land is held by this vehicle means that requirements of form found in property law become more relevant. Because the land is held by an aggregate rather than a single entity, legal title must be transferred whenever one partner disposes of its interest. In addition, since the interest of each partner is an equitable interest in land (and not merely an interest in the shares of a company) formalities in relation to the transfer of equitable interests must be complied with when a partner disposes of its share.[18]

Documentation

Although there are no requirements of formal documentation in order to establish a partnership, in practice the co-venturers will embody their joint venture arrangements in a Partnership Agreement. This will include many of the same matters covered by the Shareholders' Agreement of a JVC, although prudent co-venturers will also want to address specific issues which are peculiar to partnerships. For example:

(1) PA 1890 will apply in the absence of any express or implied agreement to the contrary. Hence, if any of its provisions are considered inappropriate or non-beneficial to the joint venture, the partners must displace them by specifically providing otherwise in the Partnership Agreement. For instance, they may wish to place limits on the authority of a partner to act as an agent of the partnership in respect of certain matters,[19] to provide their own procedures in relation to disputes[20] or to prohibit unilateral dissolution of the partnership.[21]

(2) As already referred to above, partners will usually displace the primacy of the duty to sell the development property (and thereby prevent a partner from obtaining a court order for sale under LPA 1925, s 30 without the consent of the other partners) by agreeing that the property should not be sold without the consent of all, or until a particular condition, such as completion of the development, shall have been fulfilled.

(3) The joint and several liability of partners has the consequence that the indemnity and security arrangements in the Partnership Agreement must be watertight.

(4) Since the partnership itself does not throw up a particular management structure—ie there is no pre-existing structure such as Table A in the Companies (Tables A to F) Regulations 1985 (SI No 805) for a JVC—the Partnership Agreement will need to set out itself the detailed management arrangements and the formalities to be used.

(5) Dealings by partners with their interest in the joint venture should also be closely regulated because the joint and several liability of partners make the identity of any new joint venture partner crucial.

(6) The Partnership Agreement will usually specify the only circumstances in which the partnership can be determined.

Unlimited liability

The liability of partners is unlimited. It is this feature of partnership which has contributed more than any other to its comparative under-use as a joint venture vehicle and to a preference for the use of JVC instead. However, this potential difficulty can be mitigated by using a wholly-owned subsidiary company to act as the partner.

Liability of partners to third parties   Any contractual liability of the partners is joint, while any tortious liability is joint and several. Thus the liability of the co-venturers extends beyond the capital invested by them in the joint venture and each is liable for the debts and obligations of the partnership in their entirety. If, for instance, one partner becomes insolvent or is otherwise unable to fulfil its obligations and the debts and obligations of the joint venture cannot be satisfied out of the development alone, the remaining partner(s) will have to meet such obligations out of its own personal assets which are unrelated to the joint venture project. A partnership is therefore inappropriate where one or more of the co-venturers is financially weak, where there is a significant disparity in their financial strengths, or where they are unable to develop a relationship of mutual trust. Even where the co-venturers are of relatively equal (and substantial) financial standing and have a good relationship, the indemnity and security arrangements in the Partnership Agreement will have to be foolproof. The risks attaching to the venture must therefore be fully and carefully assessed in advance. Moreover, it is in the interests of third parties wishing to sue one of the co-venturers to seek to argue that the joint venture agreement constitutes a partnership and so acquire the benefit of rights of action against all the participants. This potential should be recognised when formulating any contractual joint venture.

The unlimited liability associated with partnership can be avoided by using single purpose subsidiary companies as the partners. It is prudent for a co-venturer to insist that the subsidiary of its counterpart be a 'clean' company which has never traded before and to obtain warranties to this effect. More comprehensive warranties will be required where it is necessary to use a company which has traded. However, even the use of limited liability companies may not be an entirely effective method of mitigating the consequences of unlimited liability.

A central feature of partnership which has added significance for the question of liability is the ability of each partner, as an agent of the partnership, to bind the other(s) by its actions in the normal course of the partnership business. This is a further reservation which co-venturers may have about selecting the partnership route for their joint venture, especially if they have no previous experience of working together and have not therefore built up a relationship of trust.

Liability of partners inter se   The relationship between partners is one of the utmost good faith. Partners are fiduciaries as far as their dealings with the other co-venturers are concerned, both during the continuance of the partnership and after its dissolution until it is wound up. Strict duties may even exist in relation to the pre-contractual negotiations between the parties.

In the context of joint ventures, perhaps the most significant aspect of this fiduciary relationship is the duty to have regard for the interest of the partnership and to avoid conflict between it and the partners' private interests.

Funding

A partnership does not enjoy the same flexibility for raising finance as that of a JVC. This, together with the relative ease with which capital may be withdrawn, results in joint venture partnerships frequently being funded by the co-venturers themselves.

A partnership cannot, for instance, create a floating charge over the partnership property—although where limited liability companies have been set up in order to enter the partnership, each can do so in respect of its interest, and the floating charge would then be over the assets of each co-venturer. This could include a charge over the co-venturer's interest in the partnership. A potential lender would need to bear in mind, for example, the provisions of PA 1890, s 31(1) which stipulates that it has no automatic right to:

> 'interfere in the management or administration of the partnership business or affairs, or to require any accounts of the partnership transactions, or to inspect the partnership books.'

However, appropriate provisions in the Partnership Agreement can cater for the normal requirements of lenders.

Nor can a partnership come to the stock market as a JVC is able to do. This may well have implications for investors who see flotation as an exit route in the future. The partners could, however, agree to incorporate the partnership business at some future date and to seek a quotation on the stock market, but this may involve adverse tax consequences compared with starting out as a limited company in the first place. Finally, some pension funds are unable, by virtue of their constitution, to enter into a partnership and this therefore precludes them as a particular source of finance in such relationships.

Distribution policy

The profits of the joint venture are distributed in the proportions and at the time agreed upon in the Partnership Agreement. This normally corresponds to the parties' beneficial interests in the land.

Similar considerations to those which apply in relation to a JVC are relevant in determining distribution policy. However, it should also be noted that:

(1) there are no statutory restrictions on the withdrawal of capital from partnerships and capital can be repaid at any time;

(2) partnerships provide flexibility in terms of the accessing of funds by drawings; and

(3) in respect of losses, the liability of partners is joint.

Management structure

Section 24(5) of PA 1890 provides that, subject to their Partnership Agreement:

'Every partner may take part in the management of the partnership business.'

The Act does not however provide partnerships with a ready-made management framework (such as Table A in the Companies (Tables A to F) Regulations 1985 (SI No 805) for a JVC) and the Partnership Agreement must itself set out the structure to be adopted and the formalities to be used. This allows the co-venturers some flexibility since they may develop management arrangements which suit their own specific requirements.

A common form of management structure used by joint venture partners is management by committee or through a board of managers who carry out the same functions as a board of directors in a JVC. Once again, co-venturers should consider the implications which the management structure they adopt has for accounting purposes. It will be difficult, if not impossible, to have a partnership liability treated as off balance sheet. Indeed, because of joint liability the whole of a partnership borrowings might be treated as a liability of each partner. This can be mitigated by special provisions in the loan arrangements or for example by each partner borrowing its share of capital separately and lending it on to the partnership (but this may have tax consequences).

A further consideration is that in some circumstances, if there are more than two partners, there is a danger that the inclusion of detailed provisions as to management in the Partnership Agreement may result in the partnership being treated as a collective investment scheme, with tax and FSA 1986 consequences. For example, if the property venture is structured as an investment, ie not trading, and all the partners are not actively involved, then FSA 1986 may apply. It is therefore always necessary to consider the provisions of FSA 1986 so as to be aware of whether or not the partnership arrangements constitute 'a collective investment scheme'. Normally all the partners will take part in the management of the ventures so that the exemption in s 75 (2) applies.

As already mentioned, PA 1890, s 31 states that if a partner assigns its interest, the assignee has no right to:

'interfere in the management or administration of the partnership business or affairs, or to require any accounts of the partnership transactions, or to inspect the partnership books.'

In these circumstances, a separate agreement with the remaining partner(s) would have to be reached.

Dealings with interests

A partner who proposed to deal with its interest in the partnership could do so either by retiring and arranging for the appointment of a new partner or by assigning its share in the partnership. If the partnership deed is silent then the consent of all the interested parties is needed for the admission of a new partner.[22]

A related question is transfer of title to the property. Because the partners are joint tenants at law, any new prudent partner will wish also to be a legal owner and not merely an equitable owner (unless the site is held by a nominee company or there are more than four partners or unless the property is held by a trust corporation). It should be noted that a transfer of the legal title is required when a partner disposes of its interest, and that partner is one of the holders of the legal title. This necessarily requires the participation of all the legal joint tenants, and therefore gives the remaining co-venturer(s) some automatic control over dealings by one partner with its individual share.

New partners　A measure of control over the identity of any new partner is desirable because of the joint and several liability of partners—the remaining partner(s) will wish to be satisfied as to the financial stability and reputation of the new partner. However, the requirement that the legal joint tenants join in a transfer does not give complete protection to co-venturers. For example, it does not prevent a partner from obtaining an order under LPA 1925, s 30. It will be recalled that for this reason it is usual to include in the Partnership Agreement a provision that the land, or a partner's beneficial interest in it, will not be sold without the consent of the other partner(s).

Nevertheless, the difficulty in transferring one's interest in the joint venture is disadvantageous from the point of view of a co-venturer who would like some freedom in the matter. For example it may want a possible exit route from the joint venture if this seems desirable at some point in the future. Indeed, it is in the interest of the remaining co-venturer(s) that a partner who is in difficulties should leave the joint venture. Partnership Agreements might, therefore, include such exit routes, allowing a partner to sell its beneficial interest once it has first offered that interest to its co-venturer(s) at the price offered by the third party purchaser. Put and call options may be included in addition to pre-emption rights, and in this respect the Partnership Agreement will be similar to the Shareholders' Agreement of a JVC.

Finally, PA 1890 itself places some limits upon the transfer of a partner's interest. Section 24(7) provides that, subject to the Partnership Agreement:

> 'No person may be introduced as a partner without the consent of all existing partners.'

If the partner does not retire but instead assigns its interest in the partnership then s 31(1) provides that an assignee of a partner's share does not, by virtue of the assignment, become entitled to:

> 'interfere in the management or administration of the partnership business or affairs, or to require any accounts of the partnership transactions, or to inspect the partnership books, but [is entitled] only to receive the share of profits to which the assigning partner would otherwise be entitled.'

In practice, therefore, any incoming partner will itself wish to be assured of the approval of the existing partner(s).

Dissolution

The dissolution of a partnership is far less complex than the winding-up procedure of a JVC. However, the fact that partnerships can disappear without formality can cause practical difficulties and the Partnership Agreement should aim to circumvent them by specifying the circumstances in which the partnership may be determined.

Where a partnership is entered into for an undefined length of time, it may be dissolved by any partner giving notice to the other(s) of its intention to dissolve the partnership.[23] Despite PA 1890, s 32(*b*), it seems that this is possible even in the case of a joint venture where the participants have entered into the partnership 'for a single adventure or undertaking', as is illustrated by the decision in *Walker West v. Emmett*.[24] In order to avoid the joint venture being frustrated in this way, a Partnership Agreement will usually state that the partnership is to continue for a specified period, eg for six months following completion or (if earlier) until the property is sold.

However, it should be noted that this is not an absolute guarantee that the joint venture will not be dissolved at an earlier date. For example, partners can apply to the court for a dissolution of the partnership under PA 1890, s 35.

Moreover, duties associated with partnership do not immediately come to an end on dissolution. For instance, the partnership, can still be sued or have a bankruptcy petition presented against it. Basic fiduciary duties *inter se* also continue to apply.

Nevertheless, a well-drafted Partnership Agreement can usually anticipate most of these potential difficulties. And despite the need for detailed provision, the dissolution of a partnership still entails far less formality and expense than the winding up procedure of a JVC.

Tax treatment

Generally The tax treatment of a partnership is derived from a relatively small amount of specific legislation combined with Inland Revenue and Customs & Excise practice. It is important to appreciate that a partnership formed in England and Wales (unlike one formed in Scotland) is not a legal person as distinguished from the partners who are the members of it. Nevertheless, the specific tax legislation and practice have gone some way towards giving partnerships a separate identity, at least for some tax purposes.

Financing

(1) The structuring of ownership of a partnership is far more straightforward than it is for a JVC. This is merely because the percentage of the whole held by each partner is not generally of significance from a taxation point of view and can therefore follow commercial reality. However, when the structure is in place, it is necessary to take great care over any subsequent changes. Broadly speaking, where such subsequent changes do not involve withdrawals of cash or assets or payments between partners (or incoming partners), or revaluation of assets within the partnership's accounts, the taxation effects will be negligible in most circumstances because of Inland Revenue practice. However, where those provisos do not apply (or where there are only partners who are individuals and a partner joins or departs) the knock-on taxation effects of any changes need careful consideration.

(2)   The obtaining of tax relief in respect of interest costs should be easy to arrange. It will be the partners themselves who will receive the benefit of this relief, either as a proportion of the partnership's interest costs or on interest they pay on monies lent to the partnership.

Operation of the partnership
(1)   As in the case of a JVC (see chapter two), it is important to decide from the outset whether the venture is to be a trading or investment one.

A subsequent change from an investment to a trading venture can in practice be made without adverse consequences. However, the reverse process risks crystallising a tax charge based on the then current market value of the property less its stock cost.

(2)   The partners will pay tax on the partnerships profits and not on their drawings. Where there is at least one corporate partner, the profits are apportioned for tax purposes on a current profit-sharing basis. However, where there are only individual partners, the split in partnership profits between partners for tax purposes is not necessarily the same split as that accorded in the partnership accounts because of timing differences.

(3)   A partnership, although not a separate legal person, normally requires separate VAT registration.

The provision of services between the partners (including between the partners and the partnership as a whole) will need to be carefully reviewed from a VAT point of view. Such supplies made by the partners, in their capacity as partners, will not constitute supplies for VAT purposes. However, other services may give rise to VAT even though the supplier and person supplied are in partnership.

(4)   The taxation treatment of capital gains made by partnerships is complex.

Each partner is treated as owning a proportion of each chargeable asset and will have its own related base costs for capital gains tax/ corporation tax purposes.

Every change made in a partner's sharing ratio as it applies to capital assets will theoretically give rise to a capital gain or loss. However, unless such a change follows an accounting revaluation (up or downwards), a withdrawal of capital, or payments between the partners, there will be no tax effect because the disposal/acquisition will be treated as taking place at a price such that no gain or loss is generated.

(5)   Partnerships have an unusual stamp duty treatment.

Although a document forming a partnership gives rise to no duty, the acquisition from an existing partner of a partnership share is dutiable at 1 per cent of the price paid. An incoming partner taking on a proportion of the partnership debt by becoming a partner may also be treated as acquiring an asset for consideration (the proportion of debt), the document effecting the joining of the new partner therefore being rendered stampable.

The end of the venture   Where there are no corporate partners, the dissolution of the partnership will require careful planning because of the timing difference between profits/losses for accounting and taxation purposes. However, the dissolution itself is a relatively informal and straightforward procedure.

It will not normally be feasible to avoid sale of the property by the partnership once the venture is over.

Summary of advantages and disadvantages

The relative absence of formality associated with the partnership vehicle makes it a simple and flexible one to employ. It may also be more tax efficient in certain circumstances than a joint company. However, its unlimited liability may be a major disadvantage, and the fact that the partners themselves (rather than the partnership as an entity) must hold the land means that general property law becomes more relevant and may give rise to additional difficulties.

Advantages
(1) Informality and flexibility—little formality is needed in order to establish or operate a partnership. It provides flexibility and allows the partners to conduct the relationship in a way which more readily reflects their individual needs. It also minimises the costs of establishment and administration. Conversely, a partnership may be held to exist even though the co-venturers did not in fact consider themselves to be partners. This may result in parts of the PA 1890 being applicable to their relationship with disadvantageous effects.
(2) Tax efficiency—because the partnership itself is largely tax transparent, each partner is taxed individually. This is advantageous where the tax status of the partners differs. A partnership is also beneficial for tax purposes where the joint venture objective is investment, because of the ability of the partners to access the partnership losses in circumstances where a JVC could not offer that opportunity.
(3) Confidentiality—there are no requirements of registration, nor that accounts be disclosed or that annual returns be made. A partnership therefore enjoys more privacy than does a JVC.
(4) Direct interest in land—providing greater security. This factor can also give rise to problems, however.
(5) Extraction of profit—partners have the ability to access funds by drawings and there are no statutory restrictions on the withdrawal of capital.
(6) Management arrangements may be tailored to the parties' specific needs—because there is no pre-existing structure which must be used. Legal and practical difficulties may arise however where the partners are numerous.
(7) More control over dealings with interests in the joint venture—because of the power, as a trustee, to refuse to join in a transfer. But there is less control for partners whose names do not appear on the legal title.
(8) Simplicity in dissolution—there are no formalities to be observed in dissolution, rendering partnerships easy to terminate.

Disadvantages
(1) Problems arising out of the trust for sale—in theory, as has been seen, assets may be sold against a partner's wishes. The duties of trustees could conceivably give rise to possible conflict with the co-venturers' interests. One would, however, expect this problem to be overcome by drafting adequate provisions in the partnership agreement.

(2) Unlimited liability—the most significant disadvantage associated with partnership. A partner has the ability to bind the others by the transactions it enters into and the resulting liability to third parties is joint. Extensive guarantees and indemnity provisions are therefore needed, although these may not protect a co-venturer entirely. Nor is the use of limited liability companies as partners a completely satisfactory means of escaping unlimited liability.

(3) Funding—a partnership has less capacity for raising finance than a JVC. It is unable to create a floating charge and some pension funds, and others, cannot be partners.

(4) Partnership may be disadvantageous where there are a large number of participants:

  (a) because only four of them may be legal owners of the property, leaving the others less adequately protected;[25] and

  (b) because the Partnership Agreement will not then be able to set out the management arrangements in detail, for fear that the joint venture may be regarded as an unauthorised unit trust with undesirable tax consequences and FSA 1986 implications.

(5) Interest less easily marketable—fragments of ownership are less readily marketable than shares in a company and the transfer of an interest is also more complicated.

Limited partnership

General

If co-venturers value the tax transparency of partnership and yet wish to limit their liability, they may decide instead to use a limited partnership as the joint venture vehicle—at the price, however, of surrendering control.

Despite its popularity in the US, the limited partnership has been little used in the UK. Private companies were introduced in England and Wales in the same year as limited partnerships,[26] but with additional privileges regarding publicity and with the advantage of separate corporate personality. The ready and easy availability of companies, as an alternative form of business organisation, is perhaps the principal reason why limited partnerships have so far remained under-utilised. However, in recent years the limited partnership has grown in popularity in the UK especially among venture capitalists. Moreover, if companies are in the future subjected to greater legal regulation, limited partnerships may be resorted to more than previously.

Limited partnerships are governed by the Limited Partnership Act 1907, as well as by PA 1890 and relevant case law. Section 4(2) of the Limited Partnership Act 1907 provides that a limited partnership:

> 'must consist of one or more persons called general partners, who shall be liable for all debts and obligations of the firm, and one or more persons to be called limited partners, who shall at the time of entering into such partnership contribute thereto a sum or sums as capital or property valued at a stated amount, and who shall not be liable for the debts or obligations of the firm beyond the amount so contributed.'

A limited partnership, then, is essentially an ordinary partnership but with some of its partners (ie the limited partners) enjoying limited liability. They do so, however, in return for a loss of control since limited partners may take no part in the management of the partnership. It is the general partner who is liable without limit but who has the exclusive right to control the partnership's affairs. A limited partnership therefore involves a clear distinction between active and passive participants in a joint venture. One consequence is that it is perhaps best regarded as a financing joint venture vehicle—very often a participatory rather than a co-operative joint venture.

Since a limited company may be used as the general partner, the practical result can be limited liability for all those participating in the joint venture. Limited partners who wish nevertheless to be involved in management can be shareholders in the limited company which is the general partner and appoint directors to its board. This is often the form, therefore, that joint venture limited partnerships take.

Capital must be contributed by limited partners at the outset, (ie actual money or the equivalent of money in the form of property must be contributed by the limited partner. A bank guarantee in respect of the partnership's debts, for example, will not suffice). This might seem to be a disadvantage as compared with JVC shareholders, who are not necessarily required to pay the full nominal value on their shares when they are issued. The parties could, however, agree on quite small initial contributions to be supplemented by further contributions at a later date. In common with ordinary partnerships, a limited partnership shall consist of no more than 20 partners. This is unlikely to be significant as far as joint ventures are concerned, which often involve only two or three participants.

Co-venturers must comply precisely with the requirements of the Limited Partnership Act 1907 in order to establish a limited partnership—if they do not, their arrangement will be regarded as an ordinary partnership instead, and they will have failed to secure the limited liability which was one of the main reasons for selecting the structure.

Circumstantial factors

Limited partnership may well be appropriate for a co-venturer which cannot carry on trading activities. The interest of a limited partner is treated as being an investment.

Formalities and regulatory requirements

A limited partnership may be established and operated with less cost and formality than a JVC, but there are more formalities to be complied with than is the case with an ordinary partnership.

The requirements of the Limited Partnership Act 1907 must be followed exactly, otherwise co-venturers who believe themselves to be limited partners, and act on that basis, may in fact find themselves in an ordinary partnership with unlimited liability.[27] Moreover, the terms of the Act receive a strict construction by the courts because it constitutes an exception to the common law principle of unlimited liability.

The Act requires registration, which is effected by sending a simple form of statement to the Registrar of Companies. This contains certain details, including, for example, the general nature of the partnership business, the name and place of the business of the partnership, the names of the partners, the term for which the partnership is entered into and its date of commencement, and the sum contributed by each limited partner.[28] Certain changes, such as those in the nature of the business, the partners, the terms or character of the partnership and the liability of any partner, must also be registered.[29]

In addition, notice of transactions under which a partner becomes a limited, instead of a general partner, or under which the share of a limited partner is assigned, must be advertised in the *Gazette*.[30] These transactions are deemed to be ineffective until they have been so advertised, but the obligations are rarely met in practice.

The Registrar of Companies files all statements received under the Limited Partnership Act 1907 and issues a certificate of registration. Any person may inspect the statements so filed.[31] As a result, limited partnerships do not enjoy quite the same degree of confidentiality as do ordinary partnerships. However, there are no statutory requirements regarding the preparation of financial statements or annual audits and limited partnerships remain considerably more private than JVCs.

Finally, a limited partnership is likely to constitute a collective investment scheme under FSA 1986. This means that, in addition to the minimal formalities referred to above, the general partner will need to be authorised by IMRO. This could take as long as eight weeks and will involve very much more by way of formalities. It is this (possibly unintended) result of FSA 1986 which means that limited partnerships are unlikely to be used except for fairly major transactions which warrant the expense of complying with the difficult and time-consuming obligations of the Act.

Since the introduction of the Partnership and Unlimited Companies (Accounts) Regulations 1993 (SI No 1820), where the general partner is a limited company it must file accounts for the partnership.

Documentation

There are no requirements as to the documentation of a limited partnership, apart from those relating to registration and, as stated above, to the filing of accounts. However, co-venturers will usually enter into a Limited Partnership Agreement which will be very similar to an ordinary Partnership Agreement.

Liability

To third parties General partners are liable for all the debts and obligations of the partnership in their entirety[32] and have the power to bind the partnership by their acts in the same way as partners in an ordinary partnership are able to.[33]

In contrast, limited partners are only liable to the extent of their contribution and have no authority to bind the partnership. The price of this limited liability is an inability to participate in the management of the partnership business—if they do so, they will become liable for all the debts and obligations of the partnership as though they were general partners.[34]

The limited liability of the limited partners is, however, subject to three qualifications:

(1) it is lost if they take part in the management of the partnership business;
(2) if the limited partnership is not registered in accordance with the Limited

Partnership Act 1907, it is deemed to be an ordinary partnership so that the liability of all the partners is unlimited; and

(3) a limited partner who draws out or receives back any part of its contribution during the continuance of the partnership will be liable for the debts and obligations of the partnership up to the amount so drawn out or received back.[35]

The limited liability of some of the partners is an important advantage associated with limited partnership. However, few co-venturers may be prepared to act as the general partner. For this reason, co-venturers often set up a limited company as the general partner, so that their liability is then limited.

Inter se   The liability of the partners *inter se* will be determined by their Limited Partnership Agreement, the Limited Partnership Act 1907, PA 1890 and relevant case law.

Funding

Because of the inability of limited partners to take part in the management of the partnership business, limited partnerships are perhaps more a joint venture property development vehicle by nature.

Distribution policy

The Limited Partnership Agreement should set out the interest of the co-venturers in capital and in the partnership property. Otherwise, PA 1890, s 24(1) applies and all the partners are entitled to share equally in the capital and profits of the joint venture.

The general partner will often take a first charge on the profits as remuneration. Furthermore, a limited partner which draws back or receives, either directly or indirectly, any part of its capital contribution during the continuance of the partnership remains liable for an equivalent amount. If it does so, the limited partner *pro tanto* forfeits its right to limited liability.[36] There is some doubt as to whether this precludes a limited partner from receiving interest on capital or a share of the profits during the life of the partnership,[37] but the safer view is that it does not since the usefulness of limited partnerships would otherwise be greatly diminished.[38]

Finally, limited partners are not liable for losses, including deficiencies of capital, beyond the amount of their capital contributions.

Management structure

Limited partners must take no part in the management of the partnership business if they are to preserve their limited liability and it is therefore the general partner only who manages the partnership. Hence limited partnerships may involve a loss of control over the joint venture development and it should only be adopted where the limited partners have complete trust and confidence in the general partner or are represented on the board and at general meetings.

However, limited partners do have the right to inspect the books of the partnership. The Limited Partnership Act 1907 provides that they may examine into the state and prospects of the partnership business, and be consulted.

In exercising this right, limited partners must be careful not to do anything which could be regarded as participating in the management of the partnership business. Similarly, any provisions in the Limited Partnership Agreement as to the resolution of disputes should also be careful not to cross this threshold.

Dealings with interests

Subject to any agreement between the co-venturers, a limited partner may assign its share in the partnership only with the consent of the general partner.[39] The assignment is only effective if notice of it is advertised in the *Gazette*.[40] Once this is done, however, the assignee becomes a limited partner with all the rights of the asssignor.

Dissolution

A limited partnership may be dissolved in the same way as an ordinary partnership, save that a limited partner is not entitled to dissolve the partnership by notice (unless the Limited Partnership Agreement so provides). In the event of dissolution it is the general partner who winds up the partnership's affairs.

The bankruptcy of a limited partner does not automatically dissolve the limited partnership. If the co-venturers wish this to be the case, they will need to provide for it in their Agreement.

Tax treatment

The tax treatment of a limited partnership broadly follows that accorded to a general partnership. The major distinction is in relation to losses of a limited partner, which are restricted for tax purposes to the actual amount contributed to the partnership by that partner.

Summary of advantages and disadvantages

Advantages
(1) Limited liability of some partners—where limited liability is important, a limited partnership may be preferable to an ordinary partnership. The use of a limited liability company as the general partner enables everyone's liability to be limited.

Disadvantages
(1) Loss of control—for those who are limited partners, since they must take no part in the management of the partnership business.
(2) Loss of confidentiality—to some limited extent due to the limited requirements relating to registration and notice, and more importantly, through the liability of the general partner to file accounts. However, the limited partnership is still a more private and less formal vehicle than the JVC.
(3) Effects of the withdrawal of capital by limited partners—during the continuance of the partnership (see above).
(4) Limited partnerships will usually constitute collective investment schemes—within the FSA 1986, requiring authorisation accordingly.

[1] But not in Scotland, where a partnership is recognised as having legal personality: Partnership Act 1890, s 4(2).

[2] PA 1890, s 1(1).

[3] Lindley and Banks, 'On Partnership' (1990, 16th edn), at 5–24.

[4] See, eg, Megarry J in *Stekel v Ellice* [1973] 1 WLR 191, at 197.

[5] See, for instance, Brett LJ in *Smith v Anderson* (1880) 15 Ch D 247, at 277.

[6] *Re Abenheim* (1913) 109 LT 219, *per* Phillimore J; *George Hall & Son v Platt* (1954) 35 TC 440; *Gardner & Bowring, Hardy & Co v IRC* (1934) 15 TC 602; *Winsor v Schroeder* (1979) 129 NLJ 1266. Also PA 1890, s 32(*b*) seems to envisage that an agreement in relation to a single project can amount to a partnership.

[7] See, for example, *Walker West v Emmett* (1979) 252 EG 1171, where the defendant builders sold the development land to the plaintiff property developers, agreeing at the same time to build houses upon it, and it was not suggested that the defendants retained any equitable interest in the property. The agreement between the plaintiffs and the defendants to share the net profits of the project was, however, regarded by the Court of Appeal as giving rise to a partnership, and this was despite the fact that it contained no provision that losses would also be shared.

[8] PA 1890, s 2(1).

[9] PA 1890, s 20.

[10] PA 1890, s 39.

[11] Bankruptcy Act 1914, s 33(6).

[12] Bankruptcy Act 1914, s 33(6).

[13] PA 1890, s 22.

[14] The 1925 property legislation imposes a statutory trust for sale in almost all cases of co-ownership. Where it does not strictly do so, the courts have managed to fill the gap.

[15] Unless the contrary intention appears: Law of Property Act 1925, s 25(1).

[16] See *Re Mayo* [1943] Ch 302, at 304.

[17] See *Re Buchanan-Wollaston's Conveyance* [1939] Ch 217, at 738.

[18] LPA 1925, s 53(1)(*c*).

[19] See PA 1890, s 5. Note, however, that this limitation will not affect third parties dealing with a partner whose authority is limited.

[20] See PA 1890, s 24(8). See also Chapter 8.

[21] See PA 1890, s 32.

[22] PA 1890, s 24(7).

[23] PA 1890, s 32(c).

[24] (1979) 252 EG 1171.

[25] Although the legal title may instead be held by a nominee company.

[26] In 1907.

[27] Limited Partnership Act 1907, s 5. Cf the Uniform Limited Partnership Act 1916 in the US, which does not subject persons who erroneously believe themselves to be limited partners to the obligations of a general partner, provided they at once renounce their interests in the profits of the partnership on discovering the mistake.

[28] Limited Partnership Act 1907, s 8.

[29] Limited Partnership Act 1907, s 9(1).

[30] Limited Partnership Act 1907, s 10.

[31] Limited Partnership Act 1907, s 16(1).

[32] Limited Partnership Act 1907, s 4(2).

[33] Limited Partnership Act 1907, s 7 and Partnership Act 1890, s 5.

[34] Limited Partnership Act 1907, s 6(1).

[35] Limited Partnership Act 1907, s 4(3).

[36] Limited Partnership Act 1907, s 4(3).

[37] See, for example, Lindley & Banks, 'On Partnership' (1990, 16th edn).

[38] Drake, 'Law of Partnership' (1983, 3rd edn), at p 344.

[39] Limited Partnership Act 1907, s 6(5)(b).

[40] Limited Partnership Act 1907, s 10.

Chapter 4

Profit-sharing leases

General

Profit-sharing lease arrangements can be classified as joint ventures because they may be used—by exploiting legal estates in land—as a method for undertaking development in association with others and sharing the profit. They fall, therefore, within the wider definition of 'joint venture' and should be regarded by co-venturers as a further possible option available to them when selecting the legal vehicle for their joint venture.

From the 1960s onwards, extensive use has been made of sales and leasebacks as a means of raising development finance. Various forms of sale and leaseback were themselves developed as the lease structure became more pervasive in the property market. Often the lease itself is preceded by an agreement for lease containing development obligations on the satisfaction of which the lease is granted. From a developer's point of view, this is by no means fatal to funding so long as the banker's needs are accommodated. In the case of an investing institution, the enabling agreement also prescribes for the provision of finance.

A typical development sale and leaseback arrangement involves the sale of the freehold or long leasehold title to land by a landowner, or developer, to an investor—typically, an institution—with the former simultaneously taking back a lease from the latter. The vendor-developer is then obliged to find sub-tenants who will occupy the property, once it is developed, and who will generate its income. Meanwhile, during construction, the investor will cover all, or part of the costs of development. On completion, the developer enjoys its profit by way of the difference between the rent it receives from its own sub-tenants and the rent it pays to the landlord. Thus, by using a lease arrangement of this type, co-venturers can share the profits of their joint venture via an agreed percentage of rental income of the property to which they are entitled under their agreement.

Form of lease arrangement

There are, of course, many variations to the basic structure outlined above and every lease arrangement will be different. For instance, the developer may find a suitable site, with the institution taking a long lease from the freeholder and the developer a sub-lease. In this way, landowner, institution and developer all share in the income of the property. There are, moreover, many variations in the form of sharing arrangement according to the way in which the rent is shared. Frequently these can be complex, and the sharing arrangements layered with each layer perhaps housing a different share.

In its earliest form, the sale and leaseback often involved a 'top slice' arrangement. Here, the institution would receive its share of the rent first and was guaranteed a minimum return by the developer. Any shortfall in the rent was therefore borne by the developer alone. Many were, in effect, 'geared' leases whereby the developer's proportionate share of the income would increase as the total rental income grew, typically through occupational rent reviews. In these early agreements, rent reviews were at infrequent intervals between the investor/head landlord and developer.

More modern sharing arrangements involve side-by-side (or vertical) leases in which any shortfall is met by both the institution and the developer in the same proportions as their entitlement to the rent. The investment risk is therefore shared between them, although the terms of the agreement may also provide for a mimimum guaranteed rent to the provider of the finance—irrespective of the level of occupational rents.

Co-venturers' relationship

Profit-sharing lease arrangements are thus investment, rather than trading, joint ventures and, by nature, involve a long-term relationship between co-venturers. For developers, the leaseback can be a method of raising finance which eliminates the problem of initial income shortfall (when, as has frequently been the case, long-term interest rates are above property investment yields) as it enables them both to make an adequate return and to retain an interest in the completed development. For landowners, it can be a way of enjoying the increased value of their land following development without parting with the freehold and is therefore more secure than a purely contractual arrangement. For institutions, using a lease arrangement as the joint venture vehicle enables them to obtain the developer's expertise and access to opportunitites as well as subsequent management skills.

While lease arrangements clearly involve close co-operation on the part of those engaging in them, the co-venturers do not unite in the way that they do in combinative joint ventures, such as a JVC or partnership. Yet although the participants retain their separate identities, interests are not as distinct as the interests of those who collaborate in participatory joint ventures. Rather, participants in lease arrangements are more effectively 'locked together', by reason of their concurrent interests in the same land.

However, they retain a clearly-defined degree of control over, and identity of interest with, the other participants so as to ensure that the venture continues as a going concern.

Profit-sharing lease arrangements have also been described as 'quasi-partnerships'. However, there are certain features of the structure which may make it an awkward joint venture vehicle.

(1) The landlord-tenant relationship is an inherently antagonistic and unequal one. The lease structure is not capable therefore of creating, or even accommodating, a complete identity of interest which can be so important to the success of a joint venture.

(2) The interests of the co-venturers are likely to diverge as the term runs. The developer-lessee holds a wasting asset, whereas the institution-lessor is able to look forward to the increased marriage value of the property once the term ends.[1]

(3)   Linked to this, disputes are likely to—and, in fact, frequently do—arise over the refurbishment or rebuilding of the property. This problem stems from the long-term nature of the relationship, which is usually intended to last for a longer period of time than the building itself. Given changes in technology, design and fashion, it can therefore be expected that the building will need to be altered or even rebuilt during the term. Yet at the stage where this is necessary, the developer-lessee may only have a few years of its term left and may be content to take what income it can from the property during those remaining years. This is especially the case where there is insufficient time of the lease left over in which to amortise the refurbishment or redevelopment costs. In contrast, the landlord has a keener interest in refurbishment and the future rental growth of the property. The issue is further complicated by the need to agree the proportions in which the necessary capital will be invested, and how this may affect the rent sharing formula.

(4)   There is potential for conflict even at the start of the venture. For instance, in order to maximise its profit from the development, the developer will wish to see it let as quickly as possible and at as high a rent as can be agreed. But an institution, as a long-term investor, will be more interested in ensuring that the sub-tenants are financially reliable and that the rents are realistic. There may be similar conflict over questions concerning the quality and cost of the construction, equipment and finishes. These areas of conflict will need to be confronted and carefully resolved in initial negotiations if the lease structure is to form the basis of a successful joint venture relationship.

It is problems such as these—which may only emerge at a late stage in the relationship when a number of years of the term have passed—which have led to attempts to unscramble many of the sales and leasebacks entered into in the past. Nevertheless, provided these problems can be adequately addressed by the parties at the start of their relationship, leases can, and do, prove to be a valuable form of joint venture vehicle.

Sales and leasebacks can allow off balance sheet financing.[2] This may be a particularly attractive feature now that the redefinition in CA 1989 of subsidiary undertakings makes it more difficult to avoid consolidation by using a JVC or partnership structure. Despite some dissatisfaction with the stucture, profit-sharing lease arrangements will remain an option in selecting an appropriate vehicle for collaborating in property development, especially for those interested in long-term investment in land. They are also a well-established vehicle for public/private sector joint ventures.

Circumstantial factors

Because profit-sharing lease arrangements are often a form of investment joint venture, they are typically entered into between developers and investors such as pension funds, charities, insurance companies and local authorities. Alternatively, they are entered into between landowners, developers and investors, since a lease arrangement enables a landowner to share in the development profit, while at the same time safeguarding its interest in that profit and retaining a right to participate in the future growth of the value of the property. Sales and leasebacks are also used extensively by businesses owning property, such as retail store groups, who need to release capital tied up in buildings, rather than in the business itself.

Formalities

Creation

The formalities which must be complied with in order to create a legal lease are not peculiar to joint ventures. A legal lease for a period of more than three years must be created by deed, but a legal lease for a period of three years or less can be created in writing or even orally.[3] However, sale and leaseback transactions typically involve the grant of long leases for a term of 99 or 125 years and will therefore always require a deed,[4] and be registerable at HM Land Registry accordingly.

Assignment

The assignment (transfer) by the lessee of its legal lease must be effected formally by deed, whatever the length of the term.[5]

Regulation: the law of landlord and tenant

The use of profit-sharing lease arrangements by co-venturers involves them in the manipulation of an existing, and heavily regulated, proprietary relationship, namely that of Landlord and Tenant. Co-venturers exploit the legal relationship for their own investment ends . However, because the relationship plays such a pivotal role in the provision of premises for business and commercial enterprise, in the regulation of land use for agricultural purposes and in the provision of residential accommodation, it is one which is extensively controlled both by the common law and by legislation.

(1) A lease gives its holder an interest in the land itself which is binding on a purchaser of the freehold reversion. This is in contrast to pure contractual arrangements which a developer may enter into with a landowner, but which will not bind (except in exceptional circumstances) a purchaser.[6] To have an interest in the land itself therefore provides greater security and is a valuable asset on which finance can be raised. Indeed, LPA 1925 identifies the lease, or 'term of years absolute' as an estate.

(2) Legislation provides a measure of protection to occupational tenants who constitute business tenants within the Landlord and Tenant Act 1954, Pt II.[7] The Act provides such tenants with security of tenure[8] and prevents their tenancy from being determined except in accordance with the special machinery of the Act. It also enables a tenant to obtain compensation from its immediate landlord (eg the developer) in certain circumstances. This includes cases where the tenant has made improvements to the property, provided it has satisfied the requisite statutory conditions contained in the Act.

(3) In the absence of express contrary agreements, the lease impliedly imposes certain obligations on both landlord and tenant. These include, for instance, the landlord's covenants for quiet enjoyment and against derogation from grant; and the tenant's covenant not to commit waste. Co-venturers must

therefore displace the obligations which they do not wish to be a feature of their relationship when drafting the lease. However, they are also subject to certain other statutory obligations—for example, a tenant may be subject to rights of entry reserved by statute on behalf of the landlord.

(4) A combination of common law and statutory rules governs the enforceability of leasehold covenants and therefore determines (in part at least) the liability of the co-venturers.

(5) The law of landlord and tenant provides particular remedies for the breach of leasehold covenants, and also dictates the manner of their enforcement. Particularly important here, as far as co-venturers are concerned, is the landlord's right to re-enter the property and forfeit the lease. In the case of breach of covenants other than the covenant to pay rent, the landlord must follow a special statutory notice procedure in order to forfeit the lease, but the remedy of forfeiture still represents a fairly draconian remedy, particularly from the point of view of the developer/lessee and the occupying sub-tenant. However, a tenant may apply to the courts for relief from forfeiture, and the courts have a discretion to grant or withold relief as they think fit. Nevertheless, the possibility of forfeiture is a significant hazard of the lease route for developer co-venturers. If the landlord forfeits the head lease, the sublease is likewise destroyed (although the sub-tenant has an independent right to seek relief against forfeiture). More significantly, forfeiture destroys any mortgage over the leasehold estate.

Although a legal mortgagee may also seek relief, the risk of forfeiture clearly renders leasehold property generally unacceptable security to mortgagees in the specific case where there is a clause which provides for forfeiture in the event of the tenant's liquidation or insolvency.[9] (It should be noted that full rack rent leases (which by implication are not intended to have a capital value) will invariably contain such a clause and are therefore effectively unmortgageable. Being occupation leases, however, neither will they feature as profit-share leases but will comprise the most inferior leases in the chain producing the entirety of the income.)

It is clear that lease arrangements still involve significantly less formality than is required in the case of a JVC. While both are heavily regulated, the regulation of leases is predominantly that of the substantive relationship rather than an imposition of a procedural form or framework, as with a JVC. This substantive regulation may make the lease structure less attractive to some co-venturers. Nevertheless, the law does allow them room to structure or create the precise details of the relationship.

Documentation

The documentation in a leasehold arrangement will consist of the joint venture agreement/agreement for lease, the lease and the draft underlease.

The joint venture/finance agreement

This will contain, *inter alia*, the developer's undertaking to complete the development and to sublet on terms approved by the institution, and the institution's undertakings in relation to the financing of the development. Both parties will agree to enter into the sale, followed by the grant of a lease if not immediately, then on completion of the development. Depending on the quality of head landlord, if it is not an institution providing finance, such an agreement is often mortgageable. It is important to remember that the matters contained in the joint venture agreement are binding in contract only (although the agreement to sell may give rise to a constructive trust). If the agreement comprises also an agreement for lease it is registerable and thus binding on successors to the reversion. It may in that event also be construed as a lease, despite assertions to the contrary.

The lease

The lease will contain the letting policy agreed by the parties, the rent-sharing arrangements (including a method for calculation) and the provisions relating to the management of the property. All these matters are usually the source of keen negotiations between the parties, highlighting the antagonistic nature of the relationship and the conflicts of interest built into the lease structure. The investor will wish to exercise as much control as possible over the development and subsequent letting and management of the property. In contrast, the developer will seek to retain as much independence as it can. However, where the lease arrangement involves side-by-side leases—so that both parties are sharing the investment risk and are true (if unequal) partners in the economic sense—it is to the benefit of both that they compromise and genuinely take into account the other's needs and concerns.

As regards letting policy, the following covenants are typically found in the lease granted to the developer:

(1) By the developer-lessee that it will use its best/reasonable endeavours to ensure that the property is fully let and that it will consult the institution-landlord at all times on its letting policy.
(2) By the developer-lessee that it will not sublet the property, except on terms that:
    (a) the institution-landlord's approval of the sub-tenant is first obtained;
    (b) the rent payable under the sub-lease is the full open market rent, with no fine or premium;
    (c) the term of the sub-lease is not less than 25 years;
    (d) the rent reserved by the underlease is reviewable on an upwards-only basis at intervals of at least five years.
(3) By the developer-lessee to use its best/reasonable endeavours to sublet the building only as a whole or in specified units.
(4) By the developer-lessee to impose a standard form of sub-lease (usually supplied by the head landlord).

It must be recognised however that in particularly difficult market conditions, when tenants are in a position to demand concessions, and inducements, in return for signing a lease, these 'ideal' head-lease terms may well have to be modified to suit market circumstances. Moreover, the typical 'institutional' term of 25 years with upwards-only five year reviews is under attack, although in post-recession Britain it appears attractive to foreign investors.

The lease will also set out the basis upon which the present and subsequent rental growth is to be shared, the way in which it is to be calculated, and the management structure which is to be adopted.

The underlease

In 'normal' market conditions, the terms of the head-lease will not leave much scope for the developer to negotiate (occupation) under-leases in accordance with its own desires. A standard form of sub-lease, acceptable to the institution-landlord, is usually imposed, containing fairly predictable covenants. But, as noted above, adverse market circumstances may well require a more flexible set of rules.

Liability

Participants in lease arrangements hold their own separate interests in the land and maintain their own identities. In general, therefore, they are liable to third parties only in respect of their own acts/omissions. If they wish to allocate certain risks between themselves in a particular way, they must do so through covenants and guarantees.

However, a lease structure raises special questions of liability because the co-venturers are in a proprietary, and not merely a contractual, relationship. This means that:

(1) a co-venturer may be liable to its partner's assignees, despite the absence of privity of contract; and
(2) a co-venturer continues to be liable to its original partner even after it has disengaged itself from the joint venture.

In addition, a tenant and any sub-tenant are subject to the landlord's remedy of forfeiture in the event of a breach of covenant by them.

Liability between the original landlord and tenant

The liability between the original landlord and tenant is contractual. Of particular importance to co-venturers is the consequence that both parties remain liable to each other, in the absence of a contractually-agreed release, throughout the term— even after one of them has assigned its interest and left the joint venture. (This, however, remains under review by the government.)

Because of the institution's typically superior bargaining position as landlord and as provider of the development finance, it is, moreover, unusual for the landlord-institution to agree that the developer-lessee's liability should not survive the assignment of the term. Thus a tenant remains liable to the landlord in respect of breaches by its assignee, or any subsequent assignees, of all of the covenants contained in the original lease. The tenant may even be liable on the covenants as amended by agreement between the landlord and a subsequent assignee of the term—for instance, for rent fixed under a later rent review.[10] And although the tenant has a right of indemnity (both at common law and under statute)[11] against the assignee in default, this is of little use where the latter becomes insolvent. It may be prudent for the developer-tenant, if it does assign the term, to expressly reserve a right of re-entry against the assignee in respect of any breach of covenant for which the developer is made liable.[12]

The institution-landlord's contractual liability to the original tenant similarly survives its assignment of the freehold reversion, unless otherwise agreed (but see below).

Liability to assignees

Whether assignees of the freehold reversion are liable to the original tenant in respect of the landlord's covenants, and whether assignees of the lease are liable to the landlord in respect of the tenant's covenants, depends on whether the lease is legal or equitable. However, it has been seen above that a lease arrangement between co-venturers will almost certainly contain a legal lease.

Under LPA 1925, s 141(1), the developer-lessee is liable to the (landlord) institution's assignees for breach of all those covenants 'having reference to the subject-matter' of the lease. This means those covenants which at common law 'touch and concern' the land. In other words, the tenant is liable to the assignee only in respect of those covenants which intrinsically affect the lessor in his capacity as landlord and the lessee in his capacity as tenant. The 'touch and concern' requirement excludes covenants which are exclusively of personal or private significance for the parties to the lease.

The liability of the institution/landlord to the developer's assignees exists at common law only, provided that the covenant which the assignee seeks to enforce 'touches and concerns' the land and that 'privity of estate' exists between it and the institution. Privity of estate exists between those persons who currently stand in the position of landlord and tenant *vis-à-vis* each other.

Liability of assignees

Under LPA 1925, s 142(1), assignees of the freehold reversion are liable to the developer-tenant in respect of all those covenants 'having reference to the subject-matter of the lease'. Again, this means those covenants which 'touch and concern' the land. An option to renew the lease is regarded as such a covenant. However, rights of pre-emption and an option to purchase the reversion at a pre-fixed price have—somewhat surprisingly—been held by the courts not to constitute covenants which 'touch and concern' the land. In the case of unregistered land, the option to renew the lease will only bind an assignee of the reversion if it has been registered as an estate contract under the Land Charges Act 1972. In the case of registered land, registration of the lease against the superior title is required to secure the same end.

Assignees of the developer-tenant are liable to the institution-landlord at common law in respect of those covenants which 'touch and concern' the land, and provided that privity of estate exists between them.

Liability to sub-tenants to the institution as landlord

Neither privity of contract nor privity of estate exists between landlord and sub-tenant. However, if the sub-tenant has notice of the existence of a restrictive covenant in the head lease, the landlord may be able to obtain an injunction restraining it from committing a breach of that covenant. Furthermore, acts by the sub-tenant which are in breach of the covenants in the head lease may entitle the landlord to forfeit the lease against the intermediate tenant. This, in turn, brings about a forfeiture of the sublease also, although as mentioned above, a sub-tenant may have rights of relief from forfeiture.

Funding

Profit-sharing lease arrangements are themselves a form of funding arrangement. If the developer owns the land already, there will be a sale of the freehold or long lease-hold title by the developer to the institution, on terms that the institution grant to the developer a lease. This releases the cash necessary for financing the start of the development. Typically, the developer will have an option or contract to purchase the land, which it will assign to the institution, who then completes the transfer. This avoids a double stamp duty charge. A lease arrangement thus enables financers of property development to take an equity, rather than a debt, position in relation to the properties which they finance.

Distribution policy

The profits of the development are distributed by way of the receipt of the rent payable by the occupying sub-tenants. It is the rent-sharing arrangements which therefore embody the distribution policy agreed to by the co-venturers.

Basis on which rent is shared

It is the different bases on which rent may be shared which distinguish the various types of sale and leaseback structure. For example:

(1)   Top slice (horizontal) arrangement. Here, the institution is typically guaranteed a minimum return, after which the rent is shared in agreed proportions: for example, 50/50. It is the developer, therefore, who meets any shortfall as the sharing relates only to the investment income from the completed development. The rents from the development project are effectively shared as the 'profit-rent' is divided between the developer and the institution. From the developer's point of view, therefore, the top slice lease arrangement is somewhat unattractive because of the greater risk attaching to the developer's share of the income, which in turn renders the interest less marketable. Hence, most arrangements make provision for either party to buy the other out, often at a price calculated on the basis of a pre-agreed formula, should either decide to sell its interest, via a put or call option.

Although early sales and leasebacks took this form, side-by-side arrangements became increasingly popular as a result of increased frequency of rent reviews and the institutions' willingness to become more involved in the development and in its risks; and as a result of their recognition that many developer's guarantees were often worthless in adverse market conditions.

(2)   Side-by-side (vertical) leases. In the case of true side-by-side leases, the institution and the developer share both the losses and the profits of the completed

development in pre-agreed proportions (unless there is, in addition, a minimum guaranteed rent). The investment income/risk is therefore shared. However, in some agreements where the institution receives a minimum 'priority return' it is necessary to distinguish between the sharing in the investment returns and the sharing of the development profit. These sharing arrangements may be different because of the greater risk which attaches to the development. Thus, if the developer guarantees the institution an initial return, it is still the developer who bears most of the risk of the development project, despite the fact that the rental income is shared side by side following completion.

Calculation of the rent reserved

Regardless of the way and the proportions in which the rent is shared between the co-venturers, it must first be calculated. The net rental income of the property is reached by subtracting certain costs and other agreed deductions from the gross income of the property. It is therefore important that what constitutes 'gross income' and what are permissible 'deductions', is carefully defined and set out in the lease.

(1) Gross income—this might include, for instance, not only rents but also advertising revenues, insurance monies arising from loss of income claims, mesne profits and damages received from occupiers, licence fees, service charges paid by occupiers, insurance commissions, deemed rent and VAT.

(2) Costs/deductions—this might include the costs of complying with leasehold covenants, the supply of services for the property, statutory compliance, costs incurred in the grant of underleases, legal and surveyors' fees, the cost of collecting rents and management costs. The lease will usually provide also for the landlord's approval of undefined costs.

(3) Payment on account—it is usual for a co-venturer/financier to provide payments on account. Thus the developer will commonly agree to pay on account quarterly in advance a sum equal to the difference between the net income for the period and its own share of that income. There will also be provisos to ensure that a balancing-up process takes place at the end of the relevant accounting year. If the net income flow is negative, it is the landlord who will make the relevant payments to the tenant.

The nature of this arrangement is also characterised by whether the rental income upon which the calculations are based is deemed receivable (usually, but not necessarily, associated with top-slicing) or received (side by side).

Management structure

It is one of the benefits of profit-sharing lease arrangements, as far as institutions are concerned, that they are thereby relieved of the management of the completed property. It is the developer (or other intermediate lessee) who assumes responsibility for management. However, because of its interest in the income and rental growth of the property, an institution will clearly wish to exercise a degree of supervision.

The co-venturers may decide to establish a committee of management, on which they are each entitled to sit. However, this can increase costs and cause delay. It also allows more scope for disagreement. Operational decisions and the day-to-day management of the property will therefore often be left to the developer. But strict controls will be exercised over the development itself and the institution is likely to reserve its consent to major decisions affecting the property, such as the identity of sub-tenants and alterations to the property.

Hence the lease structure, unlike the JVC or partnership, is not really conducive to joint management. Instead, one party—the developer—assumes responsibility for this aspect of the joint venture. In this respect at least, profit-sharing lease arrangements are closer to being participatory joint ventures than they are to co-operative joint ventures.

Refurbishment

A problem which is peculiar to the lease structure is that of the eventual need to refurbish or even to demolish and rebuild the property which is the subject-matter of the joint venture.[13] Because the relationship between the co-venturers is long term, the need to refurbish may and often will arise before the termination of that relationship. And yet, at the point at which the question arises, the term of the lease may be near its end, or be so reduced that amortising the costs of refurbishment may make the work unviable to the tenant and hence the interests of landlord and tenant are likely to diverge. The question of refurbishment is often therefore a major source of potential disagreement between the participants in this form of joint venture vehicle. It is also one of the most difficult problems to provide for, despite its being anticipated.

If it is the tenant who wishes to alter the property, it at least has the ability to obtain vacant possession (albeit at a cost) of the property, but is still likely to need the landlord's consent to the alterations. The lease may provide for a payment to be made by the tenant to the landlord which covers any temporary loss of the latter's income from the property. However, following refurbishment, the rental income should be increased and thus the lease may also provide for a variation in the proportions in which the parties are entitled to share in the income in order to reflect this. The landlord may, further, reserve to itself an option enabling it to provide the finance for the alterations, which would similarly be reflected in an adjustment to the rent-sharing provisions.

More often, it is the landlord who wishes to carry out redevelopment. The developer/tenant may have no interest in alterations because its lease is about to terminate through the expiry of the term. For the landlord to insist on carrying out refurbishment and then to require a higher proportion of the rent as well, is contrary to the normally established relationship between a landlord and tenant. The inclusion of break clauses, coupled with an option on the part of the tenant to take a new lease following redevelopment, is an unsatisfactory means of addressing the problem. A better way, perhaps, is simply to include options allowing either party to buy out the other's interest under a pre-arranged formula which takes into account the marriage value which will accrue to the purchaser and which is otherwise inadequately reflected in the price of an interest standing on its own.

Dealings with interests

In principle, each party to a lease arrangement is able freely to dispose of its interest as it wishes and without the consent of the other—there are no in-built constraints to a lease structure. However, in practice, the landlord will often reserve its consent to an assignment of the lease. It will also seek to control further dealings by the tenant, such as the variation of underleases, the acceptance of surrenders or the granting of options, by which the rental income from the property would in any way be reduced or prejudiced. Sales and leasebacks sometimes contain options enabling either party to buy the other out under certain conditions. The basis on which a valuation for this purpose is to be carried out will also normally be found in the lease.

Termination

The leasehold relationship between co-venturers may be terminated in a variety of ways:

(1) Expiry of the term—if the joint venture runs its 'natural' course, the relationship will only come to an end on the expiry of the term, at which time the lease terminates automatically, without any need on the part of the landlord to serve a notice to quit.[14]

(2) Forfeiture—the landlord may re-enter the property on the tenant's breach of leasehold covenants and forfeit the lease, subject to compliance with a statutory notice procedure and the tenant's right to relief against forfeiture via an application to the court.

(3) Notice to quit—where the co-venturers have expressly agreed that the lease should be terminated by a notice to quit to determine the lease, then this method may be used to end the relationship. However, given the nature of a joint venture, it is highly improbable that co-venturers would include such a provision in their agreement and thereby allow one party to unilaterally terminate the relationship.

(4) Surrender/merger—the lease ends on the surrender by the tenant of its interest to the landlord, or by the acquisition by the tenant of the reversion.

(5) Disclaimer—if the tenant becomes bankrupt its trustee in bankruptcy may disclaim the lease if it relates to property which is 'unsaleable or not readily saleable' or which is likely to give rise to a 'liability to pay money or perform any onerous act'.[15] Such a remedy is more often used by a liquidation of a tenant under a rack rented lease (if the landlord under it has not sought forfeiture on grounds of liquidation). Otherwise, a lease having some capital value may not be considered inherently onerous.

(6) Frustration—in *National Carriers v Panalpina*[16] the House of Lords held that a lease can be frustrated, although this would be 'exceedingly rare'.[17] It is difficult to imagine situations in which a lease between co-venturers would be frustrated.

Tax treatment

Introduction

There are no specific features of the relevant tax legislation and practice that differentiate between a landlord and tenant relationship with a joint venture background and any other landlord/tenant relationship.

Financing

In a sense, the financing arrangements are straightforward because there is no joint venture vehicle for tax purposes, only the separate parties. However, it is more important as a result that both institution and developer will be in a position to obtain tax relief on any interest costs separately borne. This may well affect the structure of the lease(s) used.

Operation of the leasing structure

(1) The retained property interests will normally constitute investments in the hands of the institution and/or developer. Any initial sale of the property to the institution by the developer, however, will usually be a trading transaction.
(2) Special rules apply to sales and leasebacks:
  (a) There are provisions that prevent an owner of land from obtaining a tax deduction on artificially high rent following a sale and leaseback; and
  (b) A tenant of a short lease (50 years or less still to run) who assigns or surrenders it to its landlord for a capital sum and takes a lease for a term not exceeding 15 years is liable to be taxed on a proportion of the capital sum received as if it were income.
(3) Stamp duty planning is important in the context of leases—the duty can be at rates of up to 24 per cent.
(4) VAT is also an important factor in the context of leases, in particular, the use of the option to tax (or election to waive exemption for VAT purposes) is very important and requires careful planning.

Summary of advantages and disadvantages

Advantages

These include the following:

(1) The parties are able to maintain their separate identities and are given separate interests in the land—the co-venturers are thus able to manage their own affairs without reference to the other and to freely alienate (subject to any agreement between them) their interest in the joint venture. However, 'separateness' can be regarded as inimical to joint ventures and as productive of conflict.
(2) The provision of finance—is an advantage of the lease structure as far as developers are concerned, as, hopefully they are able to make a profit as a result.
(3) Management—from the point of view of developers, profit-sharing lease arrangements give them control over the management of the property. For

institutions, despite a loss of control, they are relieved of this aspect of responsibility for the property.

(4) Equity participation—lease arrangements allow providers of finance to take an equity position, rather than a mere debt position, in relation to the property which they finance.

(5) Landowners can participate in development profit without parting with the freehold title—a lease also provides them with greater security than does the imposition of covenants or the reservation of options.

(6) Off balance sheet—profit-sharing leases may allow off balance sheet accounting.

Disadvantages

(1) The leasehold relationship is inherently antagonistic and unequal—the structure itself can generate conflicts of interest and the landlord is invariably in a superior bargaining position.

(2) Economic interests are likely to diverge as the term runs—as the landlord can look forward to an undivided investment, whereas the tenant holds only a wasting asset which reduces in value over the course of the term.

(3) Potential for conflict generally is greater than some of the other structures.

(4) Need for refurbishment—will become necessary during the term and is likely to be a major source of disagreement. It is a problem which is difficult to deal with adequately by express provision as its arrival is far distant and so much can change.

(5) Extensive legal regulation—the landlord-tenant relationship is one which is heavily regulated, both at common law and by legislation.

(6) Hazard of forfeiture—the developer is subject to the landlord's right to forfeit the lease for breach of leasehold covenants, even in respect of conduct by sub-tenants.

(7) Extended liability—due to the running of leasehold covenants. (This can also be seen as a benefit, from the point of view of a co-venturer with rights of enforceability.)

(8) Marketability—although leases are freely alienable, co-venturers' interests can be difficult to value and may not realise a fair price when one considers the underlying marriage value of the lease and the reversion.

---

[1] A lessee in occupation may have a right to a new lease under the Landlord and Tenant Act 1954, but this is not guaranteed and the term of the new lease must not exceed 14 years.

[2] Provided that the lease does not constitute a 'finance lease' (as to which, see SSAP 21).

[3] LPA 1925, ss 52(1), 52(2)(d) and 54(2).

[4] Even if the requirement of a deed is not complied with, the lease may take effect in equity—although after the Law Reform (Miscellaneous Provisions) Act 1989 it will have to be in writing signed by both parties. However, it is most improbable that co-venturers would embark upon a joint venture without proper legal advice and legal documentation.

[5] Assignment is usually made subject to the landlord's consent.

[6] Options, rights of pre-emption, restrictive covenants, contracts to purchase the land, and mortgages not secured by deposit of title deeds are all contractual arrangements which will bind a purchaser if properly protected by registration.

[7] Ie tenants who occupy the premises for the purposes of a business carried on by them or for those and other purposes: Landlord and Tenant Act 1954, s 23(1).

[8] Landlord and Tenant Act 1954, Pt II, s 24(1).

[9] A forfeiture clause *per se* will not render the lease an unacceptable security. It is a clause which provides for forfeiture on insolvency/liquidation which is objectionable to mortgagees. All rack rent leases will contain such a clause and are therefore effectively unmortgageable.

[10] *Selous Street Properties Ltd v Oronel Fabrics Ltd* (1984) 270 EG 643; *Centrovincial Estates v Bulk Storage* (1983) 46 P & CR 393.

[11] LPA 1925, s 77; Land Registration Act 1925, s 24(1)(*b*).

[12] Cf *Shiloh Spinners v Harding* [1973] AC 691.

[13] The need to refurbish is common to all long-term, investment joint ventures. But it is a peculiar problem to lease arrangements because of the usual covenant against alterations found in the lease.

[14] Note, however, the rights of business tenants under the Landlord & Tenant Act 1954, who may request the grant of a new lease.

[15] Insolvency Act 1986, s 315(1), (2)(*b*).

[16] [1981] AC 675.

[17] [1981] AC 675, at 692B–D and 697A.

Chapter 5

Profit-sharing mortgages

General

This relatively new (to the UK) financing technique enables providers of finance to share in the increase in value of property consequent on development, via a profit-sharing mortgage. As a form of joint venture vehicle, it may be considered as an alternative to forward funding, sale and leasebacks and other methods of raising finance.

There are two forms of profit-sharing mortgage. Both differ from a conventional mortgage by effectively giving the lender an interest in the equity, and by allowing it to share in the increase in capital value of the property during the term of the loan.

(1) A participating mortgage requires the profit share to be made by a specified point in time: it usually involves the payment of a fixed sum, expressed as a percentage of the increased value of the property.

(2) A convertible mortgage gives the lender an option to convert some or all of the loan into an equity interest in the property (or into shares in a special purpose company owning the property). The terms on which a convertible mortgage is given vary—for instance, according to the time at which the option may be exercised, or whether all or part of the loan is convertible, and whether the amount of the conversion payment is fixed or variable.

Hence, the profit-sharing mortgage involves a legal mortgage, coupled with either a form of overage payment (the 'equity payment') or an option to convert into the equity of the property. The adoption of a profit-sharing mortgage may be attractive to both developer and financier alike, especially if the provision of straight debt is unattractive. If developers sell their projects on completion, they lose the chance of benefiting from any future upturn in values. For those who are willing to take a longer-term view of the property market, the profit-sharing mortgage represents a potential alternative funding technique. It enables a developer to obtain finance with a higher loan-to-value ratio and at a lower rate of interest than conventional debt and may avoid losses on untimely disposal. It also permits the developer to retain ownership of the project.

The providers of finance are attracted by the prospect that they can share in any increase in the value of the property without being exposed to a substantially greater risk. Furthermore, with a convertible mortgage, the lender can defer its decision on whether or not to invest significant equity in the property until it has been able to evaluate how the property is performing. If the value of the property appreciates, the lender can exercise its option to share in capital growth. If, on the other hand, the value depreciates or is static, the lender can remain in the position of a pure lender.

This in effect gives the lender some protection against the devaluation of money in times of high inflation. At the same time a guaranteed return is ensured.

Primary use as investment/financing techniques

The participating and convertible mortgages are therefore primarily investment/financing techniques. Yet the lender's participation in the equity of the property (economic only in the case of a participating mortgage, but proprietary also in the case of a convertible mortgage) means that they are regarded as a form of joint venture. The profit-sharing mortgage lies between equity and debt. It is a participatory joint venture, namely one in which the participants share the profits of the joint venture project, but not the immediate practical responsibilities and management of the project itself. In other words, although the provision of finance is vital to enable the project to be undertaken at all, it is in another sense incidental or peripheral to the development, which remains the developer's project alone. The project is not co-active: there is no combined effort. Although the financier will take a keen interest in the success of the project and will want to exercise a measure of control over it, its role is essentially passive.

Hence there is not the same identity of interest which exists in a JVC or partnership. The participants maintain their distinct roles and interests. Although developer and financier have in common an economic interest in the success of the development, the relationship is essentially unequal and potentially hostile: if the project failed, they would not stand or fall together. Rather, the financier would retrieve what it could and would leave the developer to its own devices. However, these features may make the structure appealing to parties who value their independence, or to developers who value control, since it allows those interested in property development to come together, without having to join together.

Circumstantial factors

The profit-sharing mortgage is an attractive financing technique from the point of view of developers, especially if there is any undervaluation in the (particular) property sector, which may in the future correct itself. Thus developers are unwilling to sell properties into a depressed market and thereby lose the opportunity of benefiting from any rise in property values. By using a profit-sharing mortgage instead, they preserve that opportunity; and although they share the upturn in value with the provider of finance, they at least manage to retain part of the profit. This type of joint venture vehicle may be particularly suited to weak market conditions.

Since mortgages are by nature typically a long-term financing technique, profit-sharing mortgages are appropriate in the case of major, long-term development projects. This is particularly so as regards convertible mortgages, because apparent legal problems surrounding their enforceability may necessitate the adoption of a corporate finance structure and this is only really justifiable or worthwhile where the size of project, and therefore the sums of money involved, are large. In addition, because the participating mortgage envisages a fixed time at which the profit share will take place, it is perhaps suitable only where there is a planned disposal of the property, or where at the start of the joint venture the developer is confident of having presold the project, at the required date, (when it must, of course, pay over to the lender the appropriate share of the uplift in value).

A profit-sharing mortgage can be appropriate in the case of both trading and investment joint ventures. However, the likelihood of the latter form of profit-sharing mortgage being considered a collective investment scheme within FSA 1986 may restrict profit-sharing mortgages to projects which the developer intends to trade on completion. Nevertheless, they remain of interest to both institutions and banks, offering the advantages of a secured loan with that of equity returns.

Formalities and problems of legal enforceability

Creation

The profit-sharing mortgage involves a legal mortgage coupled with either a fixed payment calculated by reference to the increase in value of the property during the mortgage, or an option to convert the loan into an equity interest in the property.

The LPA 1925, s 85(1) provides that a legal mortgage of freehold land can only be created:

> 'by a demise for a term of years absolute, subject to a provision for cesser or redemption, or by a charge by deed expressed to be by way of legal mortgage.'

In other words, it is created by the grant of either a long lease or a charge. Similarly, LPA 1925, s 86(1) provides that a legal mortgage of leasehold land may be created by either a sublease or a charge. Thus with a straightforward legal mortgage, legal title to the property remains with the developer throughout.

(1) In the case of a participating mortgage, the provisions relating to the equity payment could in theory be contained in the loan/mortgage document, but, for the reasons discussed below, they will usually be found in a separate document. The profit share is not expressed as a charge over the equity, but simply as a cash payment payable on a specified date and representing a percentage of the increased value of the property concerned.

    It is therefore merely a contractual arrangement and does not purport to confer a proprietary interest on the lender. As such, there are no particular formalities to be complied with.

(2) In the case of a convertible mortgage, however, the legal mortgage is coupled with an option which is an enforceable interest in the equity. The option is regarded as a 'contract for the sale or other disposition of land' and as such must comply with s 2 of the Law of Property (Miscellaneous Provisions) Act 1989 (LP(MP)A 1989). This requires the contract to be 'made in writing' and to be signed by both parties. It must also incorporate all the terms expressly agreed by the parties.

The exercise of the option to convert and the Law of Property (Miscellaneous Provisions) Act 1989

Prior to the LP(MP)A 1989, contracts for the sale or other disposition of land had only to be evidenced in writing[1] and signed by the obligor alone, and in practice both the grant and the exercise of the option were sufficiently evidenced in writing to satisfy the requirement. However, after the 1989 Act, such contracts have to be in writing and signed by both parties. This gave rise to some debate about the nature of options. If the grant of an option and its exercise both constituted contracts for the sale or other disposition of land, then the formalities contained in LP(MP)A 1989, s 2 would have to be observed at the time the option was exercised as well as at the time it was granted. However, if an option instead represents a single contract for the sale or other disposition of land, conditional upon the option holder giving notice of its exercise, then s 2 is considered relevant only at the time the option is granted. This is of some importance, since a requirement that both the grantor and the grantee put their signatures to the exercise of the option would prevent it from being a unilateral act, as has hitherto been the case.

In *Spiro v Glencrown Properties* [1991] 1 All ER 600, Hoffman J, as he then was, held that where the option was essentially conceived as a conditional contract, s 2 need be complied with only at the time of the grant of the option, and that it was not necessary to observe its requirements at the time of exercising the option. This should mean that the lender need comply with no particular statutory formalities when exercising the option to convert. The case has not been appealed and the result seems a satisfactory compromise. Pre-existing options are thought not to be tainted by the statute.

Registration

Both the legal mortgage and, in the case of the convertible mortgage, the option to convert, must be registered; as to the latter in the case of unregistered land as an estate contract (a class C (iv) land charge) pursuant to ss 1(1) and 2(4) of the Land Charges Act 1972 and, in the case of registered land, as a notice under s 4(6) of the Land Registration Act 1925. The effect of registration is that subsequent purchasers of the land take their title subject to the mortgage (registered where appropriate) and the option. All mortgages of registered land must be registered in order to be effective. However, in the case of unregistered land only the second or a subsequent legal mortgage, not supported by the title deeds, must be registered (as a 'puisne' mortgage—land charge class C (i)) in order to be effective, but a first legal mortgage supported by title deeds requires no registration at all!

The Financial Services Act 1986

If the profit-sharing mortgage constitutes a 'collective investment scheme' within FSA 1986, its operator will have to be authorised under the Act (s 3 and para 16 of Sched 1).

Problems of legal enforceability

The law relating to mortgages raises doubts about the legal enforceability of profit-sharing mortgages. Historically, the courts have been concerned to protect the mortgagor (borrower) from harsh terms or unconscionable dealing. In particular, they have insisted that no 'clogs or fetters' should be imposed on the mortgagor's right to redeem. In its extreme form, the doctrine invalidated any provision in a mortgage transaction which might inhibit the realistic possibility of redemption of the mortgage or prevent the mortgagor from regaining in full an unencumbered status by the repayment of all monies due.

This would seem to invalidate profit-sharing mortgages. However, in later cases the doctrine was qualified, to the point that there is now no general rule prohibiting all collateral advantages.

A collateral advantage is only impermissible where it is:

(1) unfair and unconscionable; or
(2) in the nature of a penalty, clogging the equity of redemption; or
(3) inconsistent with or repugnant to the mortgagor's contractual and/or equitable right to redeem.[2]

The courts' scrutiny may today be influenced, instead, by a more flexible test of fairness. Nevertheless, the rule against collateral advantages has raised doubts about the legal enforceability of profit-sharing mortgages.

It is likely that the courts' disapproval of oppressive terms is reserved particularly for the case of residential mortgages or where the parties are clearly of unequal bargaining power, and that a commercial mortgage (such as those discussed here) negotiated between business parties at arm's length would not be treated as within the doctrine. However, even if this is the case, the amount of money likely to be involved in profit-sharing mortgages makes the risk of having the interest in the equity of the property set aside one which, although perhaps small, a lender may be reluctant to take.

Avoidance of the rule against collateral advantage   A number of ways have been suggested for avoiding the rule against collateral advantages. It is thought that if the provision for the equity payment in the participating mortgage, or the option in the convertible mortgage, were contained in a separate document to that representing the legal mortgage, it would satisfy the rule. This is because, technically, the loan is not then subject to the collateral advantage, even if in practice they could both take place at the same time. Indeed, the House of Lords held valid an option to purchase part of the secured property in *Reeve v Lisle*[3] precisely because it was contained in a transaction separate and independent from the original mortgage transaction, having been granted ten days after it. However, this avoidance technique will not necessarily succeed, since the courts will always ask themselves whether the two documents represent, 'in substance a single and undivided contract or two distinct contracts'.[4] The mere fact that the mortgage and the provision for the equity payment/option are in separate documents will not necessarily save the profit-sharing mortgage. It should be noted, however, that convertible mortgages in the US are based upon this structure and that there is case law in the US which confirms that an option is not a clog on the equity of redemption.

Another method for protecting the lender's interest is the use of a corporate finance structure. Here the borrower would set up a special purpose company to hold the property. The legal mortgage would then be granted over the property within the company and the option would be an option to convert, not into the equity of the property, but instead into the shares of the company. The loan documentation would also contain covenants controlling further borrowing by the company without the lender's consent, thereby protecting the option from being at risk from any act which might dilute or reduce the equity in the property.

Residual uncertainty   Despite such techniques, until profit-sharing mortgages are actually tested in the courts, some residual uncertainty will continue to surround the question of their legal validity and this is clearly a drawback of this joint venture vehicle. However, the Law Commission published a report on land mortgages and a draft Bill at the end of 1991, in which they proposed that the rule against collateral advantages should be abolished and replaced by a body of more flexible statutory guidelines for variation, amendment or the reopening of terms. If these proposals should become law, the question of the legal enforceability of profit-sharing mortgages will no longer be of significance, although the exercise by the courts of their discretion in favour of varying terms will remain a possibility. If, however, the terms are varied then the court will consider whether the terms were freely negotiated. If they were, the court could order the borrower to compensate the lender. This, together with the developer requiring future loans would, it is submitted, cause a borrower to think long and hard before attempting to avoid the option. An analogy can be drawn with international syndicated loans where there has been hardly any litigation as a result of these market pressures. This is an indication of an awareness on the part of borrowers that they would be 'blacklisted' if they did litigate, or seek to avoid the option.

Documentation

The documentation of the profit-sharing mortgage involves a legal mortgage (the loan documentation) and, for the reasons already discussed, a separate document containing either an agreement for a payment fixed by reference to the increased value of the property to be made by a specified date, or an option to convert part or all of the loan into the equity of the property.

The legal mortgage

This will contain the terms of the loan, including the rate at, and the way in which the interest is to be paid, and the date on which the loan becomes repayable. Where a corporate structure is being used, the loan documentation may also incorporate the specific covenants restraining the borrower from further borrowing or from giving further security. In practice, the mortgage may be in a bank's standard form coupled with an agreement setting out more closely the commercial terms, expressly overriding where necessary the standard terms contained in the mortgage deed.

The agreement for the equity payment or the option to convert

(1) In the case of a participating mortgage, the agreement for the equity payment will contain:
    (a) the agreed percentage of the net sale price of the property to which the lender is entitled;
    (b) the date on which it will become due (usually an alternative between the date on which the loan becomes due, the redemption date, the sale date or the repayment date, whichever is the earliest);
    (c) a definition of the sale price and a mechanism for determining market value; and
    (d) a definition of allowable deductions from the sale price so as to reach the net sale price.

(2) For a convertible mortgage, the lender's option will include such terms as:
   (a) the period during which the option may be exercised;
   (b) whether part or all of the loan is convertible;
   (c) whether a further sum is payable on conversion; and
   (d) the formula for calculating the conversion payment.

Where a corporate structure is used it may also include the specific covenants referred to above.

Liability

As a self-contained financing technique in which the participants always retain their separate identities, the profit-sharing mortgage does not really raise questions as to their limited or unlimited liability. An option is an equitable proprietary interest in land which can be enforced by specific performance. A receiver will be bound by the option.[5]

Funding

The profit-sharing mortgage is itself a funding vehicle and can be regarded as an alternative to sales and leasebacks or forward funding arrangements. It enables a higher loan-to-value ratio to be considered and offers a relatively lower rate of interest than straight debt. The participation in the equity of the property (or the company owning the property) makes it a hybrid structure, standing somewhere between debt and equity.

Profit-sharing mechanism

Participating mortgage

The profit share in a participating mortgage is expressed as a percentage of the increased value of the property during the term of the loan (ie as a percentage of the net sale price). It becomes payable on a predetermined date. The definition of the net sale price and the date for repayment therefore need to be agreed.

The net sale price will be defined and a method for determining this is necessary, in case the equity payment becomes due on a date other than the date of an actual sale of the property. Allowable items will be specified, such as legal fees incurred in relation to sale (provided they are agreed by the lender), the loan, and the borrower's equity (ie the borrower's own financial contribution to the purchase of the property). The percentage of the residual sum to which the lender is entitled is, of course, a matter for prior negotiation.

The equity payment usually takes the form of a cash payment, often made following a sale of the property. However, alternative dates for repayment may be specified. For instance, the profit share could take place on the earliest of the following dates: the date on which the loan becomes repayable, the date of the actual redemption of the mortgage, the date of any sale of the property, or the equity payment date (ie a long-stop date, failing the occurrence of any of the previous dates). In practice, it may be necessary for the borrower to sell the property in order to make the equity payment. A participating mortgage is perhaps most suitable, therefore, where there is a planned disposal of the property, or where the borrower is certain of having the money available by the time of the repayment date.

Convertible mortgage

The convertible mortgage gives the lender an option to convert into the equity of the property. This may take a number of forms:

(1) the option could allow the lender to take an interest in the property directly;
(2) it could allow him a share of the profits on a disposal of the property.

The mortgage could also take a mixture of the two forms.

The value of the conversion interest and payment will need to be determined, as will the date on which the option expires. The value of the conversion payment could be expressed in a similar way to the equity payment due under a participating mortgage—that is, as the outstanding balance of the loan plus a percentage of the increased value of the property. Alternatively, it could be variable, according to a pre-determined formula.

The date on which the conversion option expires will usually be earlier than the date of the repayment of the loan. (In any event the term of an option to purchase for valuable consideration is limited under s 9 of the Perpetuities and Accumulations Act 1964 to 21 years.) This allows the borrower some time to refinance the property should the lender decide not to exercise the option. Moreover, refinancing will be easier if the property is not still subject to the option.

Management

The profit-sharing mortgage is not a co-active joint venture vehicle, and as such the management of the property itself remains the responsibility of the borrower. However, the lender has some interest in exercising controls over the borrower, in order to protect the value of its equity interest in the property. To this end, certain guidelines concerning the management of the property may be agreed to by the parties, and certain restrictions (eg in relation to using the property as further security) may be placed on the borrower, these provisions being incorporated in the mortgage deed or, as the case may be, the enabling agreement. Leasing terms provide some guidance and a similar set of undertakings and controls may be adopted. The borrower may also be required to obtain the consent of the lender to its operating and capital improvement budgets.

Market reaction

It has been argued above that the profit-sharing mortgage is particularly suited to an uncertain market. It may also be attractive to US lenders, who are already familiar with the structure. However, there are a number of factors which suggest that the market reaction of lenders may be initially cautious, perhaps unnecessarily.

(1) Lenders are understandably cautious of new financing techniques and the profit-sharing mortgage has not yet been made available on a wide-enough

basis in the market for a secondary sector to exist. This caution could recede over time as the structure becomes more familiar.

(2) Part interests in property are less readily disposable in this country and fragmentation of ownership generally results in a discount in the value of the whole. A syndicate of banks, however, could acquire the asset and would sell on at the right price.

(3) Commitment to a profit-sharing mortgage involves being prepared to take a longer-term view of the property market and depends upon the perception that there is likely to be a significant future upturn in property values.

(4) There is some uncertainty surrounding the legal enforceability of profit-sharing mortgages. Certain techniques for achieving enforceability have been advocated and used successfully in the US. Borrowers of any standing are unlikely to challenge the option for the reasons mentioned above. The bank's position is also strengthened by the knowledge that the Law Commission's proposals in relation to land mortgages could remove this uncertainty.

(It should be noted that a convertible mortgage was proposed by Stanhope Properties plc and CS First Boston in 1990 for 200 Grays Inn Road in London, with ITN as the tenant. The mortgage did not proceed due to market resistance. Particularly, it was thought that the pricing was wrong.)

Termination of relationship

(1) The relationship between lender and borrower comes to an end in the case of a participating mortgage on the repayment of all outstanding sums—ie the loan (including interest) and the equity payment.

(2) In the case of a convertible mortgage, it comes to an end on the expiry of the option or on the repayment of the loan, whichever is the later. However, if the option to convert is exercised in such a way that the lender takes an interest in the property itself, the parties will then be locked in a long-term relationship of co-ownership. That relationship will only terminate on a sale of the property, or in the event that one co-owner buys out the other.

Tax treatment

One of the most significant tax advantages with these instruments is that the borrower receives funds (albeit initially in the form of borrowings) without being liable for capital gains tax on the sale of the property (or of an interest in the property) until such a time as the option is exercised.

In England and Wales, the case of *J Sainsbury plc v O'Connor*[6] has lifted, to some extent, the concern that the existence of an option could crystallise a tax charge on the basis that it had parted with the beneficial interest in the property.[7] If the borrower anticipates that tax rates will fall or that there will be a less onerous regime in relation to capital gains tax in the future, then this could be particularly attractive.

Interest

A convertible mortgage permits the borrower to make deductions for interest payments and any allowable depreciation prior to conversion, on the basis that it is still the owner of the property. In England and Wales, the borrower should be able to obtain relief as a charge on income pursuant to s 338 of the Income and Corporation Taxes Act 1988 so that interest is set against income. Relief for depreciation should also be available in the form of capital allowances, prior to conversion, under the Capital Allowances Act 1990.

It should be noted that if the rate of interest depends upon the performance of the borrower's business (eg if the interest rate is linked to rents obtained from the property) there is a possibility that the interest may be treated as being paid as a distribution for tax purposes (although there are exceptions). As a result, it would not be deductible in computing the borrower's profits. The borrower would also accelerate its liability to tax in the form of ACT (s 14 of the Income and Corporation Taxes Act 1988) which might in turn be set off at a later date against the liability to tax on its profits. There would however be a cash flow disadvantage. It should be noted that in reality ACT may become an absolute cost if the borrower is unable to generate sufficient mainstream corporation tax to offset the ACT.

If the lender was a company resident in the UK for tax purposes and the distribution treatment applied, it would receive the distribution free of tax. The 'distribution treatment' would not apply if the consideration were not greater than the reasonable commercial return for the use of the loan principal (s 209(2)(*d*) of the Income and Corporation Taxes Act 1988). A share in the profit of a property development, to the lender, is likely to be a reasonable commercial return.

Interest paid by a company can be deducted either as a trading expense or a charge on income as mentioned above. A company can also claim a deduction for interest paid in calculating a capital gain subject to corporation tax (s 40 of the Taxation of Chargeable Gains Act 1992).

Loan redemption

Any premium on the redemption of a loan should be tax deductible if the loan is properly structured. The sum payable on redemption should be fixed in advance to provide the required return to the lender and not be linked to rental growth (otherwise, the payment could amount to a distribution). The loan could also be structured as a deep discount security pursuant to s 57 and Sched 4 of the Income and Corporation Taxes Act 1988 if it is a redeemable security at a price below its redemption value carrying a zero interest coupon. The discount must be more than 15 per cent of the redemption value or 0.5 per cent per annum of that amount each year between issue and redemption.

Corporation tax

The grant of the option is a disposal of chargeable assets for capital gains tax purposes and the consideration received by the borrower will be subject to corporation tax. Even if no consideration is attributable to the grant of the option, it may be possible that the Inland Revenue would want to attribute a market value to it on the basis that a disposal at no consideration is not an arm's length transaction.[8] This would only apply if the underlying asset is acquired at less than market value. If the option is not exercised then there is no corporation tax implication.

With a straightforward convertible mortgage, the lender does not acquire an interest in the borrowing company. Upon the assumption that the loan is a normal commercial loan,[9] the borrower company should remain in the same tax group. This will have a number of advantages. For example, the taxable losses, or profits arising from the rental surpluses or shortfall in a period can be offset against profits and losses elsewhere in the tax group in the same period under the group relief provisions. The chargeable gain arising on the disposal of an interest in the property can also be sheltered under these provisions.[10] (This is on the assumption that tax losses arise elsewhere in the group and the disposal excludes brought-forward losses so that any gain can be passed through a group company with tax losses.)

For a non-UK lender, no withholding tax needs to be applied to the interest payment if advantage can be taken of a double taxation agreement. This is on the basis that the investor is non-resident with a possibility of reducing withholding tax obligations to nil.[11] The borrower will want to ensure that the lender complies with s 349(3)(*a*) of the Income and Corporation Taxes Act 1988, whereby there is no withholding requirement on interest payable in the UK. (A recent practice statement issued by the Inland Revenue has relaxed the previous practice on withholding tax.)

Stamp duty

Stamp duty also needs to be considered. The use of a convertible mortgage would defer the timing of a 'conveyance or transfer on sale' for stamp duty purposes until conversion of the mortgage.

Value added tax

VAT may be charged on any premium paid on the grant of an option to acquire land pursuant to the Value Added Tax Act 1983 (as amended) depending on the tax arrangements of the grantor and the type of property over which the option is granted. If the grantor has waived the exemption from charging VAT by notice to HM Customs & Excise, it must charge VAT on the premium. By waiving the exemption, it is then able to claim back VAT paid out in relation to the property. The complex provisions relating to VAT on commercial property are incorporated in Sched 10 of the Value Added Tax Act 1994.

Summary of advantages and disadvantages

Advantages

(1) Higher loan-to-value ratio may be considered. In a conventional mortgage, the lender may provide up to 70 per cent of the property's value; whereas with a profit-sharing mortgage, the lender may consider a loan as high as 85 per cent.
(2) Lower rate of interest is often payable than is the case with straight debt.
(3) Protection for lenders against the devaluation of money in times of high inflation.

(4) Borrower avoids losses on untimely disposal and preserves the opportunity to benefit from any upturn in property values. It also retains some equity in the property.

(5) Lender's ability to defer the decision whether to invest in property until its actual, rather than estimated value, is known. If property values appreciate, the lender can exercise its option; if they depreciate, it can remain in the position of a pure lender.

(6) Deferral of tax.

(7) Suited to a weak market.

Disadvantages

(1) Uncertainty concerning their legal enforceability—due to the rule of mortgage law which invalidates collateral advantages. However, the Law Commission has recommended its abolition and replacement by more flexible statutory guidelines.

(2) Disposability—no established market exists for part interests in property. The interests are also likely to be valued at a discount.

(3) Market reaction—is as yet conservative and cautious.

(4) Profit-sharing mortgages may constitute 'collective investment schemes' within FSA 1986—requiring authorisation and with adverse tax consequences.

(5) The predetermined date for profit share in a participating mortgage means the 'redemption date' can become a matter of the management of the borrower's finances rather than the state of the property market—and the borrower may be forced to sell the property at an inopportune time.

---

[1] As required by LPA 1925, s 40.

[2] Per Lord Parker in *Kreglinger v New Patagonia Meat and Storage Co Ltd* [1914] AC 25, at 61.

[3] [1902] AC 461.

[4] Per Viscount Haldane LC in *Kreglinger v New Patagonia Meat and Storage Co Ltd* [1914] AC 25, at 39.

[5] *Telematrix plc v Modern Engineers of Bristol (Holdings) plc* (1981) 1 BCC 99.

[6] *Sainsbury J plc v O'Connor (Inspector of Taxes)* (1990) STC 516.

[7] See also *Wood Preservation Ltd v Prior (Inspector of Taxes)* (1968) 4 STC 112.

[8] Taxation of Chargeable Gains Act 1992, s 17.

[9] As defined in Income and Corporation Taxes Act 1988, Sched 18, para 1(5).

[10] Taxation of Chargeable Gains Act 1992, s 171.

[11] As where, for example, the borrower is resident in the US.

Chapter 6

Forward sale and forward funding arrangements (contractual joint ventures)

General

Forward sale purchase and forward funding arrangements became fairly prevalent from the 1970s onwards as development mortgage finance and then sales and lease-backs declined. They enabled institutions and other major providers of finance to participate in development and remain an important method of raising finance. They continue to be a popular vehicle, used by participants in property development.

Although developer and institution do not combine their efforts in the way that the members of a JVC or partnership do and they retain their separate identities throughout, these types of arrangement may nevertheless be regarded as joint ventures since both parties may share the profit following the completion of the development project. However, the relationship is based on ownership and the institution, as the provider of finance, will be in a much stronger position and able to insist on an entitlement to greater (if not the entire) reward.

Forward sale

In simpler investment/purchase agreements, the institutions' exposure to the risks of development takes the form of forward purchase. Here, the institution enters into a contract to buy the development before it is completed. The developer obtains short-term finance from elsewhere in order to cover the costs of development, but the fact that it already has a (forward) purchaser for the development makes the task a relatively easy one. It may also enable it to obtain the finance at more favourable rates. The contract will contain an agreed formula for calculating the purchase price perhaps by reference to the estimated net current rental values and a yield, usually just above the current investment yield. Any actual surplus beyond this, from the actual rents being achieved above estimated rents, is then capitalised and shared in agreed proportions between developer and institution.

Forward funding

The institution/fund may itself provide the interim finance in addition to agreeing to purchase the completed development. This is a 'forward funding' arrangement. Here the developer's profit may be represented by the difference between the agreed purchase price (which includes a rental formula) and the costs of development.

Rental overage may be reflected in the agreed formula in calculating the purchase/sale price. Alternatively the whole purchase and development cost may be met with the developer's entire overage based upon a rental formula, the institution's income being underpinned by a minimum income required from the developer. The risks of construction and letting are still shared (but not always on the part of the developer where the interim income is treated as part of, or merely added to, the development cost), but the developer is able to obtain the finance at a lower rate than it would be able to from other sources. The institution, too, benefits from the acquisition of an investment at a lower price than the price of the completed development in the open market. There are, inevitably, a number of variations on this basic form of forward funding arrangement, for example:

(1) A 'priority yield' provision in a forward funding agreement reduces the risk of losses to the institution by giving it a prior claim to (part of) the returns of the development.

(2) The institution may insist upon a rental guarantee, for a defined period, from the developer, and is thereby assured a minimum return (for example, as under a notional lease, imposing upon the developer in addition all the obligations of a tenant until the development is fully let for the first time). The formula for the transaction may depend upon whether it is deal driven or covenant driven. However, the developer may obtain the development finance at a lower rate as a *quid pro quo*. In practical terms, it is only substantial developers, or those supported by a substantial covenant, who are able to offer an acceptable quality rental guarantee.

(3) Whether combined with notional interest during the development period, or actual interest in lieu of rent thereafter, the institution's financial commitment will always be subject to a maximum figure.

Definitions

Both forward sales and forward funding agreements are thus primarily methods of raising finance. To this extent, they are similar to profit-sharing leases and profit-sharing mortgages but without the concept of 'debt' as such. In contrast to sale and leasebacks, the developer in a forward sale/funding arrangement does not retain an interest in the completed development. It participates in the development profit only, and not in the subsequent investment value of the property. With a profit-sharing mortgage, on the other hand, it is the institution who may (in a convertible mortgage) or will not (in a participating mortgage) have an interest in the development once it is completed.

A forward sale/funding arrangement is a contractual joint venture, although it may often be difficult to demarcate purely contractual arrangements and contractual agreements constituting partnerships. The possibility that an agreement may be regarded as a partnership, thus displacing undesirable provisions of PA 1890, should therefore be considered. In such transactions the concept of formal partnership can relatively easily be avoided in a properly constructed agreement. Moreover, because the institution's role is a largely passive one (although advance of development finance under a formal forward funding will be carefully controlled by the institution) and because there is neither joint management nor unity of effort, these arrangements are participatory, and not co-operative (genuine), joint ventures.

A forward sale/funding arrangement is a contractual relationship between a relatively passive investor or provider of finance and an active trader-developer. It enables the developer to obtain the finance necessary to undertake the project at a favourable rate, and yet to participate in the enhanced value of the project on its completion. The drawback for the developer is that the institution/fund will require a (substantial) share of the development profit as a result. For the institution, an additional advantage is that it acquires an investment suited to its particular requirements at a lower price than it would have to pay for a completed and let development in the open market. It will also be able to influence the design, specification, letting criteria etc during the negotiation stages with the developer.

The parties

However, the fact that the joint venture is participatory only, and hence that the parties maintain their separateness and that the relationship is unequal (with the provider of finance typically in a stronger bargaining position), also means that there are potential conflicts of interest between the parties, which may not be capable of entirely effective resolution. For instance, as a trader, the developer will be keen to see the development let as quickly as possible and at as high a rent as can be obtained, in order to maximise its profit. In contrast, the institution as an investor will be more interested in the strength of the tenant's covenant, in diversifying its class of tenants, and so on. (Similar conflicts of interest bedevil the landlord and tenant relationship in leasehold arrangements.) Nevertheless, despite these problems, the forward sale/funding arrangement remains an attractive means of raising development finance and continues to be widely used.

Circumstantial

Forward funding arrangements invariably involve single development projects between a developer and an investor, such as an institution, fund, trust or charity. The development itself may be phased, with the financial formula including developer's profit being treated on a like basis.

Formalities

As a purely contractual joint venture, a forward sale/funding agreement is probably the least formal of all the available legal vehicles although the documentation may be lengthy and extremely detailed. There are no particular formalities or regulatory requirements which the co-venturers must comply with. However, co-venturers should consider the possibility that their arrangement amounts to a 'collective investment scheme' within FSA 1986. The agreement to purchase the completed development, as a contract for the sale of land, need only satisfy LP(MP)A 1989, s 2, ie in writing, signed by both parties, and above all entire whether by reference or in substance.

Documentation

The documentation relating to a forward sale/funding arrangement will consist of the finance agreement, containing the undertaking by the institution to purchase the development on completion, and the detailed terms concerning the provision of finance and the way in which the development profit is to be shared. Since the final purchase price and the amount of the development profit are determined by the successful completion of the project, the letting provisions will be a fundamental part of the agreement. A similar letting policy to that followed in the case of profit-sharing lease arrangements may be adopted.

Liability

The fund will want to ensure it bears as little risk as possible and may require guarantees and additional security as well as warranties from contractors and professionals. The developer's covenant, whether or not supported by a guarantee, is pivotal, not least when the institution's investment decision is based upon a reliable income stream from the outset.

Funding

A forward sale or funding agreement is itself a method of raising finance. In a forward sale, the developer usually obtains the finance necessary to fund the development from a bank by way of debt. This is made easier by virtue of the fact that it already has a purchaser for the completed development. In a forward funding agreement, it is the institution which provides the interim finance. In return, the purchase price of the development may be lower than that which the institution would have to pay subsequently in the open market.

Distribution policy

The agreement between the parties will set out the basis upon which the development profit is to be shared. This will be further governed by any provisions in the funding agreement relating to priority yield, rental guarantee, erosion of developer's profit, etc.

Management structure

As a participatory joint venture, the forward sale/funding arrangement does not essentially involve joint management or decision-making. The institution's role is largely passive in this respect and it is the developer who will assume the day-to-day responsibilities related to the management of the development project. However, as provider of the finance, purchaser of the completed project, and co-participant in the risks involved, the institution will wish to exercise a measure of control (particularly in the case of a forward funding) and to this end will usually require all significant matters to be subject to its monitoring, inspection and approval. Approval of expenditure and quality control will have highest priority. Similar terms to those found in leasehold arrangements will also be included.

Tax treatment

Introduction

There are no specific features of the relevant tax legislation and practice that differentiate between a forward sale or forward funding arrangement and any other arrangement between a vendor, purchaser and funding party. However, the fact that a forward sale involves the sale of a building that is not yet in existence can give rise to conceptual difficulties.

Financing

In a sense, the financing arrangements are straightforward because there is no joint venture vehicle for tax purposes, only the separate parties. However, the need to obtain tax relief on any interest costs separately borne will remain of paramount significance, and it will be for each party to ensure that this is the case.

Operation of the forward sale or forward funding

(1) The developer will usually hold its interests in the land as trading stock. The other party may hold its interests as an investment or as trading stock.
(2) VAT is also an important factor in the context of these arrangements.

Summary of advantages and disadvantages

Advantages

(1) Developer obtains development finance at a favourable rate—because, at the time of obtaining the finance, it already has a contractually committed purchaser for the completed development (forward sale), or because it is the institution, who has completed its purchase at the outset, and who bears the interim costs (forward funding).
(2) The developer retains management control over the development—although the institution/fund will clearly exercise some control through a power of veto over certain decisions and, in the case of forward funding, control over advances of development cost.
(3) The institution acquires an investment suitable for its particular requirements at a price lower than that which it would have to pay for the completed development in the open market
(4) Savings on stamp duty—stamp duty is paid only once, on purchase of the site in the case of forward funding arrangements, and on completion of purchase of the finished development under a forward sale. Care is required in the preparation of documents to ensure this result actually ensues.

Disadvantages

(1) Developer must surrender a substantial share of the development profit to the institution/fund—as the price of cheaper finance, and so as to reflect the greater risk assumed by the fund.

(2) The relationship is unequal—with the provider of finance in a stronger negotiating position, able to dictate terms.

(3) Potential sources of conflict—due to differing objectives and the separateness of the parties. The interests of the parties are especially likely to diverge in relation to the letting provisions in the agreement.

(4) Relationship vulnerable to being construed as a partnership—which may lead to disadvantageous effects if the parties have drafted their agreement without taking PA 1890 into account. Furthermore, any third party wishing to sue one of the co-venturers may seek to argue that their relationship is one of partnership in order to acquire rights against both. (Under well drawn agreements for lease, an institution will safeguard its position by requiring the developer to undertake construction responsibilities direct to the tenant.)

(5) Developer retains no interest in the development—and after completion is therefore unable to participate in its future growth, but may retain obligations to secure lettings and meanwhile support the income of the purchaser/institution.

Chapter 7

Other contractual arrangements (overage payments)

General

In order to share with the developer the increased value of land following the grant of planning permission, a landowner may choose to enter into a contractual arrangement securing for itself an overage payment (ie a sum representing a proportion of the increased value and/or a proportion of the development profit), rather than enter into a sale alone. In this way, the landowner is able both to share in the development profit and to obtain a price for the land calculated on the basis of actual, and not estimated, values. Contractual overage payments are therefore a form of joint venture vehicle which may be 'forced upon' a developer by a landowner because of the latter's control over a valuable resource (ie land), vital to development. It is a joint venture which arises out of the landowner's desire to realise more—by extracting a share of the development profit—than it would do on a conventional sale. In addition, it enables the developer to hedge some of the risk, by not paying an excessive purchase price initially, before the end result of the project has been ascertained.

There are a variety of methods by which landowners may reserve to themselves an entitlement to participate in the increased value of their land if, for example, a more advantageous planning permission is granted in the future. The two principal criteria governing the choice of method will be:

(1) its tax implications; and
(2) whether the particular method provides effective security for the future payments.

As regards security, the landowner will be concerned to ensure that the structure chosen actually does enable him/her to compel the payments and that this is so even in circumstances of the purchaser's (ie developer's) insolvency, or as against the developer's successors in title. The problem here is that the right of a former owner of land to receive a proportion of its increase in value following the grant of planning permission is not recognised as a proprietary interest. It is no more than a profit-share agreement. The benefit and burden of such an arrangement is only personal to the original parties to the contract. What is needed is some additional mechanism which attaches the right to receive the payment to the land itself. A number of conveyancing devices are available to help achieve this. These include:

(1) mortgages;
(2) options;
(3) the imposition of covenants coupled with a right of re-entry (clawback);

(4)   a conditional contract;

(5)   a long lease.

Any one of these methods for participating in development profit may be chosen by a landowner contemplating disposal to a developer in preference to the joint venture vehicles already discussed. They are likely to be favoured over the alternative vehicles, such as a JVC or partnership, where the vendor landowner wishes to be a passive participant in the project and where there is longer-term development potential which is uncertain at the time the agreement is reached. Like the profit-sharing mortgage, overage payments may thus be regarded as participatory joint ventures. The landowner's role is essentially passive and the element of combination which is central to all joint ventures refers only to the sharing in the increased value of the land.

Mortgages

The inherent drawback of a mortgage in these circumstances is an inhibition on the developer/purchaser in raising finance. In practical terms, a bank mortgagee will not be attracted by such an arrangement unless given unlimited priority, and the security is thus limited. The practical result, if the developer's covenant is strong enough, is to rely only on positive covenants (see below) under a simple profit-sharing agreement.

Options

The structure

Option agreements have traditionally been viewed as advantageous to the developer rather than a landowner: the latter has its land tied up for the period of the option, while the former is under no obligation to enter into a contract to purchase the land. The decision to bring about a sale is therefore entirely the developer's alone, upon which the landowner waits. The developer's option is a 'call option', ie it is able to call upon the landowner to sell the land. A 'put option', where the landowner is able to call upon the developer to buy the land, is rare. There are advantages to an option agreement for a landowner. It is able to enhance the value of the land by obtaining the benefit of the developer's knowledge of development and planning processes. Further, a properly advised landowner may wish to induce a purchaser to perform his obligations and exercise the option by requiring a substantial option fee at the outset. This fee may, or may not, be part of the agreed purchase price.

In the case of a call option, the developer is entitled to exercise the option during its life and in accordance with the timetable laid down in the option agreement (However, it cannot exceed 21 years from the date of the grant of the option.)[1] The exercise price provided for by the option agreement will be either a fixed sum, or calculated in accordance with detailed valuation criteria contained in the option agreement. Longer-term options will often prescribe a formula to determine the price. A mere agreement to agree is void. In general, the option period should not be such that it ties up the land for too long. Nor should the period during which the overage payment is to be made be capable of easy evasion by the developer.[2]

A variant on this type of option agreement is the provision for cross-options. Here, the landowner grants the developer a call option to purchase the land during the agreed period (which should not exceed 21 years). In return, the developer grants the landowner a put option by reason of which the landowner may require the developer to purchase all or part of the land. Both options are exercisable only, for example, on the grant of planning permission or on the satisfaction of some conditions. The addition of the put option in the arrangement allows the landowner to bring about a sale, when economic circumstances may have led to an unwillingness on the part of the developer to exercise its call option. It therefore provides the landowner with some choice also over the timing of a sale. But, in both types of arrangement, the option is only realistically exercisable on an increase in value of the land, thereby enabling the landowner to participate in the enhanced value, and ultimately relies on the developer's ability to complete the purchase.

The landowner can grant an option which is only exercisable in the event that planning consent for new development or a change of use is obtained. In this case, the option agreement should describe, in as much detail as possible:

(1)   the planning consent which is to be obtained;
(2)   the timetable for obtaining it (which may need to allow some flexibility if the developer is to be allowed to appeal to the Secretary of State against a refusal by the planning authority); and
(3)   a mechanism for the resolution of disputes.

The developer will probably be required to undertake to use its best/reasonable endeavours to obtain the best planning consent. The agreement should define closely what is, and what is not, a satisfactory planning permission entitling either party to exercise its option. The agreement may cater for the involvement of the landowner in the planning process. For example, it may oblige the landowner to refrain from opposing an application for planning consent. It should also make it clear who is to meet the costs of obtaining planning consent.

Formalities

The potential difficulties surrounding the use of options as a result of LP(MP)A 1989, s 2 should be borne in mind. The cautious draftsman will include in any option agreement a mechanism to ensure the validity of the option, even in the face of the most pessimistic reading of s 2. As a result of the decision in *Spiro v Glencrown Properties*[3] (albeit at first instance only), options now granted in relation to land should be cast as conditional contracts.

Security

Provided that the trigger for the overage payment occurs prior to the exercise of the option, the landowner's security is absolute since title is retained. If the overage payment only became due on a subsequent sale of the property, after the option had been exercised, then the option arrangement would have done nothing to secure the payment to the landowner.[4] The developer should meanwhile protect its call option by registration:

- as a Class C (iv) land charge in the case of unregistered land
- by notice, restriction or caution in the case of registered land.

Otherwise, the option would not bind a successor in title of the landowner. Indeed, it is in the nature of a put option that, being in contract only, there is no interest against which the landowner can register it.

Tax treatment

Introduction For taxation purposes, there are two stages in the life of an option: its grant and its exercise. Each stage poses a potential tax charge.

Grant and exercise of the option The grant of an option is itself the disposal of an asset (the option) for tax purposes.

If the property concerned is held as trading stock, any money received on the grant of the option will normally constitute a trading receipt independent of money received upon the option being exercised.

However, if the land concerned is held as an investment, although any money received on the grant of the option will potentially generate a capital gain, upon the subsequent exercise of the option the money received on the grant of the option will be merged with the money received on the disposal of the land, which will be treated as a single transaction. Providing that the option is eventually exercised, therefore, in practice the capital gain on grant of the option will be held over.

VAT In broad terms, the VAT treatment of options over land follows the VAT treatment of the underlying land.

Imposition of covenants

An alternative method of securing the overage payment is the imposition of covenants in the freehold title, either restricting the user of the land until the overage payment is made, or permitting the developer to sell the land only on the condition that the sub-purchaser also enter into a direct covenant with the original landowner to make the payment. Restrictive and positive covenants raise different questions of enforceability and will be considered in turn.

Restrictive covenants

The structure On a sale of the land to the developer, the landowner may include in the transfer or conveyance a 'restrictive covenant' preventing the former from putting the land to any use other than its current one. This is coupled with an agreement to release or modify the covenant on receipt of the overage payment following planning permission. In practice, therefore, the developer must make the payment if it wishes to develop the land for occupation for a specific use. However, it may choose instead to sell the land, and the problem is whether the landowner can enforce the covenant against the developer's successors in title.

Security The developer remains liable under the original covenant for its breach by any sub-purchaser by reason of privity of contract. However, where the land is sold at or near its market value and/or the prospect of obtaining planning permission is speculative, a prudent developer may also insist that the covenant be expressed so as to bind it only during actual ownership. In any event, the landowner must somehow seek to ensure that the sub-purchasers can themselves be compelled to make the payment.

If the landowner retains land capable of being benefited by the covenant and the covenant 'touches and concerns' the land and is negative in substance, the sub-purchaser may be bound by the 'restrictive' covenant, without need of giving a further covenant itself, and thus be forced to pay for its release. However, it will be difficult for the landowner to retain land in a way which satisfies these conditions. Since the restrictive covenant is merely a device for securing the overage payment, it is unlikely that any retained land will be regarded as capable of being benefited by it. Moreover, the covenant looks more like a personal arrangement than one which benefits the landowner in his capacity as landowner, so that it is difficult to view it as touching and concerning the land.

A way round this problem would be for the landowner to reserve a right of re-entry on breach of the restrictive covenant. (In order to be enforceable against sub-purchasers as an equitable interest in land, a restrictive covenant must either be registered at HM Land Registry against the title (in the case of registered land), or the sub-purchaser must have notice of it by registration of a land charge class D (ii) (in the case of unregistered land).)[5] Nevertheless, even this will not provide the landowner with entirely effective security, for the sub-purchaser is entitled to apply to the court for relief against forfeiture. The Lands Tribunal also has jurisdiction to modify or set aside restrictive covenants and may discharge the covenant as impeding the reasonable user of the land once planning permission has been granted.

The right of re-entry may inhibit the developer in its ability to raise finance. However, the device is sometimes used and one body in particular, the Crown Estate, has such a mechanism apparently available to it enshrined in statute (see Chapter 12, The Urban Regeneration Agency).[6]

Tax treatment   The securing of overage payments by the use of a restrictive covenant is unlikely to have any taxation effects. Even if it is successfully argued that the overage payments are made purely for the removal of the restrictive covenant (and not as further consideration for the land), providing that the price for the land (pre overage) exceeds the capital gains base cost of the land in the hands of the landlord there will be no real tax effect. If the landowner holds the land as trading stock, there will be no effect even if the land is sold (pre overage) at a price below cost.

However, the VAT treatment accorded to the overage payments may be affected by the use of restrictive covenants. If the payments are regarded as relating to the release of the restrictive covenants, VAT at the standard rate will arise even where no VAT was chargeable on the disposal of the land.

Positive covenants

The structure   Here, the landowner imposes a positive covenant requiring the developer to make the overage payment during its ownership and, further, requiring it to ensure that any sub-purchaser enters into a direct covenant with the landowner to make the payment too. The burden of positive covenants cannot be made to run with the land, as with restrictive covenants. Some other method must be found, therefore, for securing the overage payment against the developer's successors in title.

Security   One method which has been suggested is to create a mortgage which is irredeemable until planning permission has been obtained. The landowner retains control over title and is thereby able to prevent a disposition of the land until the overage payment is made. However, inherent in every mortgage is the 'equity of redemption' which may lead to the sub-purchaser/mortgagor insisting on redemption before, for example, planning permission has been granted. The insertion of a redemption figure, index-linked to land prices, might accommodate the rule, but could entail undesirable tax consequences for the landowner. The structure is also inherently unattractive to a financier who is providing purchase monies secured by way of legal charge. Unless it is clearly seen that the particular security remains in place for a specific period only and the financier includes in his prospective advances an amount to cover payment of the overage (and release of the relevant security) and which he will see as only viable while he has priority over all other interests, it remains unattractive. It is always essential that the relevant security is specifically confined in terms of events of default which would trigger exercise of the mortgagee's rights, and banks are habitually assiduous in the pursuit of such aims.

Another possible method of ensuring the enforcement of the positive covenant is through the use of an estate rentcharge. For reasons mentioned below, however, the effectiveness of this method is strictly limited. Estate rentcharges are the only form of rentcharge which may now be created following the Rentcharges Act 1977. By s 2(4)(*a*), they include rentcharges created for the purpose of making covenants enforceable by the 'rent owner' against the owner for the time being of the land.

The rent charge deed is intended to ensure the enforceability of the positive covenant by a right of re-entry akin to forfeiture of a lease.[7] However, s 2(4)(*b*) confines the nature of the payments to matters of a management nature and, under s 2(5), any payment of more than a nominal amount, otherwise than for such purposes, effectively negates the rentcharge, and thus for practical purposes such a device is unsuitable for securing overage payments.

Both restrictive and positive covenants may therefore provide limited security for a landowner against sub-purchasers who fail to make the overage payment.

Tax treatment   The use of a rent charge will not usually have any taxation effect.

Conditional contract

The structure

The landowner may instead choose to enter into a conditional contract with the developer. The sale of the land is deferred until the condition specified, namely the grant of planning permission, occurs. This arrangement is similar to the grant by the landowner of an option, and may even be seen as conceptually identical following *Spiro*. However, the pure conditional contract is perhaps more appropriate where there appears to be an imminent likelihood of a grant of planning permission rather than where there is great uncertainty as to whether development will ever become possible and only at some indeterminate future date. The distinction, if any, is that once the essential condition (obtaining planning consent, for example) has been satisfied, there is no further requirement, save for administrative convenience, to serve notice to make the contract unconditional. The contract is then immediately enforceable by both vendor and purchaser.

Security

As in the case of an option, the landowner retains the freehold title to the land for the time being and thus its security is absolute since a sale of the land only takes place at the point when it has increased in value, in exchange for the basic price (if any) and the overage payment.

Tax treatment

For tax purposes, there will be no taxable event until the contract becomes unconditional.

Long lease

The structure

The use by the landowner of a long lease as the method for sharing in the increased value of its land is similar to the imposition of covenants. Here, the landowner might grant a lease for a period as long, perhaps, as 999 years, at a premium corresponding to the freehold value of the land. It is desirable, but not necessary, that the lease should contain restrictive user covenants, coupled with a right of re-entry. The right of re-entry also means that the developer is unable to enlarge the term into a fee simple under LPA 1925, s 153.

It should be noted that the benefit and burden of a covenant contained in a lease will only attach to the respective successors in title of the original contracting parties if the covenant touches and concerns the land.[8] This would almost certainly mean that a simple covenant by the tenant to pay a sum of money to the landlord would not run with the land. Such a covenant is thought to confer a purely personal advantage[9] (unless it is inextricably bound up with other covenants that touch and concern the land).[10]

Leases are also frequently used as a medium for sharing rents and it is not unknown for institutions to use such a method to structure a consortium of interests. Forfeiture of a superior interest is naturally prejudicial to an inferior one, requiring an inferior lessee to apply to the court for relief. However, where management effectively reposes in the first tier above occupation leases, the question is largely one of income flow alone and this tends towards allowing a broader view.

Security

In contrast to the imposition of freehold covenants, however, the landowner retains the freehold title and thus is provided with effective security for the overage payment. Furthermore, the jurisdiction of the Lands Tribunal to modify or discharge restrictive covenants is limited to applications made after at least 25 years of the term have elapsed, and the length of the lease enables the developer to raise finance. A long lease therefore affords more effective security than does the imposition of restrictive covenants and can be coupled with a tenant's option to acquire the freehold once the financial obligation has been met.

Tax treatment

There are no special taxation effects generated by the use of a long lease in this way.

---

[1] Perpetuities and Accumulations Act 1964, s 9.

[2] In *Briargate Developments Ltd v Newprop Co Ltd* (1989) 33 EG 42, an option agreement provided that the original landowner was entitled to a percentage of the sale price on a subsequent sale of the property by the developer/purchaser. However, it was only entitled to a share of the price of a sale made within 45 months of the exercise of the option. Within the period, the developer entered into an agreement to sell the property to a sub-purchaser, but under which the sub-purchaser was not to pay the purchase price until 19 days after the expiry of the 45-month period. In this way, the developer was able to avoid making the overage payment to the original landowner who, despite the misgivings of the judge, was ordered to specifically perform the contract of sale with the developer.

[3] [1991] 1 All ER 600.

[4] See *Briargate Developments Ltd v Newprop Co Ltd* (1989) 33 EG 42.

[5] See *Shiloh Spinners v Harding* [1973] AC 691.

[6] Crown Estate Act 1961, s 3(8).

[7] LPA 1925, s 121 confers a right of distress on all rentcharge owners in any event.

[8] *Spencer's case* (1583) 5 Co Rep 16 and LPA 1925, s 141 where the expression 'having reference to the subject matter' of the lease is used.

[9] *Re Hunter's Lease* [1942] Ch 124.

[10] *Moss Empires Ltd v Olympia (Liverpool) Ltd* [1939] AC 544.

Chapter 8

Dispute resolution and deadlock procedures

General

One matter common to all joint ventures is the need to provide for what is to happen in the event of a dispute or deadlock between the parties. Regardless of the structure adopted, the co-venturers should consider at the outset whether to adopt a procedure for resolving disputes. This is not to say, however, that the same dispute resolution procedures will be used on every occasion. Dispute resolution procedures nearly always confer on either party the right to refer the dispute to a third party, for determination. Within this broad framework, however, there is considerable scope for fine-tuning the drafting to meet the particular needs of the parties. Dispute procedures may also be confined to certain issues, leaving others for resolution by the court. Nevertheless, parties having considered the question may decide not to make specific provision on the basis that commercial pressures will cause them to find a practical solution. This is often a reasonable approach where the parties are of equal size or bargaining power. Where, however, one is significantly weaker than the other, failure to provide a mechanism may weigh against the weaker party.

Third party determination

The first question is whether the independent third party is to act as an expert or as an arbitrator. The disputes clause must identify the party who is to resolve the dispute, or the method by which he/she is to be appointed. It may occasionally be possible to name a specific professional person or firm to resolve the dispute. This has the advantage of reducing procedural delay to a minimum. There is clearly a risk, though, that because of death or incapacity, the person or firm is not available when a dispute arises. For this reason, it may not be appropriate to name the person or firm if the agreement is expected to endure for any appreciable length of time, and it will be more appropriate to refer to the third party generically as, for example, a solicitor, surveyor or accountant. The machinery will generally seek to determine the nature of the dispute first, so that it may be properly determined by the person or persons most concerned (see below). Indeed, the use of a generic description is preferred in nearly every case.

In the event that the co-venturers cannot agree on the third party to be appointed then the joint venture agreement will usually provide that either of them may apply to the president of a relevant professional body to make an appointment.

The disputes which can arise may be of various kinds. Interpretation of the terms of the agreement is best resolved by a lawyer while disputes relating to rentals or sale prices, for example, are more appropriately dealt with by a surveyor. Additionally if the parties cannot even agree as to the nature of the dispute then this question itself may be referred to a lawyer for determination.

Between the 'named individual' and the 'generic' approaches to the identity of the third party there lies a half-way house. This involves adding certain qualifying criteria to a generic description. For example, the clause may provide that the third party is to have been qualified for at least a given period of time. More specifically, the clause may require the individual to have exercised his or her profession in a given geographical, or specialist subject area.

Dispute resolution clauses can thus be structured in a variety of different ways. On occasion, the parties may make a decision to take a radically different approach to dispute resolution. They may, for example, make no provision for dispute resolution short of the termination of the joint venture. This option is most commonly encountered where the joint venturers have used a limited company.

Deadlock

The appropriate constitutive documents of the company (in the case of a JVC, its Articles of Association and Shareholders' Agreement if there is one) may provide for a situation known as 'deadlock'. Essentially this arises where each of the parties is given an equal say, or vote, in the management of the company, especially at Board level.

Participants frequently observe that dispute resolution clauses exist to encourage co-venturers to resolve disputes amicably. The rationale behind this is that timing is a crucial factor in any property development and disputes inevitably lead to lengthy delay. If this is the view of the co-venturers then the deadlock procedure may, perversely, suit their purposes well.

Even where the parties have identical voting rights, it is possible to provide for any deadlock to be resolved by appointment of an independent third party.

Clearly, this is a problem which does not arise in the same way in the case of participatory joint ventures where one party occupies an essentially passive role, for example that of a creditor. In other cases, although the passive partner will wish to exercise some control over the project, the element of joint decision-making is absent.

This can arise, for example, in certain circumstances, where a funder has an absolute discretion when granting or withholding its consent to some specified actions proposed by the developer. In other cases, it does not have this discretion and must be reasonable when making its decision. Such distinctions are common in development documentation and, indeed, in leases (including, not least, leases containing development obligations).

There is, however, a danger that financial institutions can often insist on retaining a power of veto that is perhaps too great and wide-ranging. This can give the impression that the financial institution is not as totally committed to the project as it was.

The stronger or dominant party is often able to impose its will on the other. Where the joint venture vehicle is a limited company, the majority voting shareholders are in a strong position in at least two respects. First, they have the advantage of being able to make decisions in the name of the company where these require ordinary resolutions. If their majority amounts to 75 per cent or more of the voting rights then they will also be able to ensure the passing of special resolutions. Secondly, minority shareholders will usually be unable to bring an action in the name of the company, in order, for example, to enforce the duties of directors and controlling members.

Minority shareholders

The otherwise unenviable position of minority shareholders may be mitigated by various actions, since a body of case law and statutory provisions has grown up to help protect them. Among the various ways in which minority shareholders may be able to obtain assistance, the following are worthy of note:

(1) The doctrine that the majority of the members must not commit a fraud on the minority.

(2) Sections 122 and 124 of the Insolvency Act 1986 confer on members a right to petition the court to wind up the company on the ground that it is just and equitable to do so.

(3) Section 459 of CA 1985 gives members the right to petition the court where the company's affairs are being conducted in a manner which is unfairly prejudicial to some or all of the members.

In addition, the rule in *Foss v Harbottle*[1] is subject to exceptions which favour minority shareholders. The exceptions concern the right of individual shareholders to bring derivative or representative actions in certain circumstances.

A derivative action is one which is brought by a shareholder to enforce a duty owed to the company.[2] It is a 'procedural device for enabling the court to do justice to a company controlled by miscreant directors or shareholders'.[3] The right to bring a derivative action does not contradict the rule in *Foss v Harbottle*. There must be some exceptional reason for permitting a minority shareholder or shareholders to bring an action on behalf of the company, which the company, acting through its Board and in general meeting, could bring for itself if it so wished. Thus, the right may arise where the behaviour of the majority amounts to a fraud on the minority.[4]

On other occasions, minority shareholders may be able to bring an action to protect some right of their own. This is known as a representative action. Such an action is brought by minority shareholders in their own name and not that of the company.[5] A representative action can be brought, for example, to prevent proposed acts where a special majority is required and has not been obtained.[6] It should be emphasised that a representative action is not available where the wrong complained of is simply a diminution in value of the shares of the company.[7]

Where, despite the existence of this protection, there is a possibility of a dispute/deadlock arising, some form of procedure for resolving it must be adopted. Certain disputes may be anticipated in advance and specifically provided for. But otherwise the co-venturers should agree upon a general mechanism which can be brought into operation in the event of unspecified disputes/deadlock. In some form or other, the mechanism used will probably be similar to one of those mentioned above.

Precautions

Co-venturers are often carried away by the optimism in which a joint venture is born and are prone to advocate a pragmatic approach to everything. They are usually critical of lawyers for being unduly pessimistic in insisting that thought should be given, at the outset, as to what is to happen in the event of dispute/deadlock. Yet to discuss and anticipate contentious areas at the commencement of their relationship can also remove areas of potential conflict and minimise the possibility of dispute between the co-venturers later. In addition, without any clear decision-making machinery there is a real risk that a participant may be locked into a joint venture which is stagnating, or has taken on a significantly different character or purpose.

Dispute resolution procedures (and an understanding of the limitations of the particular procedures adopted) are therefore essential to all joint ventures, corporate or otherwise, and the legal documentation should incorporate them as appropriate.

Minimising the possibility of dispute/deadlock

Although dispute resolution procedures are necessary, it is always preferable to ensure (or attempt to ensure) that disputes do not arise in the first place. The co-venturers can nevertheless take a number of preventative measures when structuring their relationship in order to minimise disputes.

(1) Choice of partner. The selection of partner is a vitally important matter affecting the likelihood of future disputes. The significance of the identity of a co-venturer is something which cannot be over-stressed. Having a financially powerful partner, for instance, reduces the risk of insolvency or default and is particularly important where the legal vehicle used for the joint venture is not one which is characterised by limited liability. Selecting as a partner an organisation with whom a good working relationship and a high level of mutual trust exists or is likely to develop does much to remove the possibility of future disputes. If the co-venturers have previously worked well together, this should also reduce the likelihood of future dispute/deadlock. Moreover, by ensuring at the start of the joint venture that there is a definite identity of interest, the co-venturers can contain possible sources of future conflict.

(2) Maintaining regular contact. Maintaining a regular and close contact with a partner, beyond that which is merely for the purposes of discussing the joint venture project itself, encourages a good relationship. This lessens the chances of misunderstandings or disputes. Even if disputes do arise, this may lead to them being resolved relatively quickly and amicably. Minimum requirements concerning mutual consultation can be written into the legal documents but the more important consideration is what happens in practice.

(3) Taking care over, and spending time on, the documentation. By spending time and by taking meticulous care in advance to ensure that all the terms of the joint venture are fully appreciated and well-thought through, any disputes arising out of them in the future may be more easily avoided. Co-venturers should identify issues or areas which may prove contentious and attempt to reach some agreement on them before actually embarking on the joint venture. All parties need to be fully aware of their responsibilities and should provide for the regular reporting and/or sharing of information. They might also choose to record points of principle and provide in the joint venture agreement that specific matters concerning important issues should be resolved in accordance with

those principles. This indeed is one of the most important reasons for having formal agreements.

(4) Effective management structure. The adoption of an effective management and communications structure also helps to minimise disputes.

Relevant considerations

Although there are a number of different mechanisms which may be used for resolving disputes, the procedure that co-venturers decide to use in their own particular case will be influenced by one or more of the following:

(1) The form of the joint venture vehicle. For instance, if a limited partnership has been chosen, the limited partners will be concerned to ensure that the consequences of the dispute procedure do not jeopardise their limited liability status. Indeed, not only the consequences of the dispute procedure, but the presence in the documentation of the procedure itself may affect their status if it means that the limited partners are to be regarded as able to take part in the management of the partnership business.

  The form of the joint venture vehicle may also affect the choice of a dispute/deadlock procedure in a more general way. The procedures discussed below are most appropriate in the case of genuine (co-operative) joint ventures, where there is joint management and joint decision-making. In the case of other types of joint venture, important matters of policy will usually be subject to the consent of the provider of the land or finance. Control is therefore exercised in a different way and at a different level. Although this power of veto could be seen as a potential precursor of a deadlock, in practice the greater bargaining strength of the landowner or financier (by reason of its control over essential inputs) will usually mean that the developer has to accommodate its wishes.

(2) Single or multi-project joint venture. Where there is a multi-project joint venture, the parties may prefer a deadlock procedure which enables each to retain those assets which it particularly desires, followed by a sale of the remaining assets not taken up by either/any of them. This may be preferable to winding up the joint venture and selling all its assets, or to a procedure which allows one co-venturer to buy the other(s) out. This is because it offers a more commercially viable timetable for the disposals, and for tax planning, than might be the case if there is a forced sale. It also provides the parties with the opportunity to control individual assets of the joint venture vehicle which they might wish to retain themselves, following the breakdown of the joint venture.

(3) The number of co-venturers. Where, for instance, there are an odd number of participants, and provided that unanimity in decision-making is not required, there may be no possibility of a dispute arising in the first place. Also, if there are more than two co-venturers, a dispute procedure such as the 'Russian Roulette' or 'Mexican Stand-off' procedure (which envisages only two participants)[8] is clearly inappropriate.

(4) Relative financial standing of the parties. Where the parties are of unequal financial standing, it may be that disputes cannot arise at all, because the smaller co-venturer has no choice but to comply (subject to what has already been said concerning minority protection). But where the parties do,

nevertheless, have equal decision-making power, any disparity in their wealth may render unsuitable certain dispute resolution procedures. For instance, the Russian Roulette/Mexican Stand-off buy-out procedure is capable of abuse by the stronger party in this situation, since it will be able to force a deadlock in order to gain control at a time of its choosing. The other party may therefore find itself in the unfortunate position of having its shares purchased at a price which it cannot afford to pay, but which nevertheless does not properly reflect their true value.

(5) Sale of development. The termination of the joint venture and sale of the project as a method for resolving dispute/deadlock is clearly unsatisfactory where the development is incomplete, as this will hardly secure the best price. Indeed the co-venturers are more likely to make a loss.

(6) Tax implications. Certain forms of dispute procedure may have unfavourable tax consequences. For instance, provisions giving either/both parties an option to buy out the other in the event of dispute/deadlock may in themselves threaten the availability of consortium relief.[9] Very often, implementation of a deadlock-breaking provision would produce an unsatisfactory tax position for both parties and serve to bring them to the negotiating table in order to improve the position of both.

Procedures for the resolution of disputes/deadlock

Disputes

The two main types of dispute which may arise between co-venturers are those over:

(1) The exact nature of their respective rights and obligations (ie over the construction of the documentation).

(2) The commercial policy or business strategy which should be followed.

Disputes of the first type are probably more typical, but disputes about policy will be particularly likely where supervening circumstances change the original intentions and/or alter the objectives of the parties. Where issues are likely to arise in the future, relating, for example, to design or letting, then a written policy will assist and, in the case of the examples given, should be regarded as essential.

Different procedures may be adopted according to the nature of the dispute. For instance, the parties may agree that disputes over the construction of the documentation should be resolved by referring them to an independent third party (see above). Alternatively, if the parties cannot agree on whether the rent at which it is proposed to let the building is the open market rent, this could be referred to a surveyor for determination. Matters such as type or mix of tenants, sub-division of units and so on, lend themselves admirably to a pre-determined 'letting policy' (only the implementation of which would be encompassed by dispute resolution). Again, a dispute could arise as to the amount properly payable under an overage arrangement. This might be referred to an accountant. Other types of dispute arise where what is at issue is a question of policy or commercial decision-making. It would clearly be inappropriate to refer a dispute of this type to a third party.

In the case of a funding agreement or profit-sharing lease, for example, one party or the other may have the final word on policy matters which arise, or there will be a fixed policy as indicated above. In the case of a limited company, the will of the majority is likely to prevail.

Deadlock

In the case of a deadlocked company, a variety of dispute resolution procedures are available to co-venturers.

(1) Silence/unanimity. The parties may decide not to provide in their agreement for a solution. The rationale here is that commercial pressures will be such that either or both will be forced to compromise and come to an agreement in the end. This may not be a satisfactory approach, as it could involve the joint venture project being held up for a considerable length of time. It may also allow the stronger party, for whom commercial/financial pressures will be less significant, to force its preferred course of action on the other. Instead therefore, co-ventures may provide for a 'cooling-off' period before the deadlock procedures come into operation. When a dispute arises, either party is thus permitted to serve on the other a formal notice of deadlock, after which a reasonable period is allowed in which the parties may yet seek to resolve the problem. This may be coupled with an obligation to bring in the Chairman or managing directors of parent companies so as to set a more 'distanced' view of any dispute. At the end of the period, they may then invoke the deadlock procedure chosen in their joint venture agreement.

(2) Termination and sale. The parties may provide that in the event of deadlock the joint venture should be brought to an end and the assets relating to it sold. This would normally be inappropriate where the development site is neither held by a JVC nor co-owned. Still less is it appropriate where the development is in progress and a return of capital cannot be realised. A deadlock in such circumstances will also be unattractive to a prospective funder to the joint venture. It is also a rather excessive reaction to a deadlock and, although—like silence—it might be seen as an incentive to resolve the dispute, it is unlikely to be favoured. Having said that, it is encountered in practice from time to time. As the risks of a dispute are comparatively great, selling the project is unlikely to be the way to realise the best price for it, especially if the development is incomplete. There may also be tax disadvantages to this procedure, as the distribution to the co-venturers of the net proceeds of sale probably constitutes a disposal for CGT purposes. Furthermore, termination followed by a sale of assets deprives both parties of the opportunity to bring the project to completion in the way which they had originally intended. For these reasons, co-venturers usually adopt one of the remaining deadlock procedures set out in (3)–(6) below.

(3) Referral to independent third party. This has already been discussed above. The third party may be an arbitrator or an expert, such as an independent surveyor. Arbitrators are skilled decision-makers and, acting in a quasi-judicial capacity, are thus subject to extensive control by the courts.

An expert is thus distinguished as an opinion-giver. If the clause states that his opinion shall be final and binding, it is likely to mean just that, with only manifest error being likely to avail an appellant of recourse to the court. An expert, however, is not immune from an action in negligence. Hence, he will rarely back his opinion with reasons.

The choice of whether to provide for a reference of disputes to an independent third party for resolution will depend on the type of project and the importance of the policy decisions which are likely to arise. For instance, this may be an appropriate method in the construction industry where there is little scope for policy-making, but it is essential that the project is completed on time. If the parties do favour this approach, it will be necessary to define the categories of differences and the basis upon which they can be referred to the appropriate experts. However, referral to a third party can involve considerable uncertainty and delay, and, further, requires the parties to surrender control over an important decision affecting the joint venture to an outsider. Some other procedure may therefore be preferred.

(4) Pre-emption rights. The joint venture agreement may provide that when deadlock arises, any restriction on transfer of shares is relaxed or even removed altogether. However, this will not in itself resolve the deadlock and it is questionable whether any third parties would be willing to buy into a deadlocked company.

(5) Buy out. The most common form of procedure adopted by co-venturers is a mechanism by which one can buy out the other. In choosing this procedure, the parties will have to bear in mind the possibility of unfavourable tax consequences, as buy out clauses may jeopardise the availability of consortium relief. The greater financial strength of one of the co-venturers may also be relevant. Nevertheless, they remain a popular method for resolving disputes. The exact form or terms of the buy out will vary, but the following are in common use:

(a) Russian Roulette/Mexican Stand-off. This system allows one co-venturer to offer to buy out the other at the price set by the offeror. The other party has a fixed period within which to accept. However, if it does not accept, or rejects the offer, it must instead buy the offeror's interest in the joint venture at the offeror's price. The theory is that this will result in a fair and realistic price being achieved, since the possibility that its own interest will be bought will inhibit the offeror from offering an unreasonably low price. Clearly, however, this will not work where there is a significant financial disparity between the parties so that the stronger can offer an unfair price safe in the knowledge that the other will nonetheless be unable to buy. This method is difficult (but not impossible) to implement where there are more than two participants in the joint venture.

(b) Piggyback. Here, one party offers to buy out the other at a stated price. If the other does not wish to accept the offer, it must then make a counter-offer, to which is added an increment fixed by the joint venture agreement. This process continues, with the price rising at each stage, until one party eventually accepts.

(c) Texas Shoot-out. This gives each co-venturer an option to purchase the other's interest at a price to be determined by an independent valuer. In the event of deadlock, the party with the 'fastest draw', ie the party which exercises its option first, gains control of the joint venture.

(d) Private auction. The parties may decide that the buy out should be determined by a private auction, with the highest bidder purchasing the other's interest. This, again, favours the financially stronger party.

(6) Sale of assets. Rather than sell the entire joint venture assets, or allow one to buy out the other, the co-venturers may prefer to bid for individual assets of the joint venture. Any assets which are not taken up by the co-venturers themselves

would then be sold to third parties. This method for resolving disputes/deadlock is particularly attractive where there is a multi-project joint venture between the parties, for the reasons given above. As a means of dispute resolution, this procedure must be given formal effect in the joint venture documentation.

Whatever means for resolving disputes are in fact adopted, the parties may also choose to include 'anti-abuse' provisions in their agreement, perhaps by introducing wording which renders the creation of an artificial deadlock a breach of the agreement. However, precisely what is an 'artificial' deadlock is inevitably highly subjective. Thus this type of anti-abuse provision will always be vulnerable to litigation.

---

[1] (1843) 2 Hare 461.
[2] See *Wallersteiner v Moir* (No 2) [1975] QB 373.
[3] *Nurcombe v Nurcombe* [1985] 1 WLR 370.
[4] See, for example, *Cook v Deeks* [1916] 1 AC 554.
[5] See, for example, *Hogg v Cramphorn* [1967] Ch 254.
[6] *Edwards v Halliwell* [1950] 2 All ER 1064.
[7] *Prudential Assurance Co Ltd. v Newman Industries Ltd (No 2)* [1982] 1 All ER 354.
[8] See p 104, para (5)(a).
[9] Finance (No 2) Act 1992, s 24 and Sched 6. Note an extra-statutory concession (replacing C10) will not treat 'trigger events' as 'arrangements'.

Chapter 9

The Financial Services Act 1986

'Collective investment schemes'

The provisions of the Financial Services Act 1986 ('FSA 1986') relating to the regulation of 'collective investment schemes' can have significant implications for all joint venture vehicles and must be considered closely by those who decide to engage in them. Failure to comply with the Act may, for instance, give rise to criminal liability.

Definition: the scope of the Act

By FSA 1986, s 75(1), a 'collective investment scheme' is defined as:

> 'any arrangement with respect to property of any description... the purpose or effect of which is to enable persons taking part in the arrangements (whether by becoming owners of the property or any part of it or otherwise) to participate in or receive profits or income arising from the acquisition, holding, management or disposal of the property or sums paid out of such profits or income.'

This wide-ranging definition clearly threatens to encompass all forms of joint venture vehicle, of which a central feature is always profit participation. It may even extend to profit-sharing lease arrangements, which are an important financing technique. However, the scope of the definition is limited in two ways:

(1) An arrangement will only constitute a collective investment scheme if some of its participants do not have 'day to day control over the management of the property in question'. The right to be consulted or to give directions will not, for these purposes, amount to having such control.[1]
(2) An arrangement will only be a collective investment scheme if *either* the contributions of the participants and the profits or income out of which payments are to be made, are pooled *or* the property in question is managed as a whole by or on behalf of the operator of the scheme.[2]

Co-venturers adopting participatory forms of joint venture vehicle must therefore ensure that they come within one of the exemptions specifically provided for in the Act.[3] If they do not do so, they will constitute collective investment schemes: this has the regulatory and taxation consequences set out below.

The regulation of 'collective investment schemes'

(1) Authorisation. The person operating the scheme must be authorised.[4] Membership of IMRO normally satisfies this requirement.

(2) Marketing. Significant restrictions are placed on the manner in which collective investment schemes may be marketed. For instance, advertisements marketing them must be issued or approved by an authorised person[5] and advertisements inviting persons to participate in the collective investment scheme may only be issued by an authorised person where the scheme is an authorised unit trust, or a foreign scheme, recognised under the Act.[6]

(3) Taxation. An authorised collective investment scheme will be taxed as an authorised unit trust. Capital gains made by such a unit trust are not taxable. Otherwise it is taxed as if it were a company, save that the rate of corporation tax is linked to the lower rate of income tax.

(4) Sanctions for non-compliance with the Act's provisions.[7] Non-compliance with the requirements of the Act may entail criminal liability. The penalty for operating a collective investment scheme without authorisation is a fine and/or imprisonment. It is also an offence to issue an advertisement without authorisation.

The arrangements may be unenforceable in the absence of a court order. Invariably the process of obtaining a court order is likely to be time-consuming and expensive. Furthermore, an obligation to indemnify the investors may arise out of a failure to comply with s 76 (which imposes restrictions on the promotion of collective investment schemes).

The potentially adverse tax consequences and the expense and inconvenience of having to comply with FSA 1986 will often lead co-venturers to ensure that their joint venture arrangements either cannot be regarded as collective investment schemes, or come within one of the Act's exemptions. Alternatively, if this cannot be avoided, they should ensure that they have fulfilled the Act's requirements in order to escape criminal liability and/or the unenforceability of their scheme.

Exclusions and exemptions

Most co-venturers will prefer to structure their joint venture so that it either falls outside the definition of a collective investment scheme, or comes within one its exclusions/exemptions, rather than have to comply with the Act. The limitation in s 75(2), which means that the definition of collective investment scheme includes only arrangements where some of its participants do not have day-to-day control over the property, will prevent most joint ventures (ie genuine joint ventures), coming within the Act's regulatory provisions. This means that genuine (ie co-operative) joint ventures, such as the JVC and partnership, will escape the Act's regulatory provisions since these forms of joint venture vehicle involve joint management and decision-making. Furthermore, companies are in any case excluded from the Act under s 75(7), although the marketing restrictions do apply to companies. The marketing of shares in companies is subject to its own regulatory regime.[8]

Those engaging in participatory joint ventures, however, will have to look to the exemptions contained in s 75(5) and (6) and try to bring themselves within one of them. However, limited partnerships will not be saved by this provision as the limited partners are not permitted to take part in the management of the partnership business. Participatory joint ventures are also vulnerable to the Act, since these are characterised precisely by the absence of joint management (the passive participant(s) in practice having no rights in relation to the day-to-day management of the joint venture).

As regards joint ventures, the most relevant of the exemptions is contained in s 75(6)(*b*), which provides that 'arrangements where each of the participants carries on a business other than investment business[9] and enters into the arrangements for commercial purposes related to that business', are not collective investment schemes. Most participants in property joint ventures will not be regarded as carrying on investment business since the majority of joint ventures have a trading objective. However, the exemption may not cover all participatory joint ventures, which often involve at least one participant (a landowner or financier) who has an investment objective. It may also be difficult to view a landowner, or a co-venturer participating in a joint venture for the first time, as carrying on a business other than investment business. Furthermore, pension funds and investment funds taking part in joint ventures may also fall outside the subsection.[10] A possible way round this problem is the argument that a collective investment scheme does not arise unless there are two or more participants, ie the party who would otherwise be entitled to 100 per cent of the profits shares its returns with two or more other participants. This, if correct, might provide an escape route for most participatory joint ventures, but it is, as yet, uncertain whether such an argument would impress the courts.

Implications for joint ventures

(1) JVC. Companies are not regarded as collective investment schemes for the purposes of FSA 1986 and participants in this form of joint venture vehicle need only take note of the restrictions in the Act relating to the marketing of shares.

(2) Partnership. If the partnership is a co-ownership partnership and detailed provisions are included in the trust deed, the joint venture could be deemed to be an unauthorised unit trust with FSA consequences. Moreover, unless all the partners are actively engaged in the management of the joint venture project, the partnership could constitute a collective investment scheme and this may therefore be of concern where a pure investor wishes to be a 'sleeping' partner. However, in most partnerships all the partners will be involved in the day-to-day management of the property and/or each of them will carry on non-investment business and the partnership will therefore escape the Act's provisions.

(3) Limited partnership. A limited partnership will usually be regarded as a collective investment scheme for the purposes of the FSA because its participants 'do not have day-to-day control over the management of the property in question'. The general partner will therefore need to be authorised under the Act.

(4) Profit-sharing leases. Profit-sharing leases would, on a literal interpretation of FSA 1986, seem to fall within the Act's provisions on collective investment schemes. However, it seems unlikely that the Act was intended to cover such arrangements.

(5) Profit-sharing mortgages. Profit-sharing mortgages, especially participating mortgages, would also seem to constitute collective investment schemes. If participants wish to avoid the consequences of this, they will therefore need to ensure that the exemption concerning those carrying on non-investment business applies.

(6)   Contractual overage arrangements. These too may be deemed to be collective investment schemes. Again, participants will either have to try to include themselves within one of the statutory exemptions, or comply with the Act's regulatory provisions.

In general, most joint venture vehicles will escape the FSA provisions on the basis that they are not carrying on 'investment business' or because each co-venturer exercises day-to-day control over the management of the property. However, *all* profit-sharing arrangements must be carefully considered with the Act in mind. In particular, participatory joint ventures are especially vulnerable to the wide-ranging definition of 'collective investment scheme' contained in s 75(1) and (2), and it may be difficult to structure them so as to avoid the Act, if this is an overriding objective.

---

[1] FSA 1986, s 75(2).
[2] FSA 1986, s 75(3)(*a*) and (*b*).
[3] FSA 1986, s 75(6).
[4] FSA 1986, s 3 and Sched 1, para 16.
[5] FSA 1986, s 57.
[6] FSA 1986, s 76(1).
[7] FSA 1986, ss 3, 57.
[8] See FSA 1986, Pt IV and V.
[9] As defined in FSA 1986, s 1(2).
[10] There is an argument that the joint venture business could be construed as a separate business from that of the fund's investments, but it is far from clear that the Act allows such a distinction to be drawn.

Chapter 10

Taxation

The very different structures of joint ventures (different from a legal if not an economic point of view) give rise to a varied range of tax treatments. The difficulty is to summarise those different tax treatments in a digestible form.

The approach adopted is to focus on the different stages in the life of a joint venture, highlighting the differing tax effects in the use of the principal available structures. (It is not possible to consider every ramification but this chapter provides an overview of the main issues involved.)

Formation of the joint venture vehicle

Introduction

In practice, there are two quite separate tax dimensions to consider and resolve at this stage:

(1) How it is anticipated that the joint venture itself will be conducted (and this will include the plans of the joint venturers themselves in relation to the undertaking, the way in which they anticipate that the profits will be generated as well as how they envisage that the joint venture will deal with the property over the life of the venture itself).

(2) The effect that the joint venture will have on the pre-existing tax position of the joint venturers themselves, including in particular the effect of transferring any existing property interests into the joint venture at the outset.

Conduct of the joint venture

It is conceivable but unlikely that a property joint venture will be entirely tax-driven. It is therefore assumed that the potential venturers have a clear idea of the way in which they propose that the joint venture will deal with the property in order to generate profit. This does not mean that they are uninterested in retaining as much flexibility as possible to allow for a change of plan in the future should it be necessary.

By far the most important decision to make at this stage is whether it is anticipated that the joint venture will be undertaking a trading or an investment activity.

Trading v Investment—the initial dilemma   Although whether an undertaking is one of trading or investment has little, if any, effect on the VAT and stamp duty position, it does have fundamental significance for the corporation tax/income tax position.

It is important to appreciate that it is not possible for a single property to be held by the same person at the same time as both an investment asset and a trading asset. Nor is it possible to hold a single property as neither a trading nor an investment asset. Moreover, using a single joint venture vehicle to hold a mix of trading and investment assets is possible but not recommended, because it is likely to provoke continuous scrutiny by the Inland Revenue and serious errors in accounting treatment are more likely to occur with a knock-on tax effect.

In practice, the best starting point for resolving this issue is for the joint venturers to ask themselves whether they see the main thrust of the venture as related to profit generated from sale of the property or from rental income derived from its retention or an interest therein. In this way, it is frequently possible to determine with relatively little difficulty whether trading (ie sale) or investment (ie letting) is primarily to be involved. The only further caveats required, at least in very straightforward cases, are that the route chosen should be properly documented and followed consistently for accounting and other purposes and that no change should be made in the chosen route without first taking proper further tax advice.

Unfortunately, there are many occasions when such a straightforward approach is simply not possible and in those cases it will be necessary to delve more deeply into the distinctions between trading and investment.

The distinction between trading and investment is based on intention. Therefore, if intention is clearly and consistently recorded at the relevant time and nothing is done subsequently to undermine that record of intention, the undertaking will be regarded accordingly as one of trading or investment. If a different intention is subsequently recorded or the behaviour of the parties is such that it is clear that there has been a change of intention, the status of the undertaking as one of trading or investment will be regarded as having changed as of the relevant time. This change in itself may generate a tax charge and is not to be contemplated lightly.

Where the status is not clear and in deciding if or when there has been a change of status, other factors become important in order to determine the issue. These include:

(1) the objects clause (if the joint venture vehicle is a company);
(2) extraneous evidence regarding intention (eg type of valuations carried out);
(3) financing arrangements (eg short-term finance may not appear compatible with an investment strategy);
(4) the net income producing profile of the property (eg does the arrangement 'stack up' as an investment strategy?);
(5) period of ownership (a short period gives the impression of dealing and not investing);
(6) immediate reason for disposal of property (eg shortage of funds, alternative strategy, etc);
(7) the track record of the joint venturers (it is assumed that past traders tend not to become investors and vice versa); and
(8) other extraneous factors such as applications for planning consent etc which may throw light on real intentions.

To illustrate some of the issues involved, the following cases were decided by the courts on the distinction between trading and investment.

(1) *Tempest Estates v Walmsley* (1975) 51 TC 305 . Land with development potential and some rental income was purchased in 1946 without any intention
regarding that land being clearly recorded (although the land was shown in the
company's accounts as an investment). In 1963, part of the land was transferred
to trading stock in the company's books and then sold. It was confirmed by the
court that it was reasonable for the Special Commissioners to have found that
the whole of the land had always been held as trading stock because it was clear
that the directors had always intended to hold the land only until such time as
its full development potential could be realised (and the rental income generated in the meantime was relatively small).

(2) *Tebrau (Johore) Rubber Syndicate v Farmer* (1910) 5 TC 658. The intention to
develop the land and then hold it as an investment was well documented. In the
event, the land was sold because, on appraising the cost of development, it was
found that the company would be unable to fund the operation. The decision
of the General Commissioners was overturned by the court, who found that the
company had not undertaken a trading transaction.

(3) *Commissioners of Inland Revenue v Toll Property Co Ltd* (1952) 34 TC 13. The
intention to sell the land once the price was right had been documented. Even
though the land was then held for about six years, during which time it
yielded a very good rental income indeed, the decision of the General
Commissioners was overturned by the court which found that the rental
income was irrelevant given the original intention, and the company had
therefore been trading.

(4) *Lionel Simmons Properties Ltd (in liq) v Commissioners of Inland Revenue* (1980)
53 TC 461. The intention to build up an investment portfolio of properties was
well documented. This was achieved by selling properties and reinvesting the
proceeds in better properties and so on. Eventually, all of the properties were
sold and the company wound up. The court overruled the General
Commissioners and found that all of the transactions (including final sale) were
investment and not trading transactions.

There are many other relevant cases but the above should assist the reader in
appreciating some of the danger areas.

Where the dilemma cannot be resolved In circumstances where the venturers are
unsure of their intentions regarding the land, it is safer to commence as an investment joint venture and change later to a trading venture than it is to undertake the
reverse process. This is because of the effect of the decision in *Sharkey v Wernher*
(1956) 36 TC 275 combined with Taxation of Chargeable Gains Act 1992, s 161
(2). The consequential effect is that a trading property becoming an investment
property is treated as having been disposed of at that point at market value for
corporation tax or income tax purposes.

However, in the case of an investment property changing to a trading property,
there is a similar tax charge, but also an election under s 161 (3) that can be used
effectively to merge the tax charge into the base cost of the property, so that no tax
is payable until actual disposal (when tax will in any case be payable on normal principles).

Investment (but not trading) properties are eligible for indexation relief on cost.
However, there are also circumstances where expenditure is allowable for trading but

not investment purposes and, if sufficiently substantial, this could militate against the use of an investment treatment, despite the points made above.

The tax position of the joint venturers

The joint venturers will want to know what tax effect their entering into the joint venture will have on their own pre-existing tax positions.

A joint venturer that is a property trader in its own right Where one or more of the joint venturers is (or has been) a trader in its own right, it is particularly important that the joint venture is clearly documented from the outset if the presumption that it is a trading joint venture is to be avoided. By contrast, the fact that a property trader has entered into an investment joint venture will not normally have a tendency to recharacterise its other trading activities as investment activities.

If one of the joint venturers introduces property that it has held as trading stock into a joint venture where the property will be held as an investment, then for corporation tax and income tax purposes there will always be a deemed disposal by that venturer of the property at market value.

However, where the joint venture will be continuing to hold the property as a trading asset, there are circumstances where such an initial charge can be avoided in whole or in part:

(1) where the joint venture arrangements do not involve an actual disposal of the property from one venturer to the other or to a legally distinct vehicle, such as a JVC; and

(2) Where the venturers are entering into a partnership with each other (but it is necessary here to rely on Inland Revenue practice, which is to a substantial extent unpublished, and it is therefore necessary to proceed with great caution).

A joint venturer that is a property investor in its own right Where a joint venturer which is (or has been) a property investor in its own right enters into a trading joint venture, it should take particular care to fully document its intention so that the joint venture does not have the effect of recharacterising its other activities as trading.

If a joint venturer introduces property that it has held as an investment into a joint venture where the property will be held as trading stock, there will always be a deemed disposal for corporation tax and income tax purposes by that venturer of the property at market value. An election to postpone such a charge to tax is possible only if the joint venturer is the same legal person carrying on the trading activity. In the case of a 'joint venture' in the form of a trading partnership, such an election must be made by all of the partners and not merely by the partner contributing the property (Taxation of Chargeable Gains Act 1992 s 161 (4)).

However, where the joint venturer will be continuing to hold the property as an investment, an initial charge may be avoided on a similar basis to that appertaining to continuing trading stock (see above).

Generally The actual transfer of property into the joint venture will potentially be subject to stamp duty (normally at 1 per cent of consideration). However, the position is complex and it is sometimes possible to avoid stamp duty altogether by careful structuring.

VAT will also be a factor where an actual transfer of the property is involved. In addition to the possibility that VAT must be charged on the property transfer, it will frequently be necessary to seek a separate VAT registration for the joint venture vehicle. Such a registration will certainly be required for a JVC (unless, unusually, the JVC can be included in a VAT group registration and that is felt to be desirable) or a partnership. Registration will normally also be required for joint ownership and similar arrangements that fall short of constituting a partnership.

Ongoing operation of the joint venture vehicle

Introduction

Most joint ventures are entered into in the anticipation that they will not run on more or less indefinitely. However, some are expected to generate ongoing profits, perhaps over a relatively long period, while others are entered into with a view to profit arising only at the end of the life of the joint venture (for example on the construction and sale of a single property).

Even if profits are not anticipated to arise until the end of the venture, there may be accounting losses arising in earlier tax years which in themselves can be utilised by the joint venturers and therefore give rise to economic value derived from the enterprise. Consequently, unless a joint venture is of sufficiently short duration as to take place within a single tax year or tax accounting period (as appropriate) of all those involved, there will be tax issues related to the ongoing operation of the joint venture as well as its final stage.

Financing

From a taxation point of view, there are two major issues:

(1) Whether the joint venture vehicle (if a legally distinct entity) is entitled to a tax deduction for interest and similar costs.
(2) Whether losses generated within the joint venture vehicle can be utilised by the venturers themselves for tax purposes.

Deductibility of interest in the hands of the joint venture vehicle Where the form of the vehicle is such that there is no separate legal entity, there is no question of that entity obtaining a tax deduction for interest paid and the venturers must look directly to their own tax positions. A partnership straddles this situation because, although not strictly a separate legal entity in England and Wales, it is effectively treated for tax purposes (including VAT but not stamp duty) as if it did have a legal identity apart from the partners.

Where the vehicle does have a separate legal identity, it is important to determine precisely how (and when) it will be entitled to such tax deductions. Again, the question of whether a trading or investment activity is involved is an important ingredient. If the venture is a trading one, the interest must be treated as a trading expense following the decision in *Wilcock v Frigate Investments Ltd* (1981) 55 TC 530 even if an alternative basis of deduction is also technically available. Normally, the trading deduction treatment is preferable for timing reasons (although, in the rather unusual circumstances of the *Wilcock* case referred to above it was not).

Generally speaking, the most important point about interest treated as a trading deduction is the inclusion of accrued interest independently of its being debited to an account (let alone actually paid, as opposed to accrued, during the period concerned).

The alternative basis of deduction (which is the only basis available to an investment vehicle) is restricted in timing terms to actual payment of interest (or actual debiting of interest in the case of certain bank interest). Unfortunately, the rules under this basis of deductibility are also complicated by the concept of 'short' as opposed to 'annual' interest.

In the case of interest paid by companies, partnerships in which a company is a partner, or (generally) to a person whose 'usual place of abode' is outside the UK, it is also important to establish from the outset whether income tax at the basic rate should be deducted from the payments made, taking into account the detailed legislation, relevant double tax treaty, etc.

Use of joint venture tax losses by the venturers   If a joint venture is ongoing and involves substantial costs (including interest) during the early stages, the venturers will normally wish to utilise those losses against their own tax liabilities. Obviously, if the joint venture vehicle does not have a separate legal identity, the losses will be those of the joint venturers, with no further ado. However, where the vehicle has its own legal identity (eg a JVC), the position is more complex.

Losses generated by partnerships other than limited partnerships will flow through to the partners as one would expect (providing that there is at least one partner that is a company, otherwise losses are not necessarily shared between the partners in the expected proportions). In the case of limited partnerships, the availability of tax losses to the limited partners is itself limited to the extent of their respective financial contributions to the partnership, even though their participation in taxable profits may well be uncapped.

In the case of a trading JVC, its tax losses will be available (upon a formal claim and surrender) to corporate joint venturers only, broadly speaking in proportion to their shareholdings. There are complex rules restricting the availability of such losses effectively where the financial structure of the JVC is such that real participation in it is not fully reflected in a single class of ordinary shareholdings. The existence of options over shares, loans that entitle the lender to participate etc must all be carefully considered when establishing the structure of such a JVC.

In the case of an investment JVC, the ongoing losses cannot be surrendered even to corporate joint venturers. In those circumstances, an investment partnership is often the preferred vehicle.

Other considerations

Rental Income   Rental income (ignoring that derived from fully serviced office accomodation and similar, where property is really only a small part of what is being provided, and temporary lets of a trader's own premises) is invariably investment and not trading income, even where that income is received by a joint venture vehicle in respect of property held as trading stock.

Furnished letting has its own regime but otherwise rental income is chargeable to tax (ie corporation tax or income tax) under Sched 1 of the Income and Corporation

Taxes Act 1988. It is important to appreciate that, technically if not always in practice, rental income is taxable on an entitlement basis, rather than upon actual receipt of the rent concerned. Rent is also classified according to whether a full rent is being charged and whether it is being charged under a tenant's repairing lease for the purpose of deciding whether net losses under one lease can be set against net profits on another for tax purposes.

It should also be borne in mind that VAT is chargeable on rent in respect of non-residential property if the relevant landlord has elected to Customs & Excise that the property is to be treated as subject to VAT.

The amount of rent can also be an important feature of a lease in determining how much stamp duty is payable on the relevant document.

VAT   VAT is an important tax in the property world, because the amounts can be very substantial and the rules relating to VAT in a property context are particularly complex. In the course of operating a property joint venture, it is very likely that the question of recovery of a substantial amount of VAT will arise at some stage and the venturers will want to be sure that such VAT will indeed be recoverable by the venture, and promptly.

Full coverage of the VAT treatment of property transactions is outside the scope of this book but a very broad appreciation of the main issues likely to be involved can be obtained by understanding the following:

(1)   The VAT legislation starts from the premise that transactions in land (including the letting of land) are exempt for VAT purposes.

(2)   There are, however, major exceptions including the sale of the freehold of a newly-constructed commercial building (standard rated, currently 17½ per cent) and the sale of the freehold or grant of a long lease of a newly constructed residential building (zero rated).

(3)   Even more importantly, it is possible for the owner of a commercial building to choose to render it taxable at the standard rate. This is usually done because the making of exempt (but not zero rated) supplies renders the supplier unable to recover the VAT costs that it has incurred in respect of that property.

(4)   In some circumstances, mainly involving commercial buildings with sitting tenants, it is also possible to arrange matters so that a taxable property is transferred without VAT actually being charged on the purchaser. These transfers are known as 'transfers of a going concern' or 'TOGCs'.

Stamp duty   Stamp duty is also particularly relevant to the property world, again because the amounts involved tend to be large and also because the effective rates of charge can in some circumstances be particularly draconian, eg on a lease the rate can be as much as 24 per cent of the annual rent payable as well as 1 per cent of any premium paid. The relevant rules are also among the most complex and the requirement to register certain types of transactions in land, combined with the general requirement by lenders that there be no possible doubt regarding legal status and documentation in relation to the relevant land, makes stamp duty on property amongst the more difficult to avoid in practice.

The main charge to duty arises at 1 per cent on the conveyance or transfer of land on a sale. In some circumstances, duty can arise on a mere agreement to sell an interest in land without an actual transfer or conveyance taking place.

The premium charged on the grant of a lease is similarly charged at 1 per cent of the premium. However, there is also duty charged on the rent payable under the lease. The rate of duty chargeable increases (to a maximum effective rate of 24 per cent) in bands according to the length of the lease. The longer the lease, then (subject to the banding) the higher the rate of duty.

There have been important changes recently (the Finance Act 1994) to the way in which documents effecting transactions where the consideration, rent etc cannot precisely be evaluated at the time the documents are stamped. Very broadly speaking, such transactions are now stamped based upon the property values involved. Previously, it was often possible to avoid any substantial duty.

There is an important relief available under Finance Act 1930 s 42 where transfers of assets (including land) are made between associated companies. A 90 per cent shareholding test must be passed and there are important anti-avoidance measures. It is nevertheless a very important and frequently used relief, which must be formally claimed using a statutory declaration as the sworn evidence that the relief is due.

The end of the joint venture

Introduction

The end of the venture and its timing may have been carefully planned from the outset or it may have been effectively forced by events. Clearly, it is easier to ensure that the winding up of the venture is carefully planned so that it is carried out in the most tax efficient way, if it is part of a long term strategy.

Where the joint venture is not a separate legal entity

In such circumstances, the end of the joint venture may well consist of the sale of the respective interests in the property. Alternatively, the end of the venture may simply consist of the ending of a business relationship with no financial effect other than that profits from that source will come to an end. In either case, the taxation arrangements will be primarily a matter for the venturers on their separate tax bases, although the question of timing may still be of importance to all involved and that, in itself, may require some serious joint planning.

Where the joint venture is a separate legal entity

In these circumstances, the planning required can become particularly complex. Not only is the timing and form of the end of the joint venture of importance to the venturers in terms of their respective tax positions, it is also of great importance that the joint venture vehicle itself bears the minimum amount of taxation so that the maximum profits are available to be passed in the planned form on to the joint venturers themselves.

Partnerships Broadly speaking, when a partnership is wound up, each partner will be treated as if it had disposed of a proportion of each asset owned by that partnership. In other words, profits or losses will usually be generated which will fall directly to the account of the partners. If certain assets are disposed of before the partnership comes to an end, the effective split of those profits and losses between the partners may be different (if only because the partnership deed may deal with ongoing profits in a different way from the position on dissolution). Furthermore, the timing of capital withdrawals may also effect the individual positions of the partners. Where there are no corporate partners, the position is likely to be even more complex.

If a partner wishes to take assets in satisfaction of its share of profits (or return of capital), it is necessary to ascribe a market value to the asset taken both for partnership accounting and for taxation purposes. (The VAT and stamp duty implications will also need to be watched carefully.)

The most important point, however, is that there is no second tier of taxation as there is in the case of a JVC.

JVCs   The end of the venture may or may not involve the winding up of the JVC itself. However, if the JVC is a trading vehicle, the end of the venture will normally involve cessation of trading and there is little attraction from a taxation point of view in retaining a UK company as a cash depository in any event.

Although, if successful, the JVC will realise a trading profit or capital gain on disposal of the property upon which it will have to pay corporation tax, it is important to appreciate that there will also potentially be tax payable by the joint venturers on the disposal or deemed disposal of their shares in the JVC, if it is wound up or sold.

One of the issues to address is whether to dispose of the property and pay up the profit to the venturers by way of dividends, subject to ACT. This is frequently advantageous but depends on the nature and circumstances of the joint venturers and it is necessary to make the relevant comparative calculations on the basis of the particular circumstances. There are also cashflow implications, as well as the question of the absolute tax charges involved.

General

It would seem particularly appropriate at the end of a chapter on taxation to point out that the forgoing constitutes a very broad overview. In addition, given that taxation is sufficiently complex (and convoluted) to render it almost impossible to make a statement to which an exception cannot arise in some circumstance or another, the reader is warned not to take any action without first obtaining specific professional advice.

Chapter 11

Local authority partnerships

General

Where a local authority owns land, various alternatives are available to achieve implementation of a project. Not all the available alternatives will necessarily be suitable for all sites, but depending on the circumstances there will be a degree of choice with advantages and disadvantages attached to each.

The alternatives range from outright freehold or long leasehold disposal to the private sector in return for a capital payment, to direct development with no private sector involvement at the other extreme. In between there are a variety of possible different partnership arrangements which in themselves cover a spectrum of local authority risk taking. These include 'four-slice' arrangements (traditionally used in many town centre and prime office schemes), where most of the risk is taken by the private sector; to two-slice lease arrangements where most, if not all, risks are taken by the local authority.

There have been yet other arrangements which do not neatly fall into any of these categories where, for example, the local authority had no land ownership but yet guaranteed a rental income to the developer, or took a head lease (ie pre-let) itself.

The most common form of partnership agreements are ground lease or profit-sharing arrangements and therefore much of this chapter will be applicable to these arrangements, as the local authority is no more than a particular type of freehold landowner, governed by statutory regulations rather than purely market forces. Furthermore, a developer may enter into some form of separate joint venture with a funder, as described in earlier chapters in order to implement the partnership development with the local authority.

Types of partnership arrangement

Most partnership agreements involve a division of responsibilities at different stages of the development process and risk is rarely shared equally. The term 'partnership' is used to embrace any agreement between a freehold landowner (freeholder) and a developer (leaseholder) where the risks and returns of development are shared in some way, however unequally. A general rule is that risk and return go hand-in-hand, but this is an over-simplification.

Early partnership agreements in the immediate post-war period were usually 99-year leases at a fixed rent or with infrequent rent reviews. The word partnership was therefore somewhat of a misnomer. From the late 1960s onwards, however, more sophisticated arrangements became commonplace in town centre redevelopment and 'four-slice' arrangements were subsequently used for industrial and office developments and are still used today.

Three- or four-slice arrangements

The question of financial return is a complex one and is inextricably tied up with risk. Different types of partnership agreements must often be considered separately before any conclusions can be made. For well-located institutionally acceptable office and industrial schemes, three- or four-slice partnership agreements, or increasingly side-by-side agreements, subject to a minimum ground rent, will usually be possible. Here the freeholder receives a secure ground rental income which is a first charge out of income generated by the development (see Diagram 6). This rent will be regularly reviewed, sometimes in an upwards only direction. In this situation the freeholder will participate in future rental growth, which in part it will help create. Ultimately, when the lease ends, the whole development will revert to the freeholder who will then receive the full rental directly from the occupational tenants, with no payments to any intermediate leaseholders.

Diagram 6

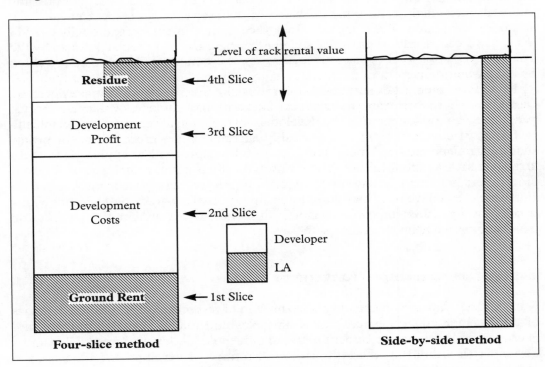

This type of agreement should enable the freeholder to achieve a secure ground rental income without undertaking the risks of development, which are borne by the private sector, almost entirely. Where local authorities are the freeholder they can therefore be seen to control development more effectively for the benefit of the community and participate in its rewards without taking many risks. However, whether the financial return will be as high as an outright freehold disposal is questionable. During a development boom, where land values are rising rapidly, a local authority may ultimately achieve a better financial return by retaining a regularly reviewable ground lease with an equity participation clause—but where land values are not rising significantly, the greater benefits to a developer/investor of freehold ownership and greater control over the development and subsequent investment may well result in a higher return from outright disposal.

However, for industrial development particularly, unless the development and its location are good, this type of partnership agreement may not attract private sector developers, mainly because they would have to shoulder most of the risk. The main worry is the strength of tenant demand and quality of covenants. Even in a prime scheme it is unusual to find developers willing to pay a ground rent which is more than about 10 per cent of full rental value (unless it is a side-by-side agreement). Any excess would normally be capitalised and paid as a premium.

One possible solution is not to have a horizontally divided three- or four-slice arrangement, but a vertical side-by-side arrangement with risks shared more equally and actual income, whether it rises or falls, split between the parties in some predetermined way. But this too has its problems, although it is increasing in popularity for prime projects. As there is no clear division of management authority, particularly over letting, problems can arise over approval of tenants and whether covenant or the level of rent is more important.

Two-slice arrangements

The most common form of partnership agreement in poor locations and high risk types of development, such as small unit industrial schemes or workspace developments, was some form of horizontal two-slice agreement where the local authority took the more exposed top slice, partially guaranteeing the developer a reasonable, or sufficient, return on costs (see Diagram 7 overleaf). In its simplest form the developer would have received a stated percentage return on costs with the residue going to the local authority when the scheme was (typically) sold on to an investor or to the occupiers. But in many inner-city areas finding an investor on these terms was often difficult!

In the 1980s, therefore, local authorities often retained the freehold and took a leaseback from the developer of the completed scheme and were themselves responsible for sub-letting. The developer achieved a pre-let to one tenant of undoubted covenant, which reduced development risks and made funding easier. The leaseback rent was usually geared to full rental value and reviewed in an upwards-only direction, thus ensuring a reasonable return if costs were properly controlled. The local authority took most of the risk because if rental income fell, due to voids (almost inevitable in small unit schemes), its profit rent would decline, but on the other hand it achieved total control over letting. In theory it could choose which tenants to accept, the terms of the lease and the level of rent.

Under the 1989 Local Government and Housing Act, income received would be counted as income (rather than capitalised and counted as a capital receipt), but the rent paid would be capitalised and counted as capital expenditure. Therefore there would be no notional capital receipt against which to offset the capital expenditure, making this approach difficult for local authorities to pursue.

Because of capital finance and other problems, and especially because of the

Diagram 7

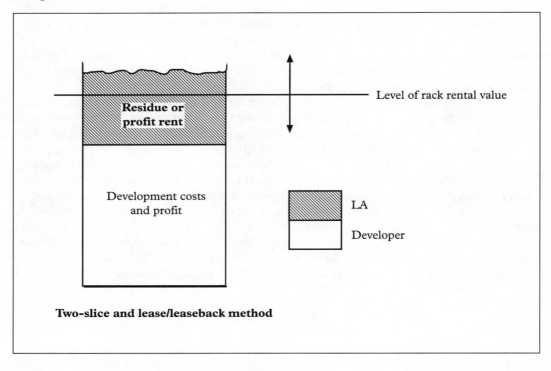

Two-slice and lease/leaseback method

private sector's unwillingness to develop due to the location, type or size of schemes, or the state of the property market, direct development by local authorities or public sector agencies was often the only solution. In the present climate of reductions and greater controls over local authority capital expenditure and grant/tax incentives to the private sector, this option of direct development is rarely feasible. Thus the partnership route has grown in importance and frequency of use.

Advantages and disadvantages of partnership schemes

Advantages

Private sector developers are prepared to be involved in partnership arrangements for the following reasons:-

(1) They can utilise local authority powers of compulsory purchase. These can often, but not always, make land acquisition quicker and cheaper or indeed enable it to occur at all. Occasionally without compulsory purchase order powers (or the threat of their use), land assembly might be impossible if a key landowner refused to sell. Compulsory purchase order powers are perhaps most useful in large town-centre schemes where there is often a myriad of land ownerships. They can also be helpful in other areas, for example, on inner-city sites where it may be desirable to marry a number of separate ownerships to obtain a larger development site with better access.

(2) The developer will be working with rather than against the local authority. This should lessen conflict, enable the developer to access a wealth of background information and research, ensure local authority backing for the scheme and a virtual guarantee of planning permission.

(3) The local authority has a financial stake in the development. This encourages it, through land ownership, to be more commercially minded and support a more market-orientated approach to development.

(4) Where local authorities ground lease a site (rather than dispose of it outright for a capital sum) the developer will have a lower capital outlay. Thus the developer will not have to incur site acquisition expenditure up front. This will mean a reduced borrowing requirement and possibly reduced risk.

(5) The local authority can assist the developer on marketing. By actively promoting the project through its property database, an authority with an active economic development unit will often receive enquiries which can be directed towards the joint venture project.

(6) The private sector looks to the public sector to assist in the provision of off-site infrastructure. This is often needed for major planning regeneration projects, and the local authority's role, as Highway and Planning Authority, is vital.

The advantages of a partnership to local authorities include the following:

(1) Partnership agreements enable them to act positively, ie by taking steps to initiate planning policies and implement development, rather than merely preparing plans and waiting for developers to respond. In many cases partnership agreements not only give control over the timing of development but they enable initiation of schemes which otherwise would not have started due to the uncertainties and risks involved, or the type of development and its location. Occasionally however, where a developer owns a large part of a potential development site, it could be in a very strong bargaining position to resist the compulsory purchase of its landholding and to force the authority to nominate it as developer (possibly on advantageous terms as there would then be no competitive tender).

(2) Land ownership gives them greater powers of control. Not only over the form of development, including its letting, and over any future reletting, but also refurbishment or redevelopment during the period of the lease. Greater control is achieved as a landlord, rather than through planning legislation. Many local authorities cite lack of control as the major drawback of freehold disposal. They fear that once land has been disposed of, different uses or mix of uses, or even size of units within the same planning use class, will be applied for. Even if planning permission is initially refused it may well be achieved on appeal. The Use Classes Order has undoubtedly reinforced these worries because of the greater freedom given to landlords within the new business use class (Class B1) and the ability to transfer from Class B2 to B1 (given by the General Development Order).

(3) While partnership arrangements should ensure greater local authority control over developments, local authorities still retain the benefits. These include private sector finance, expertise and experience in the development process. By nominating a development partner, perhaps after a selective competitive process, the authority gains choice as well as expertise. This should also encourage the best overall scheme in terms of layout and design as well as in financial

terms. This, in turn, brings possible advantages over direct development (where greater control compared to outright disposal is also achieved) because the private sector has greater experience in development and has access to finance which is uncontrolled by central government.

Disadvantages

There can be a number of disadvantages from the private sector point of view:

(1) Dealing with some local authorities can be a frustrating experience. Their bureaucratic nature and the often lengthy committee process of securing decisions can lengthen the development process. The need for public accountability must be balanced against the developer's need for speed and the maximisation of profit.
(2) Loss of control. The need to consult a partner at any stage when a decision is needed can be difficult for a developer used to making its own decisions.

From the local authority point of view there can also be disadvantages:

(1) Their lack of experience. Being involved in development as a partner with a direct legal interest is a unique experience for many councils.
(2) The potential conflict between planning and financial policies. Tensions often arise between the two, causing delay.
(3) Ultra vires: eg a guarantee given by a local authority may be unlawful and, in consequence, unenforceable.[1]

The development brief and selection of a partner

Development briefs

The objectives of a development brief[2] can be summarised as being to:

(1) promote interest in the development of a site;
(2) provide positive planning guidance over land;
(3) give the landowner reasonable control over the form and content of the scheme;
(4) provide a clear basis for the design of a scheme on which developers can work;
(5) set out the main financial terms required by the landowner;
(6) inform the developer of what plans and written material should be submitted;
(7) provide a common basis for comparing developer's proposals; and
(8) minimise the scope for renegotiation after tender date.

As mentioned earlier, one of the main benefits of partnership arrangements compared to freehold disposal is the greater control over the form and content of development. One of the objectives of the development brief is to spell out to prospective developers the type of uses, their floor space, site coverage and design principles including aspects such as access points, landscaping and circulation. This is important, not just to ensure that the development proposals conform to the local authority's wishes, but also to provide a common basis for comparing developers' proposals. However, whilst this detailed specification is desirable in most cases, it may not always be acceptable to the local authority. It may not want to constrain a developer's entrepreneurial flair and ideas. The problem with the more flexible approach is trying to select the best scheme where so many different criteria are involved.

Alternative types of development brief

Sometimes, particularly for large schemes, the development brief may not be specific (as discussed above) as to the quantification of different uses to be included in the development or even the uses themselves. This gives prospective developers greater scope to be imaginative and provide a scheme tailor-made to what they interpret market demands to be. This gives developers a free reign, but can make it difficult for the local authority to compare alternatives and weigh up the difference in financial returns with the difference in design, layout and use terms.

In contrast, at the opposite extreme, the local authority can design the scheme itself and ask the development partner merely to submit a financial bid. This makes comparison relatively easy but is rarely used because developers dislike it as there is no scope for any layout or design flair to enable one developer to produce a better scheme and therefore outbid competitors.

Another alternative, again rarely used, is for the local authority to fix the financial terms—ground rent, premium etc and let developers compete on layout/design grounds. This approach is disliked by local authorities as they cannot be certain that they are achieving the best possible financial terms. If the terms are pitched too high, potential bidders will be put off; if the terms are pitched too low, either excess profits will accrue to the selected developer or else the scheme will be built to an unnecessarily high specification. The financial terms contained in development briefs, relevant to partnership schemes, are discussed subsequently.

Criteria for selection of a development partner

The process of selecting a development partner is crucial to the success of a partnership scheme. There are various criteria that need to be employed in selection since it should not simply be a question of the highest financial offer. The criteria are:

(1) the financial offer (ground rent and/or premium) and equity share;
(2) the sustainability of the financial offer (ie is it an overbid, are costs and rents reasonable, etc);
(3) the layout/design/appearance of the proposal from an architectural, planning and estate management point of view;
(4) analysis of developer's previous schemes;
(5) the track record of the developer, its financial standing and the extent of other commitments;
(6) the financial backing of the developer for the project;
(7) the developer's team of advisers and consultants;
(8) the personalities of the development team and particularly of the key personnel of the development company; and
(9) any pre-lettings, or forward sales that the developer may introduce.

Clearly, therefore, even with a detailed development brief, the financial offer is only one aspect to be considered. The above criteria are more applicable to a competitive tender, although they are also relevant when negotiating with a single developer. In most cases it is desirable to have a restricted competitive tender to ensure the best possible scheme and the best financial offer, thereby complying with s 123 of the 1972 Local Government Act. However, there are occasions where it may be appropriate for the local authority to negotiate with just one developer, for example where that company has a substantial ownership in the proposed site, or where there is insufficient interest from other developers to make a competition worthwhile. Where one developer has particular expertise and is well known to the authority, direct negotiation may also be preferable.

Process of selection

Assuming a reasonable market and a project which is likely to be of broad interest to a range of developers, a two-stage process is normally adopted. Firstly, following a period of marketing, expressions of interest should be sought with developers putting forward their credentials and track record with an outline of their approach to the project. No financial bid should be sought at this stage but sufficient information should be secured to enable a shortlist of no more than six developers (ideally three or four) to be drawn up who would then be invited to submit detailed financial bids. A limit on the number of developers preparing schemes and financial offers is necessary, unless the scheme is simple and small in size, otherwise the time, effort and expense would deter established developers becoming involved if their chances of selection were less than about 20-25 per cent. At this stage it is important to establish the track record of the company and the method by which it would finance the project.

Having agreed on a shortlist, detailed bids would then be sought, within a specific timescale, and based on fixed criteria (depending on the form of the development brief). At this stage, the emphasis on architectural quality or financial returns should be clearly stated and the degree to which one will dominate the other depends upon the circumstances of each scheme.

It is at this point essential to combine the expertise of a property consultant with that of a property lawyer. Establishing the legal framework of a development partnership, prior to selecting the chosen developer, will save time and potential disagreements once the developer has been selected. Throughout the selection process, and before, the method of disposal and the way in which it will be documented should be clearly defined. The lawyer's role at this stage is to clarify title, identify any restrictive covenants, easements, title defects, or rights of light and to draw up a legal framework within which the joint venture will be established.

The financial terms of partnership

The basic differences between an appraisal to calculate ground rent rather than the capital site value are that first, the calculations are undertaken on an annual rather than a capital basis and second, from the developer's point of view, capital costs are obviously reduced as the site is not being acquired, no capital is at risk and no site finance charges are incurred. Although a rent (annual cost) would be paid for the site, this is normally not payable until completion of development when the project should be revenue producing. For these reasons, in certain locations, some developers prefer such an arrangement to outright freehold ownership, particularly as the landowner becomes an investor in the scheme. However, it is probably true to say that developers in many other cases would prefer freehold ownership due to the greater control over development and the ensuing investment, and this factor will be reflected in the return required.

From a local authority viewpoint, the financial terms and returns are obviously important in an era of severe controls on capital and revenue expenditure. Nevertheless, it should be emphasised that criteria other than financial may also be as important in assessing a scheme. Even if a poor financial return appears probable, the local authority may well proceed with implementation in order to obtain other benefits (eg employment, environmental, highway or other socio-economic benefits). The project might act as a catalyst and stimulate other schemes to proceed which otherwise would not have occurred.

Ground rent and equity-sharing (or gearing)

Ground rent This would normally become payable after completion of the development or after a specified time limit, often equivalent to the estimated length of the development period. During the development period a peppercorn rent would be paid, so that the ground rent effectively becomes payable when income is received by the developer from letting the completed scheme. Traditionally, in many partnership agreements, the local authority's interest would be safeguarded by ensuring that the estimated ground rent was a minimum figure which would be increased if and when the rental income from the occupational tenants increased, but could not be reduced if the scheme was less profitable than the developer expected. In this way the local authority's income was the first charge, or slice, out of the total income.

If the ground rent, or gearing ratio, was not set at a minimum figure, there would be a danger that the developer would overbid initially to win nomination and then reduce the ground rent subsequently when actual costs and rents were known. Nevertheless, in certain situations where tenant demand is less strong and the development risks are perceived to be greater, developers may be reluctant to take the risk of offering a guaranteed minimum ground rent. In this situation the local authority may be faced with either having to abandon the scheme or else enter into a true side-by-side partnership, sharing the development risk with the developer. Even where risks are not great, developers may still make offers on a side-by-side basis in return for a more attractive gearing ratio to the local authority.

Equity-sharing This arrangement effectively means that the initial relationship between ground rent and rack rent is maintained at every rent review. Every time the rack rent increases, the ground rent would also increase by the same percentage amount. It is important to clarify the term 'rack rent' in this context as there is obviously a difference between rental value and rental income. From a freeholder's viewpoint, the former is desirable because it ensures that ground rent is calculated as a percentage of the maximum rent income that the project could produce, if there were no voids. These voids could be caused by a downturn in the market, natural turnover of tenants, or refurbishment. A developer may try to resist the use of rental value, particularly if it is coupled with a high gearing ratio, arguing that a high development yield (and hence lower ground rent) would result, or that funding would be difficult.

Although the equity-sharing arrangement mentioned above is a common and simple method of apportioning future rental growth, it is by no means the only method. In some cases a local authority may prefer to receive a lower initial ground rent in return for a higher share of future rental growth. A developer may also prefer this arrangement in certain situations, particularly if the ground rent is to be a minimum figure, as the developer will then be guaranteeing a smaller sum (less initial risk), but giving away more equity if the development is successful. However, in this situation funding may be complicated.

Participation clauses and four-slice agreements

Four-slice agreements often contain a participation clause which involves the residual appraisal being reworked shortly after completion of the development, in order to use actual, rather than estimated, figures. This enables the local authority to participate in any excess profits. Due to possible inflation of costs and rents during the development period, it is likely that actual rents and possibly costs will differ from those estimated. The purpose of the participation clause is to reflect these changes in a revised equity share. This is particularly likely in larger and more complex schemes due to the length of time that often elapses between the tender date, when the ground rent offer is made, and completion date when the development is income producing. The revised equity share will then determine the local authority's income at subsequent rent reviews.

If the initial agreement stated that the estimated ground rent was to be a minimum figure (subject to upward-only review and therefore a first charge out of rental income), then the object of the participation clause will be to increase the ground rent once the developer has achieved its stated return required on actual development cost (ie a yield protection). If costs have increased to such an extent that the developer is unable to achieve this return, then the initially-agreed ground rent will remain as a minimum figure and any reduction in income will be suffered by the developer as this is part of the risk of development. If the scheme is not fully let at participation, then many partnership agreements allow for rental value to be used for the unlet parts, in order to obtain the total rent as mentioned earlier.

The differences between a four-slice agreement and a side-by-side agreement now become very clear. With a side-by-side agreement the calculation of ground rent on completion of the development is more straightforward. The gearing ratio, or equity share, is simply applied to the actual income paid by the occupational tenants to calculate the ground rent (although in some agreements this simplicity is complicated by the inclusion of a minimum ground rent to give some additional security to the local authority).

The four-slice agreement enables both partners to participate in excess profits generated by successful schemes. Occasionally, more complex sharing arrangements have been used where the nature of the scheme and its location warrant them. For example, the 50:50 split of the fourth slice, or excess profit, may be subject to a maximum, if the developer's return exceeds certain thresholds. Above such thresholds the freeholder may be entitled to a greater share than 50 per cent. Such clauses are particularly relevant in the event of the developer selling the completed scheme.

Grounds rents and premiums

In many partnerships local authorities prefer to receive a premium instead of an annual income, or some combination of a smaller premium and ground rent. This capital sum can then be used to supplement capital spending elsewhere within their area or possibly to help purchase the site itself. In an era of public sector expenditure and borrowing constraints, this desire may be particularly strong. A capital premium could be looked upon as being a non-site-specific planning gain. One problem with this approach is that under the Local Government and Housing Act 1989, only 50 per cent (25 per cent in the case of housing) of this capital receipt can be used to supplement local authority capital spending, the remaining 50 per cent (75 per cent) going towards debt redemption. (These percentages are periodically reviewed by central government.)

Alternatively, some element of planning gain could be incorporated within the development, or on a different site, similarly increasing the developer's costs and so reducing the ground rent payable, but possibly without the local authority suffering from the 50 per cent rule.

Another reason behind the use of premiums is to keep the gearing ratio between ground rent and rack rental value low. Where site value forms a large percentage of the total project's value (eg in high-value central locations) then funding institutions will resist an unfavourable gearing where the freeholder receives more than about 10-15 per cent of rack rental value unless the lease is not subject to upward-only rent review (ie on a side-by-side basis where actual income is shared). If a large proportion of the equity is receivable by the freeholder, then the leaseholder can be left with an exposed top-slice income in the event of a subsequent decline in rack rental income (if rents fall or there are voids) and where the ground rent is reviewable on an upwards-only basis (see Diagram 8 overleaf). A premium reduces gearing and thereby makes the basis of rent reviews less important and consequently may lead to a reduction in development yield required.

High-risk projects

Variations on the traditional approach   In some partnerships, in areas where development risks are considered by the private sector to be unacceptably high, a variety of alternative arrangements of income- and risk-sharing have evolved. The side-by-side basis mentioned above is an example of this because the developer/investor is not necessarily guaranteeing the local authority a minimum ground rent on completion of development and the local authority is sharing in actual income received from occupational tenants. This means that its income could fall as well as rise throughout the period of the ground lease.

Another alternative to the traditional four-slice arrangement is the three-slice arrangement. Here the developer guarantees a minimum ground rent, but at a lower figure (thus reducing development risks), receives an agreed return on the development costs as a second slice (or charge) then apportions the resultant profit (third slice) in some predetermined side-by-side basis with the local authority. As a lower ground rent is guaranteed, the developer is more likely to achieve a profit if the scheme is not particularly successful. In this situation, a lower gearing ratio would apply to all subsequent income received from occupational tenants of the completed development. Other permutations of the three- and four-slice arrangement exist

Diagram 8

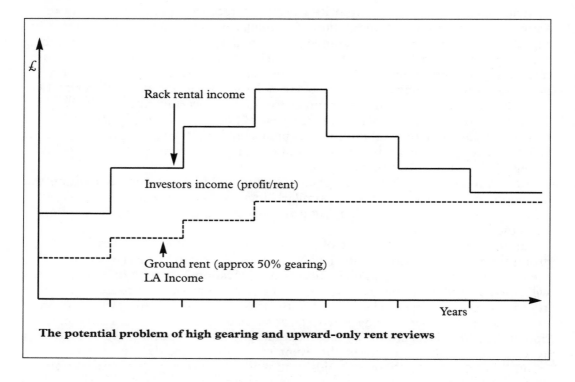

Rack rental income

Investors income (profit/rent)

Ground rent (approx 50% gearing)
LA Income

£

Years

The potential problem of high gearing and upward-only rent reviews

which all have the same objective, namely to reduce the developer's guarantees and make it more likely that an acceptable return on costs will be achieved. In its extreme form, the local authority may require no ground rent or premium but receive its land value as a share in any profits that the development achieves.

The other side of the coin obviously is that if the scheme is more successful than expected, it is the local authority who will benefit more than it would have done under the traditional four-slice arrangement.

Rental guarantees and leasebacks

Rental guarantee   In some situations, for example the implementation of small unit industrial developments in locations where demand is less certain, other arrangements have been considered where even more of the development risk is shouldered by the local authority. In the late 1970s and early 1980s this was often achieved by the local authority guaranteeing the rack rental income, but without taking back a lease of the units; or by agreeing to take an overriding lease of the scheme and then being responsible for subletting to individual tenants; or by not requiring a ground rent as a first charge out of income and in effect guaranteeing the developer a return on costs before the local authority received any income from its freehold land ownership. In these latter two alternatives the local authority would have had a much more risky top-slice income, and the developer a much more secure bottom-slice income.

In a straightforward two-slice arrangement the ground rent, rather than being a predetermined guaranteed minimum figure, would typically be calculated on completion of development, with the developer receiving a previously agreed return on actual costs incurred, but probably subject to maximum and minimum gearing to avoid the local authority receiving 100 per cent of any excess profit.

For small unit starter, or workshop, developments, even the two-slice agreement had problems, which were more related to the subsequent investment rather than the development process itself. This was obviously important to a developer because, on completion of the development, the scheme would either be sold on to an investor, or refinanced, enabling the developer to become a long-term investor. The problem concerned potential voids, tenants' covenants and the management of an investment with numerous tenants. Small unit and work space schemes by definition will be let to small companies, many of whom may well be start-up businesses with no track record. Numerous tenants with poor covenants is not an appealing investment, par-ticularly to institutional investors, who like a limited number of tenants all of high calibre and a long lease (25 years typically), with rent reviews on an upwards-only basis. Small companies will not be prepared to take long leases. They prefer short leases, ideally with 'easy in, easy out' terms. Where such leases are available, not surprisingly there will be a high turnover of tenants with potential income voids until new tenants are found.

Leasebacks The solution to these problems, in the past, was for the local authority to take a leaseback of the entire scheme and itself sublet to occupational tenants. This reduced the development risk as the developer had a pre-let at a known rent to one tenant of high calibre. It also produced a much more saleable investment and made funding easier. While the local authority was now taking a substantial risk, it did at least gain by having control over letting, in terms of choosing the tenants it wanted. In theory it received a profit rent (difference between the rent received from occupational tenants and the rent paid to the developer), admittedly as a top-slice income rather than as a secure bottom-slice income, but at least it did not have the inconvenience of undertaking the actual development.

Alternatively, to circumvent the controls on capital expenditure and borrowing, some local authorities entered into management agreements on behalf of the devel-oper, charging a fee which was equivalent to the profit rent on a leaseback basis. The local authority still controlled letting but only had to take a lease if it defaulted on the management agreement.

As mentioned above, under the Local Government and Housing Act 1989, where a local authority enters into a lease or guarantees a lease, the annual rent is capital-ised and counts as capital expenditure. This therefore often precludes this form of local authority involvement. However, in June 1993 the government relaxed these rules for development corporations which will now be able to give rental guarantees to the private sector, subject to obtaining ministerial approval. Similarly, develop-ment corporations can now put land into joint ventures without taking a payment in exchange for an equity stake. As the DOE states:[3]

'There should be a clear agreement as to how the financial risks and rewards are shaped between the partners, with the private sector partner genuinely taking on risk. The greater the degree of risk shouldered by the public sector body the greater the share of the potential rewards that should be obtained. A ceiling should, in any event, always be set on the public body's contribution.'

Control over local authority capital expenditure and receipts

Capital expenditure

Unlike the private sector, local authorities have controls imposed over their capital spending and borrowing. These controls have existed in various forms for 20 years and, in their current form under the Local Government and Housing Act 1989, they are the tightest ever.

Progressively over the last 14 years, ever since the Local Government, Planning and Land Act 1980, central government has increased its controls on local authority capital expenditure (and also annual expenditure) in order to limit the size of the Public Sector Borrowing Requirement (the 'PSBR'). One by one, the various ways which local authorities (or their advisors) devised to circumvent these controls have been eliminated, so that under the present system there is little flexibility left other than in deciding how to spend the allocation, or to use the credit-approval limit imposed on them by central government.

The 1989 Act altered the system that had existed under the 1980 Act, of cash limiting capital expenditure, to a system where the government exerts even tighter control over local authority borrowing and therefore, indirectly, spending. The new system controls credit used to finance capital expenditure and ensures a reduction in local authority debt by asset sales. Local authority capital expenditure can now be financed in three ways:

(1) borrowing, or its equivalent;
(2) government grants; and
(3) revenue, operating receipts (local authorities cannot generally trade for profit) and capital receipts (the 50 per cent, or 25 per cent in the case of the sale of local authority housing, not used to redeem debt).

The government gives each local authority a credit-approval limit for borrowing, or its equivalent, for the next financial year, and this limit can be supplemented by income from grant, revenue, operating receipts or capital receipts. However, any revenue so used will relate only to the amount raised under the new Council Tax rather than, as before, to total rates income from both domestic and commercial premises.

Capital receipts

The government also takes account of local authorities' likely ability to raise money through capital receipts when setting the credit-approval limit. Only 50 per cent (25 per cent for housing) of any capital receipts can be used to increase this limit; the remainder must be retained for debt redemption.

Many local authorities, therefore, will have a preference for receiving ground rent (income) rather than premiums (capital) when disposing of land in a partnership agreement. This means they are free to use all the income, compared to 50 per cent (temporarily increased to 100 per cent until the end of 1993) of any premium to supplement capital expenditure. However, there may be situations where capital is needed in a particular financial year rather than income spread over many years. In these situations even half a capital receipt may be preferred to income. Capital receipts also have the benefit of redeeming debt, thereby reducing interest payments and consequently the amount needed to be raised by the Council Tax.

Between 13 November 1992 and 31 December 1993, the requirement for local authorities to set aside 50 per cent of capital receipts for debt redemption was temporarily suspended, subject to a few specific exceptions. During this period, most receipts from property disposals were 'usable' and, therefore, potentially able to increase local authorities' ability to undertake new capital projects. The previous rules affecting capital receipts were reinstated on 1 January 1994.

In practice, whether this change enabled local authorities to embark on new capital projects depended on each authority's particular financial circumstances. In parallel with the suspension of the set-aside rules, the basis of central government funding was also adjusted to reflect the assumed increase in the 'usable' element of capital receipts. It is understood that the 'receipts taken into account' mechanism was adjusted for 1993/94 so as to double the amount of usable capital receipts taken into account from £375 million (in 1992/93) to around £700 million. The doubling of usable receipts may well have been achieved through the release of the obligation to set aside 50 per cent of all receipts, but the adjustment of the 'receipts taken into account' procedure means that there is an element of 'clawback' of this increased spending power.

Local authorities needed to consider a variety of factors before deciding on any disposal programmes. These included the longer-term impact on their overall financial and property strategies, having regard to current economic conditions and the somewhat uncertain prospects for an early property market recovery. The temporary suspension of the set-aside rules also impacted on land assembly, replacement of assets and notional capital receipts mentioned below.

'Capital Partnership'   Hand-in-hand with the temporary relaxation of the set-aside rules, the government introduced 'Capital Partnership' in November 1992, whereby central government grants were available for partnership projects involving the private sector, which were partially funded by capital receipts realised under the new set-aside rules. Central government estimated that the new set-aside rules would encourage £1.75 billion of capital receipts which, for projects not quite viable, could be topped up with up to £200 million of government grants and £400 million of Housing Corporation grants. This money had to be bid for and the bids were assessed on the criteria of projects best placed to stimulate growth. Capital partnership was subdivided into Housing Partnership, Urban Partnership, Environmental Partnership and Countryside Partnership.

Land assembly

Land assembly prior to the grant of a ground lease to a developer will usually require expenditure which may be difficult to finance because of the tight credit-approval limits that are imposed under the new system. Central government recognised this problem and introduced The Local Authorities (Capital Finance) Regulations 1990 (SI 1990 No 432) to assist in such situations. In particular Regulation 15—Capital Receipts to be treated as reduced; disposal of recently acquired interests—means that the capital receipt on disposal can be reduced by the cost of necessary land assembly, so that only the balance is affected by the 50 per cent debt redemption rule. The cost of land assembly is therefore financed by the capital receipt except that a period of time may intervene between acquisition and disposal over which the cost of acquisition must be financed. This period is limited by Regulation 15 to two years (three years if a contract for disposal is exchanged within two years).

Provided that all transactions are completed within the relevant period, ministerial approval will not be needed. Similar regulations under previous legislation were for only one year and required ministerial approval, so the new Regulation therefore appears to be an improvement, but is nevertheless complex. The three-year period will not always be sufficient and will make opportunity purchases and the gradual piecing together of development sites, which often occurs over several years, very difficult. This was something which many local authorities of all political persuasions have undertaken—in town centres particularly—so that they could be in the driving seat, achieving greater control over any subsequent redevelopment and reducing the need for extensive land assembly immediately before the scheme could proceed.

Another key part of Regulation 15 is that the tenure of a subsequent disposal must either be the same as the interest acquired, or superior. Where a freehold has been acquired, a long leasehold of at least 125 years is stipulated with at least 90 per cent of the capital cost of the lease being recovered before the end of the lease's first year. This means effectively that premiums must be charged because any ground rental gearing will be minimal. This should be attractive to developers and investors, but local authorities may be more reluctant to use this 'in and out' provision to facilitate development. It may also encourage disposal of parts of the overall site on separate leases with different levels of gearing. This would reduce the scheme's attractiveness to the private sector, particularly with regard to funding, although there is a strongly-held view that the 90 per cent of capital value rule applies to the capital value of the whole site, not just that part which relates to the land acquired by the local authority.

Replacement of assets

Regulation 18 of the 1990 Regulations is applicable where a local authority wants to replace part of land to be disposed of with new land. For example, if a public building such as a school is to be disposed of as part of a larger site to facilitate a viable development, the authority may require a new school to be built elsewhere on a site which either they already own or which will have to be acquired. Schedule 2 of the 1990 Regulations defines those assets to which Regulation 18 applies. They include:

- libraries;
- local authority offices;
- fire stations;
- community halls;
- training workshops;
- markets;
- bus stations;
- car parks;
- schools;
- theatres or concert halls;
- museums or art galleries.

Under a partnership agreement, the developer may have to provide the new site and pay for construction of the replacement facility with the ground rent correspondingly reduced. Alternatively, the council might acquire the new site and pay for construction out of the proceeds of the original disposal.

In either case the authority will not be penalised by having to use 50 per cent of the notional or actual capital receipt receivable on sale of the asset for debt redemption, nor will the new expenditure count as new borrowing. The only condition is that the three-year rule must be adhered to and the authority must either have spent the money or be irrevocably committed to spending it before the capital receipt is received.

The capital receipt will be reduced, for the purpose of applying the 50 per cent debt redemption rule, by the amount of the relevant replacement cost necessary to enable the scheme to go ahead. However, only the reasonable cost of an equivalent replacement building will be able to be used to offset against the capital receipt.

Planning agreements and notional capital receipts

A planning benefit arising under an agreement under s 106 of the Town and Country Planning Act 1990 will not constitute a receipt in the hands of a local authority if it is legitimately included within the s 106 agreement in accordance with Circular 16/91. Such benefits are not capable of being treated as consideration for a disposal by the local authority of its interest in land and will not therefore constitute a notional capital receipt within the meaning of s 61 of the Local Government and Housing Act 1989.

The question of what does constitute genuine planning gain has been closely examined by the courts in recent cases. In the case of *Plymouth and South Devon Co-operative Society Ltd v Plymouth City Council* (1993)[4] the judge found that there was a connection between the planning gain and the relevant site in respect of which planning permission was granted, even though the respective sites were geographically unrelated. However, the recent Court of Appeal decision relating to *Tesco Stores Ltd v Secretary of State for the Environment* in May 1994 stated that planning gain must not only be fairly and reasonably related to the property development, but also directly related. There is no hard and fast rule which can be applied infallibly to each case—it is a matter of judgment in the particular circumstances.

Joint companies

Under the Local Government, Planning and Land Act 1980 joint companies between local authorities and private developers were sometimes set up as an alternative to the long leasehold partnership agreements referred to earlier. As these companies were effectively separate from the local authority, they benefited from streamlined decision-making and administration. More importantly, they bypassed the controls on local authority capital expenditure introduced by the 1980 Act. They were, however, one step removed from the authority's direct control and they were subject to taxation which did not affect a local authority under a 'partnership' arrangement as described earlier.

Part V of the Local Government and Housing Act 1989 introduced draft regulations treating such JVCs virtually as an arm of the local authority. Local authorities will be free to enter into such JVCs, but to avoid capital expenditure problems, such companies should be neither 'controlled' nor 'influenced' companies as defined in the 1989 Act. To avoid being a 'controlled' company, the authority will only be able to have an interest in the company of 50 per cent or less and should not be involved in the company to such a degree that the local authority can be considered to be providing 50 per cent or more of the business or financial assistance to the company. Furthermore, such a joint company will be an 'influenced' company where the local authority has both a 20 per cent or greater interest in the company (as evidenced by voting rights at a General Directors' Meeting), and has a business relationship with the company. In deciding whether the local authority has a 20 per cent interest, the interest of persons associated with the local authority will be taken into account and such persons include members or officers of the local authority over the preceding four years, persons providing consultancy services for the local authority and persons who hold office in a political association.

Part V of the 1989 Act is complex, and uncertainty has been created by the Government's failure to publish the appropriate regulations (which have been in draft form since 1989). This uncertainty has been further exacerbated by the downturn in the property market.

Constraints on partnership schemes caused by central government controls

Partnership schemes and public sector pump priming are seen as vital ingredients of effective urban regeneration. The OECD,[5] the CBI,[6] the Audit Commission,[7] the National Audit Office[8] and the RICS[9] have all seen partnership as an essential part of any successful attack on urban problems.

However, the RICS, amongst others, is concerned about the obstacles which the government has put in their path. These obstacles are the regulations covering capital expenditure by local authorities and the proposed restrictions upon their ability to take an interest in private companies. The 1989 Act and the regulations made under it are extremely complex and much time and cost has been involved in determining how local authority involvement in partnership schemes might be affected. These controls have undoubtedly delayed some developments from being implemented. Indeed, in certain cases, they have prevented the implementation of partnership schemes because of the capital finance implications for local authorities.

Hopefully English Partnerships, the re-named Urban Regeneration Agency, established by the Leasehold Reform, Housing and Urban Development Act 1993, will have sufficient resources to assist in land acquisition and implementation of marginally viable urban renewal schemes. It has wide-ranging powers (to give rental guarantees or take leases under pre-let situations, for example), but only time will tell how effectively and extensively they will be used. A further encouraging sign was a change of heart by the Government in October 1993 towards rental guarantee schemes when the Inner Cities Minister allowed Merseyside Development Corporation to make 1.9 acres of land available for commercial development and give a five-year rental guarantee of income for the office space after it is completed. In return, the Corporation will share profits with the developer on a 50:50 basis. This is a two-slice agreement similar to those described earlier on pages 121 and 130. However, although the Minister is 'willing to consider further similar proposals', it is clear that ministerial approval will be needed for each scheme.

---

[1] See *Crédit Suisse v Allerdale District Council*, May 1994.

[2] *Development Briefs. Planning & Development Guidance Notes* (RICS 1985).

[3] 'Working together: Private Finance and Public Money' (June 1993).

[4] Planning Notes, Edwards, M & Martin, J, *Estates Gazette*, 3 April & 18 September 1993.

[5] Environmental Policies for Cities in the 1990s (1990).

[6] Transport in London Task Force Report (1989).

[7] Urban Regeneration and Economic Development: the local government dimension.

[8] Regenerating the Inner Cities (HMSO, 1990).

[9] Partnerships between local authorities and the private sector (1991).

Chapter 12

The Urban Regeneration Agency (English Partnerships)

General

The Leasehold Reform, Housing and Urban Development Act ('LRA 1993') was passed on 20 July 1993 and, so far as concerns the Urban Regeneration Agency (Pt III of the Act), all relevant portions of the Act are now in force. These are reproduced in the Appendix on p 153.

The Urban Regeneration Agency (since re-named 'English Partnerships') is created by s 158 of the Act and, by virtue of s 184 of the Act, The English Industrial Estates Corporation has ceased to exist, all its property, rights and liabilities in turn being adopted by the Agency (as it is called throughout the relevant provisions of the Act and thus also in this chapter). In recent years, governments have sought to revitalise certain areas of the UK through a variety of statutory measures giving rise, for example, to the creation of development corporations with particular powers over land in specific areas, and to the use of tax incentives to encourage development in, for example, enterprise zones.

To those with a detailed knowledge of this raft of statutory measures, particularly those affecting urban regeneration, the powers of the Agency as laid down by the Act will perhaps have a familiar ring. The powers of the Agency are, nonetheless, unique. They relate specifically to land in England, and not, necessarily, urban land or derelict land requiring regeneration or development. Nor indeed, despite the name of the Act, is the Agency necessarily concerned with housing. It can facilitate the provision of housing, but the Agency itself cannot provide housing, otherwise than by acquiring existing accommodation and by making it available on a temporary basis for purposes incidental to the purposes of its objects.[1-2]

Constitution of the Agency

It is expressly provided[3] that the Agency, as a creature of statute, shall not be regarded as a servant or agent of the Crown or enjoy any of its status, immunity or privilege and, in turn, that its property shall not be regarded as the property of or held on behalf of the Crown. There are exceptions to this[4] where, with the approval of the Treasury, the Secretary of State may, on terms, appoint the Agency as his agent in relation to grants for reclaiming or improving land, or bringing land into use under the Derelict Land Act 1982, and (subject to particular limitations mentioned below) in relation to financial assistance for urban regeneration, under ss 27–29 of the Housing Act 1986 (itself also amended in this respect).

The Urban Regeneration Agency (English Partnerships) is what is popularly known as a 'Quango'. The foregoing distinctions concern the creation and constitution of the Agency; the powers of the Agency are themselves to be distinguished, and can be controlled very directly by the Secretary of State.[5] Not only shall the Agency have regard to guidance from the Secretary of State in relation to the suitability of land for regeneration or development, or the exercise of any of its functions, but the Secretary of State also has power to give directions restricting the exercise of its functions or, indeed, requiring it to exercise those functions 'in any manner specified in the directions'.[6] Such directions may be 'of a general or particular nature and may be varied or revoked by subsequent directions'.[7]

The whole of Pt III of the Act has been drafted around a fundamental principle that the Secretary of State has power to intervene, and to be pro-active as well as reactive. One qualification to this principle is that the operation of certain sections of the Act is dependent upon statutory instruments which, in turn, can be annulled by either of the Houses of Parliament.

Membership and procedures

The constitution of the Agency is governed by LRA 1993, Sched 17. The Agency shall have not less than six members, all appointed by the Secretary of State. Of these, there may be one chairman and a deputy chairman. A person ceases to be a member, and in turn chairman or deputy chairman as the case may be, if he resigns or if the Secretary of State is satisfied that he is unable or unfit to carry out his appointment, has not complied with it, or has become bankrupt, or made an arrangement with his creditors. There are further provisions relating to staffing, remuneration, pensions etc, all these matters being subject to the Secretary of State's approval, including as to the appointment of a chief executive.

The Agency can devise its own procedures including the operation of committees which may be made up of members of the Agency and, with the consent of the Secretary of State, co-optees, but no committee may be constituted consisting entirely of co-optees. Whether at a meeting of members of the Agency or of a committee, members of the Agency, or members of that committee as the case may be, are required to disclose their interests in any matter brought up for consideration. If the matter in respect of which the disclosure was made is not a matter of 'contract or agreement of any description', the person in question can participate unless the rest of the members of that meeting decide 'that the interest disclosed might prejudicially affect the members' consideration of the matter'.[8] Where the matter in question is one of contract or agreement, the person cannot participate at all.

The Agency, when entering into any instrument by way of deed, does so under seal duly authenticated by the signature of any member of the Agency or of its staff duly authorised for the purpose. The Act provides, incidentally, that a transaction between a person and the Agency shall not be invalidated by reason only that it was carried out contrary to a direction given under LRA 1993, s 167(2) and, more particularly, that 'such person shall not be concerned to see or enquire whether any directions under that subsection have been given or complied with'.

Specific purposes of the Agency

The main object of the Agency shall be to secure the regeneration of land in England.[9] The kinds of land intended are, in summary, one or more of land which is:

(1) vacant or unused;
(2) in an urban area and under-used or ineffectively used;
(3) contaminated, derelict, neglected or unsightly; and
(4) likely to be become derelict, neglected or unsightly by reason of actual or apprehended collapse of the surface as the result of the carrying out of relevant operations (as described in Derelict Land Act 1982, s 1) which have ceased to be carried out.

Development

The Agency has a further object to secure development of land in England[10] which, having regard to guidance given by the Secretary of State,[11] or which the Secretary of State directs or consents to, the Agency determines to be suitable for development. Precisely how these objects are to be achieved may be inferred from what the Agency may or may not do under the Act, but in any event shall be achieved in particular, so far as the Agency considers appropriate, by:

(1) securing that land and buildings are brought into effective use;
(2) developing or encouraging the development of existing and new industry and commerce;
(3) creating an attractive and safe environment;
(4) facilitating the provision of housing and providing, or facilitating the provision of social and recreational facilities.[12]

The distinction between facilitating the provision of housing and actually providing housing is expressly limited as mentioned above.

General powers

The Agency has, subject always to advice or directions by the Secretary of State under s 167, a number of general powers. The Agency may:[13]

(1) acquire, hold, manage, reclaim, improve and dispose of land, plant, machinery, equipment and other property;
(2) carry out the development or redevelopment of land, including the conversion or demolition of existing buildings;
(3) carry out building and other operations;
(4) provide means of access, services or other facilities for land;
(5) seek to ensure the provision of water, electricity, gas, sewerage and other services;
(6) carry on any business or undertaking for the purposes of its objects;
(7) (with the consent of the Secretary of State) form, or acquire interests in, bodies corporate;
(8) act with other persons whether in partnership or otherwise;
(9) give financial assistance to other persons;

(10) act as agent for other persons;

(11) provide advisory or other services and facilities; and

(12) generally do anything necessary or expedient for the purposes of its objects or for purposes incidental to those purposes.

It is further provided[14] that these general powers relate only to the capacity of the Agency as a statutory corporation and that it is not intended that it be authorised or entitled to disregard any enactment or rule of law. Moreover, in addition to curtailment of the Agency's ability to provide housing, the Act[15] forbids it to acquire an interest in a body corporate which at the time of acquisition is 'carrying on a trade or business', if the effect of the acquisition would be to make the body corporate a subsidiary of the Agency (subsidiary in this case having the same meaning as under CA 1985, s 736).

Nevertheless, there is nothing to prevent the Agency from acquiring an influential minority interest. Section 160(2) is not inviolate, however. For example, it appears that there is nothing forbidding the Agency from entering into a joint venture arrangement under which one or more of its partners acquires further interests in the body corporate which, when aggregated, would afford control by the joint venture.

Again, when disposing of land, except with the consent of the Secretary of State, the Agency may not do so otherwise than for the 'best consideration which can reasonably be obtained'.[16] The Act is silent about plant machinery, equipment and other property but, given that the Agency may not disregard any enactment or rule of law in exercise of its object and powers, the inference seems to be that there is an implied duty of care in that respect.

Acquisition of land by the Agency

An order under s 161 (1)

The procedures to be adopted for acquisition of land by the Agency essentially depend upon whether or not that land is within the public domain. Where land is vested in a local authority, statutory undertakers or other public body, or in a wholly-owned subsidiary of a public body, it shall vest in the Agency pursuant to an order made by the Secretary of State and by the appropriate minister. An order under s 161(1) may not, however, specify land vested in statutory undertakers where the land is used for the purpose of carrying on their statutory undertakings, or which is being held for that purpose. Any order is to be made by statutory instrument, subject to a draft of the order having first been made before and approved by resolution of, each House of Parliament and shall also be subject to annulment pursuant to a resolution of either House.

Definition of 'local authority' and 'statutory undertakers'

It is important to note that the terms 'local authority' and 'statutory undertakers' are each given special meaning. The former means a county council, district council, London Borough council or the Common Council of the City of London.

'Statutory undertakers' once suggested gas, water and electricity. However, none of these are mentioned. In the Act, the definition prescribes,[17] 'except where the context otherwise requires':

(1)   persons authorised by any enactment to carry on any railway, light railway, tramway, road transport, water transport, canal, inland navigation, dock, harbour, pier or lighthouse undertaking, or any undertaking for the supply of hydraulic power;

(2)   British Shipbuilders, the Civil Aviation Authority, the British Coal Corporation and the Post Office;

(3)   any other authority, body or undertakers specified in an order made by the Secretary of State; and

(4)   any wholly-owned subsidiary of any person, authority or body mentioned in (1) or (2) above or of any authority, body or undertakers specified in an order made under (3) above;

and 'statutory undertaking' shall be construed accordingly.

An order under s 161(1) has the same effect as a declaration under the Compulsory Purchase (Vesting Declarations) Act 1981 save that for the purpose of acquisitions under the Act, Sched 19 also applies. Particularly, references to the date of service of the notice to treat are to be treated as references to the date upon which an order under s 161(1) comes into force.

Compulsory purchase

Otherwise, land may be acquired by agreement or, upon the Agency being authorised to do so by the Secretary of State, compulsorily. Compulsory purchase further extends to rights over land and, for example, Sched 20 contains relevant modifications to the Acquisition of Land Act 1981 in respect of land and rights acquired by the Agency.

Various statutory procedures relating to compulsory purchase, in cases where the Agency is involved, are modified. For example, modifications are made to s 7 of the Compulsory Purchase Act 1965 where, in assessing compensation to be paid by the Agency, regard shall be had also to the value of the land over which the right is enjoyed, and which is depreciated by the purchase, and also to the damage, if any, to be sustained by the owner of the land by reason of injurious affection of other land of the owner by the exercise of the right. Further, under para 22 of Sched 20 the Lands Tribunal can authorise the acquisition of the interest of a person's land as such, where there is a willing vendor who can demonstrate to the tribunal (where the land consists of a 'house, building or manufactory', and the right over the land cannot be purchased without material detriment to that land or, where the land consists of a park or garden), that the right cannot be purchased without seriously affecting the amenity or convenience of the house to which that land belongs. Again, where land is being acquired and forms part of a common, open space or fuel or field allotment, the Agency may, by agreement or upon being authorised to do so by the Secretary of State, compulsorily exchange land or, as the case may be, rights.[18]

In general terms all these provisions 'bolt on' to the existing framework for compulsory purchase and are not intended to remove, or restrict application of, usual procedures.

Survey of land

There are specific provisions[19] empowering the Agency to enter and survey land for the purposes of acquisition or compensation, and the term 'survey' also includes for the purpose of soil and mineral tests.

The power may be exercised as of right on not less than 28 days' notice given to the occupier by the Agency, but any authorised person must if required produce evidence of his authority. Any person who wilfully obstructs a person acting in exercise of his powers under the section shall be guilty of an offence and liable on summary conviction to a fine 'not exceeding level 2 on the standard scale'.

Where a person enters premises for the purpose of survey, and is admitted into a 'factory, workshop or workplace', and discloses to any person any information obtained by him in it 'as to any manufacturing process or trade secret', he shall be guilty of an offence.[20] The subsection in question does not apply if the disclosure is made by a person in the course of 'performing his duty in connection with the purpose for which he was authorised to enter the premises'. An offence may lead to a fine not exceeding the statutory maximum or, on conviction on indictment, to imprisonment for a term not exceeding two years, or a fine, or both. Where land is damaged in the exercise of a right of entry or in the making of a survey, compensation in respect of that damage may be recovered by any person interested in the land from the Agency.

Although powers exist for the purposes of entry to survey, the carrying out of soil and mineral tests will not be allowed unless the carrying out of such works is specifically mentioned in the notice of intention to enter. Moreover, if the land is held by a statutory undertaker who objects to the proposed works on the grounds that it would be seriously detrimental to the carrying on of that undertaking, then the authority of the appropriate minister is in addition required.

Connection of private streets to the highway

An additional weapon in the armoury of the Agency is the power by notice to require a local highway authority (as understood by the Highways Act 1980) to connect a private street to an existing highway, whether or not that highway is maintainable at the public expense.[21] The Agency must first consult with the highway authority as to the terms of the notice which will specify the private street and the highway concerned, the works required and the period for the works to be carried out.[22] The highway authority may appeal by notice within two months and, after considering any representations from the Agency and the highway authority, the Secretary of State shall determine the appeal with power to modify the connection notice. In the absence of an appeal within two months the notice becomes effective in any event.[23]

If an appeal is withdrawn before determination by the Secretary of State, the order becomes effective 21 days after the Secretary of State is notified of the withdrawal.

Once a determination is made, the highway authority must carry out the works, and is entitled to recover the cost from the Agency or, if the works are not done then the Agency may itself carry out the works or have them carried out.[24]

Sources of finance

The Agency clearly cannot operate without funds. In this respect, it is as much at the mercy of the government of the day as it is in respect of the exercise of its functions. The sourcing of funds is as important to the Agency, in respect of the ability to operate and to carry out its functions, as it is to the consequent disbursement of funds. Schedule 18 deals with financial controls and also with the provision of finance both by the Treasury and from the private sector. The financial duties of the Agency are not wholly prescribed by Sched 18. Paragraph 2 of that Schedule provides that after consultation with the Agency, the Secretary of State may, with the approval of the Treasury, determine its financial duties and different determinations may be made in relation to different functions of the Agency. Further, although notice of every determination must be given by the Secretary of State, it can be retrospective, contain incidental or supplemental provisions and be varied or revoked by a subsequent determination.

Subject to the foregoing, the Agency has a financial year which commences with the commencement of the Schedule (10 November 1993) and ends on the following 31 March and, thereafter, financial years comprising each successive period of twelve months thereafter.

Government grant

The basic source of finance is by way of government grant under para 3 of Sched 18, ie monies provided by Parliament with the approval of the Treasury in respect of the exercise of the Agency's functions and in respect of its administrative expenses, being such sums as the Secretary of State may with the approval of the Treasury determine. Payment is also on such terms as the Secretary of State may with the approval of the Treasury determine.

Borrowing

Paragraph 5 of Sched 18 covers borrowing by the Agency both from the Secretary of State and from the private sector. Where borrowing is required 'temporarily',[25] then it may be by way of overdraft or otherwise, for the purpose of meeting the Agency's obligations and exercising its functions either in sterling from the Secretary of State or, with his consent, in sterling or in a currency other than sterling, from a person other than the Secretary of State. (The word 'temporarily' is not further defined.)

Where borrowing is from the Secretary of State, there is provision for the Treasury to lend to him out of the National Loans Fund any sums necessary for the purpose. Repayment of loans from the Secretary of State shall be made to him upon such terms and at such rate of interest as he may determine. In turn, the Secretary of State must pay all sums so received, whether of principal or interest, into the National Loans Fund. All terms and arrangements for borrowing, including from a person other than the Secretary of State, require Treasury approval.

Subject to the above, where the Agency desires to borrow 'otherwise than by way of temporary loan' it may do so in sterling from the Secretary of State or, with his consent, in a currency other than sterling from a person other than the Secretary of State. The distinction, therefore, between temporary and longer-term finance is that it is only in the case of the former that, where the borrowing is from a person other than the Secretary of State, it may be in sterling or some other currency. But in the case of the latter then, unless the borrowing is from the Secretary of State, it must be in a currency other than sterling.

Guarantees of loans

Where borrowing is from a person other than the Secretary of State, then the Treasury may also guarantee that borrowing on such terms as it thinks fit. Immediately the guarantee is given the Treasury must lay a statement of the guarantee before each House of Parliament.[26] If a guarantee is called, then a statement must be made before each House as soon as possible after the end of the relevant financial year as to the issue of any sums in response to the call. Where more than one financial year is concerned, then a fresh financial statement must be issued after the end of each financial year in question. All sums paid by the Treasury in fulfilling a guarantee of this kind are to be charged out of the Consolidated Fund.

It has been and is, as a matter of general law, the rule that where a guarantee is satisfied the guarantor is entitled to indemnity by his principal. The Act is more specific in that, if a Treasury guarantee is called, the Agency may be required at such times and in such manner, to make payments to the Treasury, including as to interest in such manner, and at such rates, as the Treasury directs in respect of the sums outstanding.[27] Again, any sums received are to be paid into the Consolidated Fund.

Agency surplus and other matters

There is, of course, another side to the financial coin, in that the Agency might actually have a surplus, whether on capital or on revenue account, and Sched 18, para 6 applies where it appears to the Secretary of State, after consultation with the Treasury and the Agency, that the Agency has such a surplus, after making allowance by way of transfer to reserve or otherwise for its future requirements.

The Agency is obliged, so long as the Secretary of State with the approval of the Treasury has first consulted with it, to pay to the Secretary of State a sum not exceeding the amount of the surplus as may be specified in his direction. Payment is to be made into the Consolidated Fund. Any sums so received may be treated by the Secretary of State as principal due under loans, and, in respect of repayments due at such times, as may be so determined.[28] Where a sum is treated as repayment of part of a loan then it is to be paid by the Secretary of State to the National Loans Fund and does not go into the Consolidated Fund.

Borrowings are limited in the aggregate for the time being to £200 million, or such sum not exceeding £300 million as the Secretary of State may, by statutory order, specify.[29] No order under this paragraph can come into effect without being laid before and approved by resolution of the House of Commons.

All sums advanced by way of loan from the Secretary of State and surpluses paid into the Consolidated Fund or the National Loans Fund must be the subject of an account prepared by the Secretary of State in respect of each financial year, which he is then to send to the Comptroller and Auditor General before the end of the month of November next following the relevant financial year.[30] In turn the Comptroller is to examine, certify and report on the accounts, and lay copies of them and of his report before each House of Parliament. The form of the account itself and the manner of its preparation is nonetheless subject to Treasury direction, and is not subject to independent audit.

Accounts

The Agency must keep proper accounts and other records in relation to them, and such accounts are to show a 'true and fair view of the Agency's activities'.[31] In addition, the Agency must also prepare for each financial year a statement of the accounts, in accordance with requirements of the Secretary of State, and approved by the Treasury as to the information to be contained in it, the manner in which it is to be presented and the methods and principles according to which the statement is to be prepared,[32] and in respect of each such requirement following 'such course as may from time to time be approved by the Secretary of State with the consent of the Treasury'.[33] The foregoing distinguishes the keeping of proper accounts (which is generally unqualified) with the preparation and presentation of a statement (which is qualified).

As regards auditing of the accounts, this must be, in effect, by an independent auditor, ie one who is eligible for appointment as a company auditor under CA 1989, Pt II and who, if the Agency were a body to which CA 1985, s 384 (duty to appoint auditors) applied, would not be ineligible for appointment as a company auditor. In other words, the accounts require independent audit save for the qualification under Sched 18, para 9(1) that the auditor is to be appointed annually by the Secretary of State! Once the accounts and statement of accounts are audited, the Agency must send to the Secretary of State a copy of the statement together with a copy of any auditor's report on the statement or on the accounts. A report must also be made by the Agency to the Secretary of State as soon as possible after the end of each financial year dealing generally with its operations during that year, and including in the report a copy of the audited statement of accounts (see above) and such information as the Secretary of State may specify, he in turn laying a copy of the report before each House of Parliament.[34]

Finally, the Secretary of State has access to the books of the Agency, who must provide such explanation as the Secretary of State or his appointed representative may reasonably require.[35]

Provision of financial assistance

Funds granted or loaned to the Agency will in any event be absorbed, in part, by the cost of administration and performance of its functions. Provision is made for financial assistance to be given by the Agency,[36] subject always to the consent of the Secretary of State. Subject to such consent, financial assistance may be given by the Agency in respect only of qualifying expenditure, and on such terms as the Agency with the consent of the Secretary of State considers appropriate. Qualifying expenditure is prescribed[37] as follows:

(1) the acquisition of land;
(2) the reclamation, improvement or refurbishment of land;
(3) the development or redevelopment of land, including the conversion or demolition of existing buildings;
(4) the equipment or fitting out of land;
(5) the provision of means of access, services or other facilities for land;
(6) environmental improvements.

Subject to these specific qualifications, financial assistance may be given in any form, including grants, loans, guarantees or through the Agency incurring expenditure for the benefit of the person assisted, but the Agency shall not in giving financial assistance purchase loan or share capital in a company.[38] (This inhibition should, of course, be distinguished from the power of the Agency, under s 160, itself to acquire interests in a body corporate, albeit not so as to make it a subsidiary of the Agency if at the time of the acquisition it was carrying on a trade or business.) Provision may also be made as to the terms of repayment of loans made by the Agency, and its entitlement to recover the proceeds, or part of the proceeds, of any disposal of land in respect of which such assistance was provided.[39]

The taking of security is not expressly precluded but s 164(5) does not go so far as to afford a secured right of clawback where, for example, land has been made available by the Agency, or financial assistance has been given to improve it. In recent years the public sector in particular has had to devise ingenious means, through the use of restrictive covenants, on perhaps less than wholly sound principles, in order to recover increases in value upon onward sale following a change of use. (In this respect, by contrast, the Crown Estate is afforded a specific right to impose restrictions[40] which has at least the appearance of affording to that body more certainty in relation to the imposition of clawback conditions.) The Agency has no such special privileges save that it is, by the Act, afforded very wide powers to provide financial assistance in accordance with the existing law. The hand of the Agency is perhaps marginally strengthened, at least in contract, to the extent that any person receiving financial assistance 'shall comply with the terms and conditions on which it is given and compliance may be enforced by the Agency'.[41]

General provisions of the Act

Part III of the Act takes the opportunity to deal with a number of general provisions.

Power of Secretary of State to give financial assistance

Outside of the provisions relating exclusively to the Agency, the Secretary of State may, with the consent of the Treasury, himself give financial assistance to any person in relation to regeneration of an urban area[42] by way of substitution of a new section for s 27 of the Housing and Planning Act 1986, the activities to include in particular:

(1) securing that land and buildings are brought into effective use;
(2) developing, or encouraging the development of, existing and new industry and commerce;
(3) creating an attractive and safe environment;
(4) providing housing or social and recreational facilities so as to encourage people to live or work in the area;
(5) providing employment for people who live in the area;
(6) providing training, educational facilities or health services for people who live in the area.

Power of Secretary of State to appoint the Agency as his agent

The Secretary of State, upon terms approved by the Treasury, may appoint the Agency to act as his agent in connection with grants for reclaiming or improving land, or bringing land into use under the Derelict Land Act 1982, s 1 and to provide financial assistance for urban regeneration under ss 27–29 of the Housing and Planning Act 1986.[43] In the last mentioned case, where financial assistance is being provided then, if the Agency is acting as agent of the Secretary of State, the financial assistance which it can provide is limited only to qualifying expenditure under s 164 of the Act.

Conversely, with the consent of the Secretary of State, the Agency may appoint an urban development corporation as its own agent, but not in connection with the provision of financial assistance.[44] Additionally, the Act empowers an urban development corporation, on being requested by the Agency to assist it in carrying out any of its functions by arranging for any of its property or staff to be made available to the Agency for such period, and on such other terms, as that corporation thinks fit.[45]

Urban development corporations

Section 178 of the Act contains a substituted section for s 157 of the Highways Act 1980 (not applicable to Scotland) relating to adoption of private streets, connection of streets to the highway and traffic regulation orders for private streets. The Act modifies s 134 of the 1980 Act by adding provisions concerning the adjustment of boundaries of an urban development area, so as to exclude any area of land, by order of the Secretary of State, subject to statutory instrument.[46] Furthermore, s 165 of the 1980 Act is modified,[47] by affording the Secretary of State the right, by order, subject to consultation with each local authority in whose area all or part of the urban development area is situated, to transfer to himself any property, rights or liabilities of an urban development corporation and, reflecting s 177 of the Act, terminating the appointment of such a corporation as an agent of the Agency.

Power of the Agency to become a planning authority

A specific power is afforded whereby the Agency may become, in effect, a local planning authority.[48] The kind of land, however, in respect of which the Agency may adopt such a role is confined to that contained in a designation order identifying land in England which is in an urban area or which, in the opinion of the Secretary of State, is suitable for 'urban development'.

In such a case the Secretary of State may by order, after first consulting every local authority any part of whose area is intended to be included in the proposed designated area, designate that area ('local authority' having the same meaning as under s 161 of the Act). The order must be made by statutory instrument which shall be subject to annulment in pursuance of a resolution of either House of Parliament.[49]

Designation orders

A designation order 'may contain such savings and transitional and supplementary provisions as may be specified in the order'.[50] The effect of a designation order can be to allow the Agency to become a planning authority (see above—including that any enactment relating to local planning authorities shall apply to the Agency subject to the modifications specified in the order) or, under s 172, to serve an adoption notice in relation to street works upon private land. As regards modification of enactments, the prospects are wholly speculative.

In the case of adoption of private streets in a designated area where street works are carried out on land which becomes a private street, the Agency may serve an adoption notice under a procedure similar to that for defining a designated area, including also a provision for appeal, but without the need for consultation prior to service of the adoption notice, and upon such date as the Secretary of State specifies the street (or part as the case may be) becomes a highway maintainable at the public expense.

The Agency may make traffic regulation orders under s 173 if it submits to the Secretary of State that an order should be made in relation to a private street, and the traffic authority does not appear to the Secretary of State to intend to make an order under s 1 or, as the case may be, s 6 of the Road Traffic Regulation Act 1984 (orders concerning traffic regulations) in relation to that road.

Schedule 20

Earlier reference has been made to Sched 20 (to which effect is given by s 169 of the Act). It is divided into three parts covering, firstly, modifications to the Acquisition of Land Act 1981 in the case of compulsory purchase under Pt III of the Act, then a number of detailed supplementary provisions relating to land and, lastly, covering acquisition of rights over land, the Compulsory Purchase Act 1965 applying accordingly, subject to express modifications.[51]

Where land becomes vested in the Agency, particular note should be made as to rights over the land enjoyed by a statutory undertaker for the purpose of carrying on its undertaking (para 12) and the power to extinguish those rights, and also as to the effect of development upon apparatus which may in consequence be required to be removed or resited.[52]

An order under para 9 extinguishing a public right of way may imply the removal of telecommunications apparatus under para 11 (to be contrasted with protection of such installations where easements over land, which have been acquired by the Agency under the Act from whatever source, are overridden under para 5). With similar protection for statutory undertakers and telecommunications apparatus, private rights of way may be extinguished by para 4. In the case of extinguishment, compensation is determined in accordance with the Land Compensation Act 1961 and for interference under sections 7 or 10 (as modified) of the Compulsory Purchase Act 1965.

Finally, special provision is made under para 6 as to consecrated land and burial grounds acquired by the Agency. Use of burial grounds as such (in accordance with planning permission) is distinguished for use by the Agency under subpara (5), subject to compliance with prescribed requirements as to human remains.

Notices

A number of procedures under Pt III of the Act are triggered by notice. Section 183 prescribes the appropriate procedure to be followed including, in respect of the proper address for service, that as regards a company or partnership registered or carrying on business outside the UK, its principal office within the UK shall be deemed its principal office for that purpose. Where the proper address cannot be obtained there is a fallback upon a person apparently resident or employed upon the land, or ultimately by leaving the notice 'conspicuously affixed to some building or object on the land'.[53] Service can generally be effected by delivery to the recipient, or leaving it at his proper address or by sending it 'by post' (ie not necessarily by recorded delivery or registered post) to him at that address.

Conclusion

If the Treasury so allowed, it is clear that the Act could be used as a major engine of economic recovery. It remains to be seen what chances there are of such a hope being fulfilled. However, given that the Agency has such wide powers it may be that its greater strength will lie in being an enabler, with sufficient influence and power to bring about co-operation between elements of the public and private sectors. The Agency could, perhaps, be better contemplated as a vehicle for the prospective unlocking of difficulties which would otherwise discourage development in areas where it is most needed.

Some may see the Agency as a threat, others an opportunity. Initially, at least, it is being provided with modest funds. But it has significant statutory powers at its disposal. From the point of view of the public sector, the Agency may be seen as a means of achieving what may not have been available before. Public authorities may consider harnessing private sector skills, in conjunction with the Agency, as a means to a long-term end.

The powers of the Agency are subject always to directions from the Secretary of State but can be exercised at any time in pursuance of its objects. Both the public and private sectors can be affected, whether in their perception to their benefit or otherwise. No doubt the Agency will, in the absence of encouragement from outside, devise its own strategy and programmes. It is, accordingly, for those who see their aspirations being achievable with the assistance of the Agency, to bring their schemes and ideas forward for consideration. How they will be received remains to be seen; there will be winners and no doubt some losers. So long as there is the political will, the statute book has been enhanced by the adoption of a unique measure to facilitate development in this decade and beyond.

[1-2] LRA 1993, s 160(2)(a).
[3] LRA 1993, s 158.
[4] LRA 1993, s 175.
[5] LRA 1993, s 167.
[6] LRA 1993, s 167(2).
[7] LRA 1993, s 167(3).
[8] LRA 1993, Sched 17, para 6(3).
[9] LRA 1993, s 159(1).
[10] LRA 1993, s 159(3).
[11] LRA 1993, s 167.
[12] LRA 1993, s 159(4).
[13] LRA 1993, s 160(1).
[14] LRA 1993, s 160(3).
[15] LRA 1993, s 160(2).
[16] LRA 1993, s 160(2)(c).
[17] LRA 1993, s 161(7).

[18] LRA 1993, s 162(3).
[19] LRA 1993, s 163.
[20] LRA 1993, s 163(5).
[21] LRA 1993, s 165(1).
[22] LRA 1993, s 165(3).
[23] LRA 1993, s 156(6)(*a*).
[24] LRA 1993, s 165(8).
[25] LRA 1993, Sched 18, para 4(1).
[26] LRA 1993, Sched 18, para 5(2).
[27] LRA 1993, Sched 18, para 5(4).
[28] LRA 1993, Sched 10, para 6(4).
[29] LRA 1993, Sched 18, para 7.
[30] LRA 1993, Sched 18, para 8(2).
[31] LRA 1993, Sched 18, para 9(2).
[32] LRA 1993, Sched 18, para 9(3)(*c*).
[33] LRA 1993, Sched 18, para 9(4).
[34] LRA 1993, Sched 18, para 12.
[35] LRA 1993, Sched 18, para 13.
[36] LRA 1993, s 164.
[37] LRA 1993, s 164(2).
[38] LRA 1993, s 164(3).
[39] LRA 1993, s 164(5).
[40] Crown Estate Act 1961, s 3(8).
[41] LRA 1993, s 164(6).
[42] LRA 1993, s 174.
[43] LRA 1993, s 175.
[44] LRA 1993, s 177(1).
[45] LRA 1993, s 177(2).
[46] LRA 1993, s 179.
[47] LRA 1993, s 180.
[48] LRA 1993, s 170 and 171.
[49] LRA 1993, s 170(4).
[50] LRA 1993, s 170(4)(G).
[51] LRA 1993, Sched 20, paras 20, 23.
[52] LRA 1993, Sched 20, para 14.
[53] LRA 1993, s 183(6).

The Leasehold Reform, Housing and Urban Development Act 1993

* * * * *

The Urban Regeneration Agency

158   The Agency

(1)   There shall be a body corporate to be known as the Urban Regeneration Agency ('the Agency') for the purpose of exercising the functions conferred on it by the following provisions of this Part.

(2)   Schedule 17 to this Act shall have effect with respect to the constitution of the Agency and Schedule 18 to this Act shall have effect with respect to the finances of the Agency.

(3)   It is hereby declared that, except as provided by section 175, the Agency is not to be regarded as the servant or agent of the Crown or as enjoying any status, immunity or privilege of the Crown and that its property is not to be regarded as the property of, or property held on behalf of, the Crown.

159   Objects of Agency

(1)   The main object of the Agency shall be to secure the regeneration of land in England—

    (a)   which is land of one or more of the descriptions mentioned in subsection (2); and

    (b)   which the agency (having regard to guidance, and acting in accordance with directions, given by the Secretary of State under section 167) determines to be suitable for regeneration under this Part.

(2)   The descriptions of land referred to in subsection (1)(a) are—

    (a)   land which is vacant or unused;

    (b)   land which is situated in an urban area and which is under-used or ineffectively used;

    (c)   land which is contaminated, derelict, neglected or unsightly; and

    (d)   land which is likely to become derelict, neglected or unsightly by reason of actual or apprehended collapse of the surface as the result of the carrying out of relevant operations which have ceased to be carried out;

and in this subsection 'relevant operations' has the same meaning as in section 1 of the Derelict Land Act 1982.

(3) The Agency shall also have the object of securing the development of land in England which the Agency—

    (a) having regard to guidance given by the Secretary of State under section 167;

    (b) acting in accordance with directions given by the Secretary of State under that section; and

    (c) with the consent of the Secretary of State,

determines to be suitable for development under this Part.

(4) The objects of the Agency are to be achieved in particular by the following means (or by such of them as seem to the Agency to be appropriate in any particular case), namely—

    (a) by securing that land and buildings are brought into effective use;

    (b) by developing, or encouraging the development of, existing and new industry and commerce;

    (c) by creating an attractive and safe environment;

    (d) by facilitating the provision of housing and providing, or facilitating the provision of, social and recreational facilities.

160   General powers of Agency

(1) Subject to the following provisions of this Part, for the purpose of achieving its objects the Agency may—

    (a) acquire, hold, manage, reclaim, improve and dispose of land, plant, machinery, equipment and other property;

    (b) carry out the development or redevelopment of land, including the conversion or demolition of existing buildings;

    (c) carry out building and other operations;

    (d) provide means of access, services or other facilities for land;

    (e) seek to ensure the provision of water, electricity, gas, sewerage and other services;

    (f) carry on any business or undertaking for the purposes of its objects;

    (g) with the consent of the Secretary of State, form, or acquire interests in, bodies corporate;

    (h) act with other persons, whether in partnership or otherwise;

    (i) give financial assistance to other persons;

    (j) act as agent for other persons;

    (k) provide advisory or other services and facilities; and

    (l) generally do anything necessary or expedient for the purposes of its objects or for purposes incidental to those purposes.

(2) Nothing in section 159 or this section shall empower the Agency—

    (a) to provide housing otherwise than by acquiring existing housing accommodation and making it available on a temporary basis for purposes incidental to the purposes of its objects;

    (b) to acquire an interest in a body corporate which at the time of the acquisition is carrying on a trade or business, if the effect of the acquisition would be to make the body corporate a subsidiary of the Agency; or

    (c) except with the consent of the Secretary of State, to dispose of any land otherwise than for the best consideration which can reasonably be obtained.

(3) For the avoidance of doubt it is hereby declared that subsection (1) relates only to the capacity of the Agency as a statutory corporation and nothing in section 159 or this section authorises it to disregard any enactment or rule of law.

(4) In this section—

'improve', in relation to land, includes refurbish, equip and fit out;

'subsidiary' has the meaning given by section 736 of the Companies Act 1985;

and in this section and the following provisions of this Part references to land include land not falling within subsection (1) or (3) of section 159.

161 Vesting of land by order

(1) Subject to subsections (2) and (3), the Secretary of State may by order provide that land specified in the order which is vested in a local authority, statutory undertakers or other public body, or in a wholly-owned subsidiary of a public body, shall vest in the Agency.

(2) An order under subsection (1) may not specify land vested in statutory undertakers which is used for the purpose of carrying on their statutory undertakings or which is held for that purpose.

(3) In the case of land vested in statutory undertakers, the power to make an order under subsection (1) shall be exercisable by the Secretary of State and the appropriate Minister.

(4) An order under subsection (1) shall have the same effect as a declaration under the Compulsory Purchase (Vesting Declarations) Act 1981 except that, in relation to such an order, the enactments mentioned in Schedule 19 to this Act shall have effect with the modifications specified in that Schedule.

(5) Compensation under the Land Compensation Act 1961, as applied by subsection (4) and Schedule 19 to this Act, shall be assessed by reference to values current on the date the order under subsection (1) comes into force.

(6) No compensation is payable, by virtue of an order under subsection (1), under Part IV of the Land Compensation Act 1961.

(7) In this section—

'the appropriate Minister'—

(a) in relation to statutory undertakers who are or are deemed to be statutory undertakers for the purposes of any provision of Part XI of the Town and Country Planning Act 1990, shall be construed as if contained in that Part;

(b) in relation to any other statutory undertakers, shall be construed in accordance with an order made by the Secretary of State;

and the reference to the Secretary of State and the appropriate Minister shall be similarly construed;

'local authority' means a county council, a district council, a London borough council or the Common Council of the City of London;

'statutory undertakers', except where the context otherwise requires, means—

(a) persons authorised by any enactment to carry on any railway, light railway, tramway, road transport, water transport, canal, inland navigation, dock, harbour, pier or lighthouse undertaking, or any undertaking for the supply of hydraulic power;

(b) British Shipbuilders, the Civil Aviation Authority, the British Coal Corporation and the Post Office;

(c) any other authority, body or undertakers specified in an order made by the Secretary of State;

(d) any wholly-owned subsidiary of any person, authority or body mentioned in paragraphs (a) and (b) or of any authority, body or undertakers specified in an order made under paragraph (c);

and 'statutory undertaking' shall be construed accordingly;

'wholly-owned subsidiary' has the meaning given by section 736 of the Companies Act 1985.

(8) If any question arises as to which Minister is the appropriate Minister in relation to any statutory undertakers, that question shall be determined by the Treasury.

(9) An order under subsection (1) shall be made by statutory instrument but no such order shall be made unless a draft of the order has been laid before and approved by resolution of each House of Parliament.

(10) An order under subsection (7) shall be made by statutory instrument which shall be subject to annulment in pursuance of a resolution of either House of Parliament.

162 Acquisition of land

(1) The Agency may, for the purpose of achieving its objects or for purposes incidental to that purpose, acquire land by agreement or, on being authorised to do so by the Secretary of State, compulsorily.

(2) The Agency may, for those purposes, be authorised by the Secretary of State, by means of a compulsory purchase order, to acquire compulsorily such new rights over land as are specified in the order.

(3) Where the land referred to in subsection (1) or (2) forms part of a common, open space or fuel or field garden allotment, the Agency may acquire (by agreement or, on being authorised to do so by the Secretary of State, compulsorily) land for giving in exchange for the land or, as the case may be, rights acquired.

(4) Subject to section 169, the Acquisition of Land Act 1981 shall apply to the compulsory acquisition of land by virtue of subsection (1) or (3).

(5) Schedule 3 to that Act shall apply to the compulsory acquisition of a right by virtue of subsection (2) but with the modification that the reference in paragraph 4(3) to statutory undertakers includes a reference to the Agency.

(6) The provisions of Part I of the Compulsory Purchase Act 1965 (so far as applicable), other than section 31, shall apply to the acquisition by the Agency of land by agreement; and in that Part as so applied 'land' has the meaning given by the Interpretation Act 1978.

(7) In subsection (2)—

'new rights over land' means rights over land which are not in existence when the order specifying them is made;

'compulsory purchase order' has the same meaning as in the Acquisition of Land Act 1981.

163 Power to enter and survey land

(1) Any person who is duly authorised in writing by the Agency may at any reasonable time enter any land for the purpose of surveying it, or estimating its value, in connection with—

(a) any proposal to acquire that land or any other land; or

(b) any claim for compensation in respect of any such acquisition.

(2) The power to survey land shall be construed as including power to search and bore for the purpose of ascertaining the nature of the subsoil or the presence of minerals in it.

(3) A person authorised under this section to enter any land—

    (a) shall, if so required, produce evidence of his authority before entry, and

    (b) shall not demand admission as of right to any land which is occupied unless 28 days' notice of the intended entry has been given to the occupier by the Agency.

(4) Any person who wilfully obstructs a person acting in exercise of his powers under this section shall be guilty of an offence and liable on summary conviction to a fine not exceeding level 2 on the standard scale.

(5) If any person who, in compliance with the provisions of this section, is admitted into a factory, workshop or workplace discloses to any person any information obtained by him in it as to any manufacturing process or trade secret, he shall be guilty of an offence.

(6) Subsection (5) does not apply if the disclosure is made by a person in the course of performing his duty in connection with the purpose for which he was authorised to enter the premises.

(7) A person who is guilty of an offence under subsection (5) shall be liable on summary conviction to a fine not exceeding the statutory maximum or on conviction on indictment to imprisonment for a term not exceeding two years or a fine or both.

(8) Where any land is damaged—

    (a) in the exercise of a right of entry under this section, or

    (b) in the making of any survey under this section,

compensation in respect of that damage may be recovered by any person interested in the land from the Agency.

(9) The provisions of section 118 of the Town and Country Planning Act 1990 (determination of claims for compensation) shall apply in relation to compensation under subsection (8) as they apply in relation to compensation under Part IV of that Act.

(10) No person shall carry out under this section any works authorised by virtue of subsection (2) unless notice of his intention to do so was included in the notice required by subsection (3).

(11) The authority of the appropriate Minister shall be required for the carrying out of any such works if—

    (a) the land in question is held by statutory undertakers and

    (b) they object to the proposed works on the ground that the execution of the works would be seriously detrimental to the carrying on of their undertaking;

and expressions used in this subsection have the same meanings as they have in section 325(9) of the Town and Country Planning Act 1990 (supplementary provisions as to rights of entry).

164 Financial assistance

(1) The consent of the Secretary of State is required for the exercise of the Agency's power to give financial assistance; and such assistance—

    (a) may be given by the Agency only in respect of qualifying expenditure; and

(b) may be so given on such terms and conditions as the Agency, with the consent of the Secretary of State, considers appropriate.

(2) Expenditure incurred in connection with any of the following matters is qualifying expenditure—

(a) the acquisition of land;

(b) the reclamation, improvement or refurbishment of land;

(c) the development or redevelopment of land, including the conversion or demolition of existing buildings;

(d) the equipment or fitting out of land;

(e) the provision of means of access, services or other facilities for land;

(f) environmental improvements.

(3) Financial assistance may be given in any form and may, in particular, be given by way of—

(a) grants;

(b) loans;

(c) guarantees; or

(d) incurring expenditure for the benefit of the person assisted; but the Agency shall not in giving financial assistance purchase loan or share capital in a company.

(4) A consent under subsection (1) may be given only with the approval of the Treasury.

(5) The terms and conditions on which financial assistance is given may, in particular, include provision as to—

(a) the circumstances in which the assistance must be repaid, or otherwise made good, to the Agency, and the manner in which that is to be done;

(b) the circumstances in which the Agency is entitled to recover the proceeds or part of the proceeds of any disposal of land in respect of which the assistance was provided.

(6) Any person receiving financial assistance shall comply with the terms and conditions on which it is given and compliance may be enforced by the Agency.

165   Connection of private streets to highway

(1) For the purpose of achieving its objects or for purposes incidental to that purpose, the Agency may serve a notice (a 'connection notice') on the local highway authority requiring the authority to connect a private street to an existing highway (whether or not it is a highway which for the purposes of the Highways Act 1980 is a highway maintainable at the public expense).

(2) A connection notice must specify—

(a) the private street and existing highway;

(b) the works which appear to the Agency to be necessary to make the connection; and

(c) the period within which those works should be carried out.

(3) Before serving a connection notice the Agency shall consult the local highway authority about the proposed contents of the notice.

(4) Within the period of two months beginning with the date on which the connection notice was served, the local highway authority may appeal against the notice to the Secretary of State.

(5) After considering any representations made to him by the Agency and the local highway authority, the Secretary of State shall determine an appeal under

subsection (4) by setting aside or confirming the connection notice (with or without modifications).

(6) A connection notice becomes effective—

(a) where no appeal is made within the period of two months referred to in subsection (4), upon the expiry of that period;

(b) where an appeal is made within that period but is withdrawn before it has been determined by the Secretary of State, on the date following the expiry of the period of 21 days beginning with the date on which the Secretary of State is notified of the withdrawal;

(c) where an appeal is made and the connection notice is confirmed by a determination under subsection (5), on such date as the Secretary of State may specify in the determination.

(7) Where a connection notice becomes effective, the local highway authority shall carry out the works specified in the notice within such period as may be so specified and may recover from the Agency the expenses reasonably incurred by them in doing so.

(8) If the local highway authority do not carry out the works specified in the notice within such period as may be so specified, the Agency may itself carry out or complete those works or arrange for another person to do so.

(9) In this section 'local highway authority' has the same meaning as in the Highways Act 1980.

The Agency: supplemental

166 Consents of Secretary of State

A consent of the Secretary of State under the foregoing provisions of this Part—

(a) may be given unconditionally or subject to conditions;

(b) may be given in relation to a particular case or in relation to such descriptions of case as may be specified in the consent; and

(c) except in relation to anything already done or agreed to be done on the authority of the consent, may be varied or revoked by a notice given by the Secretary of State to the Agency.

167 Guidance and directions by Secretary of State

(1) The Agency shall have regard to guidance from time to time given by the Secretary of State in deciding—

(a) which land is suitable for regeneration or development under this Part; and

(b) which of its functions under this Part it is to exercise for securing the regeneration or development of any particular land and how it is to exercise those functions.

(2) Without prejudice to any of the foregoing provisions of this Part requiring the consent of the Secretary of State to be obtained for anything to be done by the Agency, he may give directions to the Agency—

(a) for restricting the exercise by it of any of its functions under this Part; or

(b) for requiring it to exercise those functions in any manner specified in the directions.

(3) Directions under subsection (2) may be of a general or particular nature and may be varied or revoked by subsequent directions.

168 Validity of transactions

(1) A transaction between a person and the Agency shall not be invalidated by reason only of any failure by the Agency to observe its objects or the requirement in subsection (1) of section 160 that the Agency shall exercise the powers conferred by that subsection for the purpose of achieving its objects, and such a person shall not be concerned to see or enquire whether there has been any such failure.

(2) A transaction between a person and the Agency acting in purported exercise of its functions under this Part shall not be invalidated by reason only that it was carried out in contravention of any direction given under subsection (2) of section 167, and such a person shall not be concerned to see or enquire whether any directions under that subsection have been given or complied with.

169 Supplementary provisions as to vesting and acquisition of land

(1) Schedule 20 to this Act shall have effect.

(2) Part I of that Schedule modifies the Acquisition of Land Act 1981 as applied by section 162.

(3) Part II of that Schedule contains supplementary provisions about land vested in or acquired by the Agency under this Part.

(4) Part III of that Schedule contains supplementary provisions about the acquisition by the Agency of rights over land by virtue of section 162(2).

Designation orders and their effect

170 Power to make designation orders

(1) Where, as respects any area in England which is an urban area or which, in the opinion of the Secretary of State, is suitable for urban development, it appears to the Secretary of State—

(a) that all or any of the provisions authorised by section 171 should be made in relation to the whole or any part of it; or

(b) that either or both of sections 172 and 173 should apply in relation to it, the Secretary of State may by order designate that area and either so make the provision or provisions, or direct that the section or sections shall so apply, or (as the case may require) do both of those things.

(2) In this Part 'designation order' means an order under this section and 'designated area' means, subject to subsection (5), an area designated by a designation order.

(3) Before making a designation order the Secretary of State shall consult every local authority any part of whose area is intended to be included in the proposed designated area.

(4) A designation order—

(a) shall be made by statutory instrument which shall be subject to annulment in pursuance of a resolution of either House of Parliament; and

(b) may contain such savings and transitional and supplementary provisions as may be specified in the order.

(5) The power to amend a designation order conferred by section 14 of the Interpretation Act 1978 includes power to amend the boundaries of the designated area; and where any such amendment is made, any reference in this Part to a designated area is a reference to the designated area as so amended.

(6) In this section 'local authority' means a county council, a district council, a London borough council or the Common Council of the City of London.

171 Agency as local planning authority

(1) If a designation order so provides, the Agency shall be the local planning authority for the whole or any part of the designated area—

(a) for such purposes of Part III of the Town and Country Planning Act 1990 and sections 67 and 73 of the Planning (Listed Buildings and Conservation Areas) Act 1990 as may be specified in the order; and

(b) in relation to such kinds of development as may be so specified.

(2) A designation order making such provision as is mentioned in subsection (1) may also provide—

(a) that any enactment relating to local planning authorities shall not apply to the Agency; and

(b) that any such enactment which applies to the Agency shall apply to it subject to such modifications as may be specified in the order.

(3) If a designation order so provides—

(a) subject to any modifications specified in the order, the Agency shall have, in the whole or any part of the designated area, such of the functions conferred by the provisions mentioned in subsection (4) as may be so specified; and

(b) such of the provisions of Part VI and sections 249 to 251 and 258 of the Town and Country Planning Act 1990 and sections 32 to 37 of the Planning (Listed Buildings and Conservation Areas) Act 1990 as are mentioned in the order shall have effect, in relation to the Agency and to land in the designated area, subject to the modifications there specified.

(4) The provisions referred to in subsection (3)(a) are—

(a) sections 171C, 171D, 172 to 185, 187 to 202, 206 to 222, 224, 225, 231 and 320 to 336 of, and paragraph 11 of Schedule 9 to, the Town and Country Planning Act 1990;

(b) Chapters I, II and IV of Part I and sections 54 to 56, 59 to 61, 66, 68 to 72, 74 to 76 and 88 of the Planning (Listed Buildings and Conservation Areas) Act 1990; and

(c) sections 4 to 15, 17 to 21, 23 to 26AA, 36 and 36A of the Planning (Hazardous Substances) Act 1990.

(5) A designation order making such provision as is mentioned in subsection (3) may also provide that, for the purposes of any of the provisions specified in the order, any enactment relating to local planning authorities shall apply to the Agency subject to such modifications as may be so specified.

172 Adoption of private streets

(1) Where—

(a) this section applies in relation to a designated area; and

(b) any street works have been executed on any land in the designated area which was then or has since become a private street (or part of a private street),

the Agency may serve a notice (an 'adoption notice') on the street works authority requiring the authority to declare the street (or part) to be a highway which for the purposes of the Highways Act 1980 is a highway maintainable at the public expense.

(2) Within the period of two months beginning with the date on which the adoption notice was served, the street works authority may appeal against the notice to the Secretary of State.

(3) After considering any representations made to him by the Agency and the street works authority, the Secretary of State shall determine an appeal under subsection (2) by setting aside or confirming the adoption notice (with or without modifications).

(4) Where, under subsection (3), the Secretary of State confirms the adoption notice—

(a) he may at the same time impose conditions (including financial conditions) upon the Agency with which it must comply in order for the notice to take effect; and

(b) with effect from such date as the Secretary of State may specify, the street (or part) shall become a highway which for the purposes of the Highways Act 1980 is a highway maintainable at the public expense.

(5) Where a street works authority neither complies with the adoption notice, nor appeals under subsection (2), the street (or part) shall become, upon the expiry of the period of two months referred to in subsection (2), a highway which for the purposes of the Highways Act 1980 is a highway maintainable at the public expense.

(6) In this section 'street works' and 'street works authority' have the same meanings as in Part XI of the Highways Act 1980.

173 Traffic regulation orders for private streets

(1) Where—

(a) this section applies in relation to a designated area;

(b) the Agency submits to the Secretary of State that an order under this section should be made in relation to any road in the designated area which is a private street; and

(c) it appears to the Secretary of State that the traffic authority do not intend to make an order under section 1 or, as the case may be, section 6 of the Road Traffic Regulation Act 1984 (orders concerning traffic regulation) in relation to the road,

the Secretary of State may by order under this section make in relation to the road any such provision as he might have made by order under that section if he had been the traffic authority.

(2) The Road Traffic Regulation Act 1984 applies to an order under this section as it applies to an order made by the Secretary of State under section 1 or, as the case may be, section 6 of that Act in relation to a road for which he is the traffic authority.

(3) In this section 'road' and 'traffic authority' have the same meanings as in the Road Traffic Regulation Act 1984.

Other functions of Secretary of State

174 Financial assistance for urban regeneration

For section 27 of the Housing and Planning Act 1986 (power to give financial assistance) there shall be substituted the following section—

27   'Power to give assistance

(1) The Secretary of State may, with the consent of the Treasury, give financial assistance to any person in respect of expenditure incurred in connection with activities contributing to the regeneration of an urban area.

(2) Activities contributing to the regeneration of an urban area include in particular—

(a)   securing that land and buildings are brought into effective use;

(b)   developing, or encouraging the development of, existing and new industry and commerce;

(c)   creating an attractive and safe environment;

(d)   providing housing or social and recreational facilities so as to encourage people to live or work in the area;

(e)   providing employment for people who live in the area;

(f)   providing training, educational facilities or health services for people who live in the area.'

175   Power to appoint Agency as agent

(1) The Secretary of State may, on such terms as he may with the approval of the Treasury specify, appoint the Agency to act as his agent in connection with such of the functions mentioned in subsection (2) as he may specify; and where such an appointment is made, the Agency shall act as such an agent in accordance with the terms of its appointment.

(2) The functions referred to in subsection (1) are—

(a)   functions under section 1 of the Derelict Land Act 1982 or any enactment superseded by that section (grants for reclaiming or improving land or bringing land into use), other than the powers to make orders under subsections (5) and (7) of that section; and

(b)   so far as exercisable in relation to England, functions under sections 27 to 29 of the Housing and Planning Act 1986 (financial assistance for urban regeneration).

(3) In so far as an appointment under subsection (1) relates to functions mentioned in subsection (2)(b), the terms of the appointment shall preclude the Agency from giving financial assistance in respect of expenditure which is not qualifying expenditure within the meaning of section 164.

176   Power to direct disposal of unused etc. land held by public bodies

(1) In subsection (1) of section 98 (disposal of land by public bodies at direction of Secretary of State) of the Local Government, Planning and Land Act 1980 ('the 1980 Act')—

(a)   in paragraph (a), for the words 'is for the time being entered on a register maintained by him under section 95 above' there shall be substituted the words 'for the time being satisfies the conditions specified in section 95(2) above'; and

(b)   in paragraph (b), for the words 'is for the time being entered on such a register' there shall be substituted the words 'for the time being satisfies those conditions'.

(2) In section 99A of that Act (powers of entry), subsection (2) (which precludes entry on land which is not for the time being entered on a register maintained under section 95) shall cease to have effect.

Urban development corporations

177 Power to act as agents of Agency

(1) The Agency may, with the consent of the Secretary of State, appoint an urban development corporation, on such terms as may be agreed, to act as its agent in connection with such of its functions (other than its power to give financial assistance) as may be specified in the appointment; and where such an appointment is made, the urban development corporation shall act as such an agent in accordance with the terms of its appointment.

(2) For the purpose of assisting the Agency to carry out any of its functions, an urban development corporation, on being so requested by the Agency, may arrange for any of its property or staff to be made available to the Agency for such period and on such other terms as it thinks fit.

(3) In this section 'urban development corporation' means a corporation established by an order under section 135 of the 1980 Act.

178 Powers with respect to private streets

For section 157 of the 1980 Act (highways) there shall be substituted the following sections—

'Private streets

157   Adoption of private streets

(1) Where any street works have been executed on any land in an urban development area which was then or has since become a private street (or part of a private street), the urban development corporation may serve a notice (an 'adoption notice') on the street works authority requiring the authority to declare the street (or part) to be a highway which for the purposes of the Highways Act 1980 is a highway maintainable at the public expense.

(2) Within the period of two months beginning with the date on which the adoption notice was served, the street works authority may appeal against the notice to the Secretary of State.

(3) After considering any representations made to him by the corporation and the street works authority, the Secretary of State shall determine an appeal under subsection (2) above by setting aside or confirming the adoption notice (with or without modifications).

(4) Where, under subsection (3) above, the Secretary of State confirms the adoption notice—

(a)   he may at the same time impose conditions (including financial conditions) upon the corporation with which it must comply in order for the notice to take effect; and

(b)   with effect from such date as the Secretary of State may specify, the street (or part) shall become a highway which for the purposes of the Highways Act 1980 is a highway maintainable at the public expense.

(5) Where a street works authority neither complies with the adoption notice, nor appeals under subsection (2) above, the street (or part) shall become, upon the expiry of the period of two months referred to in subsection (2) above, a highway which for the purposes of the Highways Act 1980 is a highway maintainable at the public expense.

(6) In this section—

"highway" has the same meaning as in the Highways Act 1980;

"private street", "street works" and "street works authority" have the same meanings as in Part XI of that Act.

(7) This section does not extend to Scotland.

157A   Connection of private streets to highway

(1) An urban development corporation may serve a notice (a 'connection notice') on the local highway authority requiring the authority to connect a private street in the urban development area to an existing highway (whether or not it is a highway which for the purposes of the Highways Act 1980 is a highway maintainable at the public expense).

(2) A connection notice must specify—

(a)   the private street and the existing highway;

(b)   the works which appear to the corporation to be necessary to make the connection; and

(c)   the period within which those works should be carried out.

(3) Before serving a connection notice an urban development corporation shall consult the local highway authority about the proposed contents of the notice.

(4) Within the period of two months beginning with the date on which the connection notice was served, the local highway authority may appeal against the notice to the Secretary of State.

(5) After considering any representations made to him by the corporation and the local highway authority, the Secretary of State shall determine an appeal under subsection (4) above by setting aside or confirming the connection notice (with or without modifications).

(6) A connection notice becomes effective—

(a)   where no appeal is made within the period of two months referred to in subsection (4) above, upon the expiry of that period;

(b)   where an appeal is made within that period but is withdrawn before it has been determined by the Secretary of State, on the date following the expiry of the period of 21 days beginning with the date on which the Secretary of State is notified of the withdrawal;

(c)   where an appeal is made and the connection notice is confirmed by a determination under subsection (5) above, on such date as the Secretary of State may specify in the determination.

(7) Where a connection notice becomes effective, the local highway authority shall carry out the works specified in the notice within such period as may be so specified and may recover from the corporation the expenses reasonably incurred by them in doing so.

(8) If the local highway authority do not carry out the works specified in the notice within such period as may be so specified, the corporation may themselves carry out or complete those works or arrange for another person to do so.

(9) In this section—

"highway" and "local highway authority" have the same meanings as in the Highways Act 1980;

"private street" has the same meaning as in Part XI of that Act.

(10) This section does not extend to Scotland.

157B Traffic regulation orders for private streets
    (1) Where—
    (a) an urban development corporation submits to the Secretary of State
         that an order under this section should be made in relation to any road
         in the urban development area which is a private street; and
    (b) it appears to the Secretary of State that the traffic authority do not
         intend to make an order under section 1 or, as the case may be, section
         6 of the Road Traffic Regulation Act 1984 (orders concerning traffic
         regulation) in relation to the road,
    the Secretary of State may by order under this section make in relation to the
    road any such provision as he might have made by order under that section if
    he had been the traffic authority.
    (2) The Road Traffic Regulation Act 1984 applies to an order under this
    section as it applies to an order made by the Secretary of State under section 1
    or, as the case may be, section 6 of that Act in relation to a road for which he
    is the traffic authority.
    (3) In this section—
    "private street" has the same meaning as in Part XI of the Highways Act
         1980;
    "road" and "traffic authority" have the same meanings as in the Road Traffic
         Regulation Act 1984.
    (4) This section does not extend to Scotland.'

179 Adjustment of areas
    (1) After subsection (3) of section 134 (urban development areas) of the 1980
Act there shall be inserted the following subsections—
    '(3A) The Secretary of State may by order alter the boundaries of any urban
    development area so as to exclude any area of land.
    (3B) Before making an order under subsection (3A) above, the Secretary of
    State shall consult any local authority the whole or any part of whose area is
    included in the area of land to be excluded by the order.'
    (2) In subsection (4) of that section, for the words "this section" there shall be
substituted the words 'subsection (1) above'.
    (3) After that subsection there shall be inserted the following subsection—
    '(5) The power to make an order under subsection (3A) above—
    (a) shall be exercisable by statutory instrument subject to annulment in
         pursuance of a resolution of either House of Parliament; and
    (b) shall include power to make such incidental, consequential, transitional
         or supplementary provision as the Secretary of State thinks fit.'
    (4) In section 135(2) of that Act (establishment of urban development corpora-
tions), for the words 'section 134' there shall be substituted the words 'section
134(1)'.
    (5) In section 171 of that Act (interpretation of Part XVI: general), for the
definition of 'urban development area' there shall be substituted the following
definition—
    '"urban development area" means so much of an area designated by an order
         under subsection (1) of section 134 above as is not excluded from it by an
         order under subsection (3A) of that section;'.

180 Transfers of property, rights and liabilities

(1) In subsection (1) of section 165 of the 1980 Act (power to transfer undertaking of urban development corporation), after the words 'local authority', in both places where they occur, there shall be inserted the words 'or other body'.

(2) Subsection (3) of that section (transfer of liabilities by order) shall cease to have effect; and after that section there shall be inserted the following section—

165A 'Transfer of property, rights and liabilities by order.

(1) Subject to this section, the Secretary of State may at any time by order transfer to himself, upon such terms as he thinks fit, any property, rights or liabilities which—

(a) are for the time being vested in an urban development corporation, and

(b) are not proposed to be transferred under an agreement made under section 165 above and approved by the Secretary of State with the Treasury's concurrence.

(2) An order under this section may terminate—

(a) any appointment of the corporation under subsection (1) of section 177 of the Leasehold Reform, Housing and Urban Development Act 1993 (power of corporations to act as agents of the Urban Regeneration Agency); and

(b) any arrangements made by the corporation under subsection (2) of that section.

(3) Before making an order under this section, the Secretary of State shall consult each local authority in whose area all or part of the urban development area is situated.

(4) An order under this section shall be made by statutory instrument which shall be subject to annulment in pursuance of a resolution of either House of Parliament.'

(3) In subsection (9) of that section—

(a) after the words 'this section' there shall be inserted the words 'and sections 165A and 166 below';

(b) for the words "the section", in both places where they occur, there shall be substituted the words "the sections".

(4) For subsection (1) of section 166 of that Act (dissolution of urban development corporations) there shall be substituted the following subsection—

'(1) Where all property, rights and liabilities of an urban development corporation have been transferred under or by one or more relevant instruments, the Secretary of State may make an order by statutory instrument under this section.'

(5) For subsection (5) of that section there shall be substituted the following subsection—

"(5) In this section 'relevant instrument' means an agreement made under section 165 above or an order made under section 165a above."

Miscellaneous

181 No compensation where planning decision made after certain acquisitions

(1) Section 23(3) of the Land Compensation Act 1961 (no compensation where planning decision made after certain acquisitions) shall be amended as follows.

(2) After paragraph (a) there shall be inserted the following paragraph—

'(aa) under section 104 of that Act (acquisition by the Land Authority for Wales);'.

(3) After paragraph (c) there shall be inserted the words 'or

(d) under Part III of the Leasehold Reform, Housing and Urban Development Act 1993 (acquisition by the Urban Regeneration Agency).'

(4) Subsection (2) above shall apply to an acquisition or sale of an interest in land if the date of completion (within the meaning of Part IV of that Act) falls on or after the day on which this Act is passed.

182 Powers of housing action trusts with respect to private streets

(1) In subsection (1) of section 69 of the Housing Act 1988 (powers of housing action trusts with respect to private streets), for the words "in a private street (or part of a private street) in a designated area" there shall be substituted the words "on any land in a designated area which was then or has since become a private street (or part of a private street)".

(2) In subsection (2) of that section, the words from 'on grounds' onwards shall be omitted.

Supplemental

183 Notices

(1) This section has effect in relation to any notice required or authorised by this Part to be given to or served on any person.

(2) Any such notice may be given to or served on the person in question either by delivering it to him, or by leaving it at his proper address, or by sending it by post to him at that address.

(3) Any such notice may—

(a) in the case of a body corporate, be given to or served on the secretary or clerk of that body; and

(b) in the case of a partnership, be given to or served on a partner or a person having the control or management of the partnership business.

(4) For the purposes of this section and of section 7 of the Interpretation Act 1978 (service of documents by post) in its application to this section, the proper address of any person to or on whom a notice is to be given or served shall be his last known address, except that—

(a) in the case of a body corporate or its secretary or clerk, it shall be the address of the registered or principal office of that body; and

(b) in the case of a partnership, a partner or a person having the control or management of the partnership business, it shall be that of the principal office of the partnership;

and for the purposes of this subsection the principal office of a company registered outside the United Kingdom or of a partnership carrying on business outside the United Kingdom shall be its principal office within the United Kingdom.

(5) If the person to be given or served with any notice mentioned in subsection (1) has specified an address within the United Kingdom other than his proper address within the meaning of subsection (4) as the one at which he or someone on his behalf will accept documents of the same description as that notice, that address shall also be treated for the purposes of this section and section 7 of the Interpretation Act 1978 as his proper address.

(6) If the name or address of any owner, lessee or occupier of land to or on whom any notice mentioned in subsection (1) is to be served cannot after reasonable inquiry be ascertained, the document may be served either by leaving it in the hands of a person who is or appears to be resident or employed on the land or by leaving it conspicuously affixed to some building or object on the land.

184 Dissolution of English Industrial Estates Corporation

(1) The English Industrial Estates Corporation shall cease to exist on the commencement of this section.

(2) All the property, rights and liabilities to which that Corporation was entitled or subject immediately before that commencement shall become by virtue of this section property, rights and liabilities of the Agency.

185 Interpretation of Part III

In this Part—

'the 1980 Act' means the Local Government, Planning and Land Act 1980;

'the Agency' means the Urban Regeneration Agency;

'designation order' and 'designated area' have the meanings given by section 170;

'highway' has the same meaning as in the Highways Act 1980;

'private street' has the same meaning as in Part XI of that Act.

PART IV

SUPPLEMENTAL

186 Financial provisions

(1) There shall be paid out of money provided by Parliament—

(a) any expenses of the Secretary of State incurred in consequence of this Act; and

(b) any increase attributable to this Act in the sums payable out of money so provided under any other enactment.

(2) There shall be paid into the Consolidated Fund any increase attributable to this Act in the sums payable into that Fund under any other enactment.

187 Amendments and repeals

(1) The enactments mentioned in Schedule 21 to this Act shall have effect subject to the amendments there specified (being minor amendments and amendments consequential on the provisions of this Act).

(2) The enactments mentioned in Schedule 22 to this Act (which include some that are spent or no longer of practical utility) are hereby repealed to the extent specified in the third column of that Schedule.

188   Short title, commencement and extent

(1) This Act may be cited as the Leasehold Reform, Housing and Urban Development Act 1993.

(2) This Act, except—

(a) this section;

(b) sections 126 and 127, 135 to 140, 149 to 151, 181(1), (2) and (4) and 186; and

(c) the repeal in section 80(1) of the Local Government and Housing Act 1989,

shall come into force on such day as the Secretary of State may by order made by statutory instrument appoint; and different days may be so appointed for different provisions or for different purposes.

(3) An order under subsection (2) may contain such transitional provisions and savings (whether or not involving the modification of any statutory provision) as appear to the Secretary of State necessary or expedient in connection with the provisions thereby brought into force by the order.

(4) The following, namely—

(a) Part I of this Act;

(b) Chapter I of Part II of this Act; and

(c) subject to subsection (6), Part III of this Act, extend to England and Wales only.

(5) Chapter II of Part II of this Act extends to Scotland only.

(6) In Part III of this Act—

(a) sections 174, 179 and 180 also extend to Scotland; and

(b) paragraph 8 of Schedule 17 also extends to Scotland and Northern Ireland.

(7) This Part, except this section, paragraph 3 of Schedule 21 and the repeals in the House of Commons Disqualification Act 1975 and the Northern Ireland Assembly Disqualification of Act 1975, does not extend to Northern Ireland.

★ ★ ★ ★ ★

SCHEDULE 17

CONSTITUTION OF THE AGENCY

Membership

1—(1) The Agency shall consist of such number of members (being not less than six) as the Secretary of State may from time to time appoint.

(2) The Secretary of State shall appoint one of the members to be chairman and may, if he thinks fit, appoint another of them to be deputy chairman.

(3) Subject to the provisions of this paragraph, a member of the Agency shall hold and vacate office in accordance with the terms of his appointment.

(4) A person who ceases to be a member of the Agency shall be eligible for reappointment.

(5) A member of the Agency may resign his office by notice in writing to the Secretary of State.

(6) The Secretary of State may remove a member of the Agency from office if he is satisfied that he—
    (a)   is unable or unfit to carry out the functions of a member;
    (b)   has not complied with the terms of his appointment; or
    (c)   has become bankrupt or made an arrangement with his creditors.
(7) A person shall cease to be chairman or deputy chairman of the Agency—
    (a)   if he resigns as such by notice in writing to the Secretary of State; or
    (b)   if he ceases to be a member of the Agency.

Remuneration, pensions etc.

2—(1) The Agency shall pay to its members such remuneration, and such allowances, as the Secretary of State may determine.
(2) The Agency may—
    (a)   pay such pensions, allowances or gratuities to or in respect of any persons who have been or are its members as the Secretary of State may determine;
    (b)   make such payments as the Secretary of State may determine towards provision for the payment of pensions, allowances or gratuities to or in respect of any such persons.
(3) If, when a person ceases to be a member of the Agency, the Secretary of State determines that there are special circumstances which make it right that he should receive compensation, the Agency shall pay to him a sum by way of compensation of such amount as the Secretary of State may determine.
(4) The approval of the Treasury shall be required for any determination of the Secretary of State under this paragraph.

Staff

3—(1) There shall be a chief executive of the Agency who shall be responsible to the Agency for the general exercise of the Agency's functions.
(2) The chief executive shall be appointed by the Agency but no person shall be appointed as chief executive unless the Secretary of State has consented to the appointment.
(3) The Agency may appoint such other number of staff as the Secretary of State may approve.
(4) The terms and conditions of appointment of any person appointed by the Agency under this paragraph shall be determined by the Agency with the consent of the Secretary of State.
(5) The Agency shall pay to members of its staff such remuneration, and such allowances, as it may, with the consent of the Secretary of State, determine.
(6) The Agency may—
    (a)   pay such pensions, allowances or gratuities to or in respect of any persons who have been or are members of its staff;
    (b)   make such payments towards provision for the payment of pensions, allowances or gratuities to or in respect of any such persons,
as it may, with the consent of the Secretary of State, determine.
(7) Any reference in sub-paragraph (6) to pensions, allowances or gratuities to or in respect of any such persons as are mentioned in that sub-paragraph includes a reference to payments by way of compensation to or in respect of any members of

the Agency's staff who suffer loss of office or employment or loss or diminution of emoluments.

(8) The approval of the Treasury shall be required for the giving of any consent under sub-paragraph (4), (5) or (6).

Delegation of powers

4 Anything authorised or required to be done by the Agency under this Part—
    (a)   may be done by any member of the Agency, or of its staff, who has been authorised for the purpose, whether generally or specially, by the Agency; or
    (b)   may be done by any committee or sub-committee of the Agency which has been so authorised.

Proceedings

5—(1) Subject to the following provisions of this Schedule, the Agency may regulate both its own procedure (including quorum) and that of any committee or sub-committee.

(2) The Secretary of State may give directions as to the exercise by the Agency of its power under sub-paragraph (1) to regulate procedure; and directions under this sub-paragraph may be of a general or particular nature and may be varied or revoked by subsequent directions.

(3) The validity of any proceedings of the Agency or of any committee or sub-committee of the Agency shall not be affected—
    (a)   by a vacancy amongst the members of the Agency, committee or sub-committee;
    (b)   by a defect in the appointment of a member of the Agency, committee or sub-committee; or
    (c)   by a contravention of directions under sub-paragraph (2) or of paragraph 6.

(4) With the consent of the Secretary of State, persons who are not members of the Agency may be appointed as members of a committee or sub-committee of the Agency, but any such committee or sub-committee may not consist entirely of persons who are neither members of the Agency nor members of its staff.

(5) The Agency may pay to any person who is a member of a committee or sub-committee but who is not a member of the Agency such remuneration, and such allowances, as the Secretary of State may, with the approval of the Treasury, determine.

Members' interests

6—(1) A member of the Agency or of any committee or sub-committee who is directly or indirectly interested in any matter brought up for consideration at a meeting of the Agency or of the committee or sub-committee shall disclose the nature of his interest to the meeting.

(2) Where the matter in respect of which such a disclosure is made is a contract or agreement of any description, the member shall not take part in any deliberation or decision of the Agency, committee or sub-committee with respect to the matter.

(3) Where the matter in respect of which such a disclosure is made is one other than a contract or agreement, the member may take part in any deliberation or decision of the Agency, committee or sub-committee with respect to the matter unless the rest of the members decide that the interest disclosed might prejudicially affect the member's consideration of the matter.

Application of seal and proof of instruments

7—(1) The application of the seal of the Agency shall be authenticated by the signature of any member of the Agency, or of its staff, who has been authorised by the Agency, whether generally or specially, for the purpose.

(2) Every document purporting to be an instrument issued by the Agency and to be duly sealed with the seal of the Agency or to be signed on behalf of the Agency shall be received in evidence and, unless the contrary is shown, shall be deemed to be an instrument so issued.

House of Commons disqualification

8 In Schedule 1 to the House of Commons Disqualification Act 1975 (bodies of which all members are disqualified for membership of the House of Commons), in Part II there shall be inserted, at the appropriate place, the following entry—
    'The Urban Regeneration Agency.';
and the like insertion shall be made in Part II of Schedule 1 to the Northern Ireland Assembly Disqualification Act 1975.

SCHEDULE 18

FINANCES OF THE AGENCY

Financial year

1 The financial years of the Agency shall be as follows—
  (a)   the period beginning with the commencement of this Schedule and ending with the next following 31st March; and
  (b)   each successive period of twelve months;
and references in this Schedule to a financial year shall be construed accordingly.

Financial duties

2—(1) After consultation with the Agency, the Secretary of State may, with the approval of the Treasury, determine the financial duties of the Agency; and different determinations may be made in relation to different functions of the Agency.

(2) The Secretary of State shall give the Agency notice of every determination, and a determination may—
  (a)   relate to a period beginning before the date on which it is made;
  (b)   contain incidental or supplementary provisions; and
  (c)   be varied or revoked by a subsequent determination.

Government grants

3—(1) The Secretary of State may, out of moneys provided by Parliament and with the approval of the Treasury, pay to the Agency, in respect of the exercise of its functions and in respect of its administrative expenses, such sums as he may, with the approval of the Treasury, determine.

(2) The payment may be made on such terms as the Secretary of State may, with the approval of the Treasury, determine.

Borrowing

4—(1) The Agency may borrow temporarily, by way of overdraft or otherwise, such sums as it may require for meeting its obligations and exercising its functions—
  (a) in sterling from the Secretary of State; or
  (b) with the consent of the Secretary of State, or in accordance with any general authority given by the Secretary of State, either in sterling or in a currency other than sterling from a person other than the Secretary of State.

(2) The Agency may borrow otherwise than by way of temporary loan such sums as it may require—
  (a) in sterling from the Secretary of State; or
  (b) with the consent of the Secretary of State, in a currency other than sterling from a person other than the Secretary of State.

(3) The Secretary of State may lend to the Agency any sums it has power to borrow from him under sub-paragraph (1) or (2).

(4) The Treasury may issue to the Secretary of State out of the National Loans Fund any sums necessary to enable him to make loans under sub-paragraph (3).

(5) Loans made under sub-paragraph (3) shall be repaid to the Secretary of State at such times and by such methods, and interest on the loans shall be paid to him at such times and at such rates, as he may determine.

(6) All sums received by the Secretary of State under sub-paragraph (5) shall be paid into the National Loans Fund.

(7) The approval of the Treasury shall be required for the giving of any consent or authority under sub-paragraph (1) or (2), the making of any loan under sub-paragraph (3) or the making of any determination under sub-paragraph (5).

Guarantees

5—(1) The Treasury may guarantee, in such manner and on such conditions as they think fit, the repayment of the principal of, and the payment of interest on, any sums which the Agency borrows from a person other than the Secretary of State.

(2) Immediately after a guarantee is given under this paragraph, the Treasury shall lay a statement of the guarantee before each House of Parliament; and, where any sum is issued for fulfilling a guarantee so given, the Treasury shall lay before each House of Parliament a statement relating to that sum, as soon as possible after the end of each financial year—
  (a) beginning with that in which the sum is issued; and
  (b) ending with that in which all liability in respect of the principal of the sum and in respect of interest on it is finally discharged.

(3) Any sums required by the Treasury for fulfilling a guarantee under this paragraph shall be charged on and issued out of the Consolidated Fund.

(4) If any sums are issued in fulfilment of a guarantee given under this paragraph, the Agency shall make to the Treasury, at such times and in such manner as the Treasury may from time to time direct, payments of such amounts as the Treasury so direct in or towards repayment of the sums so issued and payments of interest, at such rates as the Treasury so direct, on what is outstanding for the time being in respect of sums so issued.

(5) Any sums received by the Treasury in pursuance of sub-paragraph (4) shall be paid into the Consolidated Fund.

Surplus funds

6—(1) This paragraph applies where it appears to the Secretary of State, after consultation with the Treasury and the Agency, that the Agency has a surplus, whether on capital or on revenue account, after making allowance by way of transfer to reserve or otherwise for its future requirements.

(2) The Agency shall, if the Secretary of State with the approval of the Treasury and after consultation with the Agency so directs, pay to the Secretary of State such sum not exceeding the amount of the surplus as may be specified in the direction.

(3) Any sum received by the Secretary of State under this paragraph shall, subject to sub-paragraph (5), be paid into the Consolidated Fund.

(4) The whole or part of any payment made to the Secretary of State by the Agency under sub-paragraph (2) shall, if the Secretary of State with the approval of the Treasury so determines, be treated as made—

    (a)   by way of repayment of such part of the principal of loans under paragraph 4(3); and

    (b)   in respect of the repayments due at such times,

as may be so determined.

(5) Any sum treated under sub-paragraph (4) as a repayment of a loan shall be paid by the Secretary of State into the National Loans Fund.

Financial limits

7—(1) The aggregate amount at any time of borrowed sums shall not exceed £200 million or such greater sum not exceeding £300 million as the Secretary of State may by order made by statutory instrument specify.

(2) In sub-paragraph (1) "borrowed sums" means sums borrowed by the Agency under paragraph 4 minus repayments made or treated as made in respect of those sums.

(3) No order shall be made under sub-paragraph (1) unless a draft of the order has been laid before and approved by resolution of the House of Commons.

Grants and loans: accounts

8—(1) The Secretary of State shall prepare in respect of each financial year an account—

    (a)   of the sums issued to him under paragraph 4(4) and the sums received by him under paragraph 4(5) and of the disposal by him of those sums; and

    (b)   of the sums paid into the Consolidated Fund or National Loans Fund under paragraph 6.

(2) The Secretary of State shall send the account to the Comptroller and Auditor General before the end of the month of November next following the end of that year.

(3) The Comptroller and Auditor General shall examine, certify and report on the account and lay copies of it and of his report before each House of Parliament.

(4) The form of the account and the manner of preparing it shall be such as the Treasury may direct.

Accounts

9—(1) The Agency shall keep proper accounts and other records in relation to them.

(2) The accounts and records shall show, in respect of the financial year to which they relate, a true and fair view of the Agency's activities.

(3) The Agency shall prepare in respect of each financial year a statement of accounts complying with any requirement which the Secretary of State has, with the approval of the Treasury, notified in writing to the Agency relating to—

    (a)   the information to be contained in the statement;

    (b)   the manner in which the information is to be presented; and

    (c)   the methods and principles according to which the statement is to be prepared.

(4) Subject to any requirement notified to the Agency under sub-paragraph (3), in preparing any statement of accounts in accordance with that sub-paragraph the Agency shall follow, with respect to each of the matters specified in paragraphs (a) to (c) of that sub-paragraph, such course as may for the time being be approved by the Secretary of State with the consent of the Treasury.

Audit

10—(1) The Agency's accounts and statements of accounts shall be audited by an auditor to be appointed annually by the Secretary of State.

(2) A person shall not be qualified for appointment under sub-paragraph (1) unless—

    (a)   he is eligible for appointment as a company auditor under Part II of the Companies Act 1989 (eligibility for appointment as company auditor); and

    (b)   if the Agency were a body to which section 384 of the Companies Act 1985 (duty to appoint auditors) applies, he would not be ineligible for appointment as company auditor of the Agency by virtue of section 27 of the Companies Act 1989 (ineligibility on ground of lack of independence).

Transmission to Secretary of State

11 As soon as the accounts and statement of accounts of the Agency for any financial year have been audited, it shall send to the Secretary of State a copy of the statement, together with a copy of any report made by the auditor on the statement or on the accounts.

Reports

12—(1) As soon as possible after the end of each financial year, the Agency—

(a) shall make to the Secretary of State a report dealing generally with its operations during the year; and

(b) shall include in the report a copy of its audited statement of accounts for that year and such information as the Secretary of State may specify.

(2) The Secretary of State shall lay a copy of the report before each House of Parliament.

Information

13 Without prejudice to paragraph 12, the Agency shall provide the Secretary of State with such information relating to its activities as he may require, and for that purpose—

(a) shall permit any person authorised by the Secretary of State to inspect and make copies of the accounts, books, documents or papers of the Agency; and

(b) shall afford such explanation of them as that person or the Secretary of State may reasonably require.

SCHEDULE 19

VESTING OF LAND IN THE AGENCY: MODIFICATIONS OF ENACTMENTS

Land Compensation Act 1961 (c 33)

1 The Land Compensation Act 1961 shall have effect in relation to orders under section 161(1) of this Act with the modifications specified in paragraphs 2 to 5.

2 References to the date of service of a notice to treat shall be treated as references to the date on which an order under section 161(1) of this Act comes into force.

3 Section 17(2) (certification of appropriate alternative development) shall be treated as if for the words "the authority proposing to acquire the interest have served a notice to treat in respect thereof, or an agreement has been made for the sale thereof to that authority" there were substituted the words 'an order under section 161 of the Leasehold Reform, Housing and Urban Development Act 1993 vesting the land in which the interest subsists in the Urban Regeneration Agency has come into force, or an agreement has been made for the sale of the interest to the Agency'.

4 Section 22(2) (interpretation of Part III) shall be treated as if at the end of paragraph (c) there were added the words 'or

(ca) where an order has been made under section 161(1) of the Leasehold Reform, Housing and Urban Development Act 1993 vesting the land in which the interest subsists in the Urban Regeneration Agency'.

5 Any reference to a notice to treat in section 39(2) (interpretation) shall be treated as a reference to an order under section 161(1) of this Act.

Compulsory Purchase (Vesting Declarations) Act 1981 (c. 66)

6 In section 15 of the Compulsory Purchase (Vesting Declarations) Act 1981 (application to orders under section 141 of Local Government, Planning and Land Act 1980) after the words 'vesting declaration' there shall be inserted the words 'or under subsection (1) of section 161 of the Leasehold Reform, Housing and Urban Development Act 1993 (subsection (4) of which makes similar provision)'.

7—(1) In Schedule 2 to that Act (vesting of land in urban development corporation), in paragraph 1 after the words 'similar provision' there shall be inserted the words 'or under subsection (1) of section 161 of the Leasehold Reform, Housing and Urban Development Act 1993 (subsection (4) of which contains similar provision)'.

(2) In paragraph 3(a) of that Schedule for the words 'or, as the case may be, the housing action trust' there shall be substituted the words 'the housing action trust or the Urban Regeneration Agency (as the case may be)'.

SCHEDULE 20

The Agency: Land

Part I

Modifications of Acquisition of Land Act 1981

1 The Acquisition of Land Act 1981 (in this Part of this Schedule referred to as "the 1981 Act") shall have effect in relation to the compulsory acquisition of land under this Part of this Act with the modifications specified in paragraphs 2 and 3.

2—(1) Where a compulsory purchase order authorising the acquisition of any land is submitted to the Secretary of State in accordance with section 2(2) of the 1981 Act (procedure for authorisation), then if the Secretary of State—

    (a)   is satisfied that the order ought to be confirmed so far as it relates to part of the land comprised in it, but

    (b)   has not for the time being determined whether it ought to be confirmed so far as it relates to any other such land,

he may confirm the order so far as it relates to the land mentioned in paragraph (a), and give directions postponing the consideration of the order, so far as it relates to any other land specified in the directions, until such time as may be so specified.

(2) Where the Secretary of State gives directions under sub-paragraph (1), the notices required by section 15 of the 1981 Act (notices after confirmation of order) to be published and served shall include a statement of the effect of the directions.

3 The reference in section 17(3) of the 1981 Act (local authority and statutory undertakers' land) to statutory undertakers includes a reference to the Agency.

PART II

LAND: SUPPLEMENTARY

Extinguishment of rights over land

4—(1) Subject to this paragraph, on an order under section 161(1) of this Act coming into force or the completion by the Agency of a compulsory acquisition of land under this Part of this Act—

    (a) all private rights of way and rights of laying down, erecting, continuing or maintaining any apparatus on, under or over the land shall be extinguished; and

    (b) any such apparatus shall vest in the Agency.

(2) Sub-paragraph (1) does not apply—

    (a) to any right vested in, or apparatus belonging to, statutory undertakers for the purpose of carrying on their undertaking; or

    (b) to any right conferred by or in accordance with the telecommunications code on the operator of a telecommunications code system or to any telecommunications apparatus kept installed for the purposes of any such system.

(3) In respect of any right or apparatus not falling within sub-paragraph (2), sub-paragraph (1) shall have effect subject to—

    (a) any direction given by the Secretary of State before the coming into force of the order or by the Agency before the completion of the acquisition (as the case may be) that sub-paragraph (1) shall not apply to any right or apparatus specified in the direction, and

    (b) any agreement which may be made (whether before or after the coming into force of the order or completion of the acquisition) between the Secretary of State or the Agency and the person in or to whom the right or apparatus in question is vested or belongs.

(4) Any person who suffers loss by the extinguishment of a right or the vesting of any apparatus under this paragraph shall be entitled to compensation from the Agency.

(5) Any compensation payable under this paragraph shall be determined in accordance with the Land Compensation Act 1961.

Power to override easements

5—(1) The erection, construction, carrying out, or maintenance of any building or work on land which has been vested in or acquired by the Agency under this Part of this Act, whether done by the Agency or by any other person, is authorised by virtue of this paragraph if it is done in accordance with planning permission, notwithstanding that it involves—

    (a) interference with an interest or right to which this paragraph applies; or

    (b) a breach of a restriction as to the user of land arising by virtue of a contract.

(2) Nothing in sub-paragraph (1) shall authorise interference with any right of way or right of laying down, erecting, continuing or maintaining apparatus on, under or over land, being—

    (a)   a right vested in or belonging to statutory undertakers for the purpose of the carrying on of their undertaking; or

    (b)   a right conferred by or in accordance with the telecommunications code on the operator of a telecommunications code system.

(3) This paragraph applies to the following interests and rights, that is to say, any easement, liberty, privilege, right or advantage annexed to land and adversely affecting other land, including any natural right to support.

(4) In respect of any interference or breach in pursuance of sub-paragraph (1), compensation shall be payable under section 7 or 10 of the Compulsory Purchase Act 1965, to be assessed in the same manner and subject to the same rules as in the case of other compensation under those sections in respect of injurious affection where the compensation is to be estimated in connection with a purchase by the Agency or the injury arises from the execution of works on land acquired by the Agency.

(5) Where a person other than the Agency—

    (a)   is liable to pay compensation by virtue of sub-paragraph (4); and

    (b)   fails to discharge that liability,

the liability shall (subject to sub-paragraph (6)) be enforceable against the Agency.

(6) Nothing in sub-paragraph (5) shall be construed as affecting any agreement between the Agency and any other person for indemnifying the Agency against any liability under that sub-paragraph.

(7) Nothing in this paragraph shall be construed as authorising any act or omission on the part of any person which is actionable at the suit of any person on any grounds other than such an interference or breach as is mentioned in sub-paragraph (1).

(8) Nothing in this paragraph shall be construed as authorising any act or omission on the part of the Agency or any body corporate in contravention of any limitation imposed by law on its capacity by virtue of its constitution.

Consecrated land and burial grounds

6—(1) Any consecrated land, whether including a building or not, which has been vested in or acquired by the Agency under this Part of this Act may (subject to the following provisions of this paragraph) be used by the Agency, or by any other person, in any manner in accordance with planning permission, notwithstanding any obligation or restriction imposed under ecclesiastical law or otherwise in respect of consecrated land.

(2) Sub-paragraph (1) does not apply to land which consists or forms part of a burial ground.

(3) Any use of consecrated land authorised by sub-paragraph (1), and the use of any land, not being consecrated land, vested or acquired as mentioned in that sub-paragraph which at the time of vesting or acquisition included a church or other building used or formerly used for religious worship or the site thereof, shall be subject to compliance with the prescribed requirements with respect to—

    (a)   the removal and reinterment of any human remains; and

    (b)   the disposal of monuments,

and, in the case of consecrated land, shall be subject to such provisions as may be prescribed for prohibiting or restricting the use of the land, either absolutely or until the prescribed consent has been obtained, so long as any church or other building used or formerly used for religious worship, or any part thereof, remains on the land.

(4) Any regulations made for the purposes of sub-paragraph (3)—

 (a) shall contain such provisions as appear to the Secretary of State to be requisite for securing that any use of land which is subject to compliance with the regulations shall, as nearly as may be, be subject to the like control as is imposed by law in the case of a similar use authorised by an enactment not contained in this Act or by a Measure, or as it would be proper to impose on a disposal of the land in question otherwise than in pursuance of an enactment or Measure;

 (b) shall contain requirements relating to the disposal of any such land as is mentioned in sub-paragraph (3) such as appear to the Secretary of State requisite for securing that the provisions of that sub-paragraph shall be complied with in relation to the use of the land; and

 (c) may contain such incidental and consequential provisions (including provision as to the closing of registers) as appear to the Secretary of State to be expedient for the purposes of the regulations.

(5) Any land consisting of a burial ground or part of a burial ground which has been vested in or acquired by the Agency under this Part of this Act may be used by the Agency in any manner in accordance with planning permission, notwithstanding anything in any enactment relating to burial grounds or any obligation or restriction imposed under ecclesiastical law or otherwise in respect of burial grounds.

(6) Sub-paragraph (5) shall not have effect in respect of any land which has been used for the burial of the dead until the prescribed requirements with respect to the removal and reinterment of human remains and the disposal of monuments in or upon the land have been complied with.

(7) Provision shall be made by any regulations made for the purposes of sub-paragraphs (3) and (6)—

 (a) for requiring the persons in whom the land is vested to publish notice of their intention to carry out the removal and reinterment of any human remains or the disposal of any monuments;

 (b) for enabling the personal representatives or relatives of any deceased person themselves to undertake the removal and reinterment of the remains of the deceased and the disposal of any monument commemorating the deceased, and for requiring the persons in whom the land is vested to defray the expenses of such removal, reinterment and disposal, not exceeding such amount as may be prescribed;

 (c) for requiring compliance with such reasonable conditions (if any) as may be imposed, in the case of consecrated land, by the bishop of the diocese, with respect to the manner of removal and the place and manner of reinterment of any human remains and the disposal of any monuments; and

 (d) for requiring compliance with any directions given in any case by the Secretary of State with respect to the removal and reinterment of any human remains.

(8) Subject to the provisions of any such regulations as are referred to in sub-paragraph (7), no faculty shall be required—

 (a) for the removal and reinterment in accordance with the regulations of any human remains; or

 (b) for the removal or disposal of any monuments;

and the provisions of section 25 of the Burial Act 1857 (which prohibits the removal of human remains without the licence of the Secretary of State except in certain cases) shall not apply to a removal carried out in accordance with the regulations.

(9) Any power conferred by this paragraph to use land in a manner therein mentioned shall be construed as a power so to use the land, whether or not it involves—

(a) the erection, construction or carrying out of any building or work; or

(b) the maintenance of any building or work.

(10) Nothing in this paragraph shall be construed as authorising any act or omission on the part of any person which is actionable at the suit of any person on any grounds other than contravention of any such obligation, restriction or enactment as is mentioned in sub-paragraph (1) or (5).

(11) Sub-paragraph (8) of paragraph 5 shall apply in relation to this paragraph as it applies in relation to that.

(12) In this paragraph—

'burial ground' includes any churchyard, cemetery or other ground, whether consecrated or not, which has at any time been set apart for the purposes of interment; and

'monument' includes a tombstone or other memorial.

(13) In this paragraph 'prescribed' means prescribed by regulations made by the Secretary of State.

(14) The power to make regulations under this paragraph shall be exercisable by statutory instrument which shall be subject to annulment in pursuance of a resolution of either House of Parliament.

Open spaces

7—(1) Any land being, or forming part of, a common, open space or fuel or field garden allotment, which has been vested in or acquired by the Agency under this Part of this Act may be used by the Agency, or by any other person, in any manner in accordance with planning permission, notwithstanding anything in any enactment—

(a) relating to land of that kind; or

(b) by which the land is specially regulated.

(2) Nothing in this paragraph shall be construed as authorising any act or omission on the part of any person which is actionable at the suit of any person on any grounds other than contravention of any such enactment as is mentioned in sub-paragraph (1).

(3) Sub-paragraph (8) of paragraph 5 shall apply in relation to this paragraph as it applies in relation to that.

Displacement of persons

8 If the Secretary of State certifies that possession of a house which—

(a) has been vested in or acquired by the Agency under this Part of this Act; and

(b) is for the time being held by the Agency for the purposes of its objects, is immediately required for those purposes, nothing in the Rent (Agriculture) Act 1976, the Rent Act 1977 or the Housing Act 1988 shall prevent the Agency from obtaining possession of the house.

Extinguishment of public rights of way

9—(1) Where any land—

(a) has been vested in or acquired by the Agency under this Part of this Act; and

(b) is for the time being held by the Agency for the purposes of its objects, the Secretary of State may by order extinguish any public right of way over the land.

(2) Where the Secretary of State proposes to make an order under this paragraph, he shall—

(a) publish in such manner as appears to him to be requisite a notice—

(i) stating the effect of the order, and

(ii) specifying the time (not being less than 28 days from the publication of the notice) within which, and the manner in which, objections to the proposal may be made; and

(b) serve a like notice—

(i) on the local planning authority in whose area the land is situated; and

(ii) on the relevant highway authority.

(3) In sub-paragraph (2) 'the relevant highway authority' means any authority which is a highway authority in relation to the right of way proposed to be extinguished by the order under this paragraph.

(4) Where an objection to a proposal to make an order under this paragraph is duly made and is not withdrawn, the provisions of paragraph 10 shall have effect in relation to the proposal.

(5) For the purposes of this paragraph an objection to such a proposal shall not be treated as duly made unless—

(a) it is made within the time and in the manner specified in the notice required by this paragraph; and

(b) a statement in writing of the grounds of the objection is comprised in or submitted with the objection.

10—(1) In this paragraph any reference to making a final decision, in relation to an order, is a reference to deciding whether to make the order or what modification, if any, ought to be made.

(2) Unless the Secretary of State decides apart from the objection not to make the order, or decides to make a modification which is agreed to by the objector as meeting the objection, the Secretary of State—

(a) shall, before making a final decision, consider the grounds of the objection as set out in the statement comprised in or submitted with the objection; and

(b) may, if he thinks fit, require the objector to submit within a specified period a further statement in writing as to any of the matters to which the objection relates.

(3) In so far as the Secretary of State, after considering the grounds of the objection as set out in the original statement and in any such further statement, is satisfied that the objection relates to a matter which can be dealt with in the assessment of compensation, he may treat the objection as irrelevant for the purpose of making a final decision.

(4) In any case where—
    (a) after considering the grounds of the objection as set out in the original statement and in any such further statement, the Secretary of State is satisfied that, for the purpose of making a final decision, he is sufficiently informed as to the matters to which the objection relates; or
    (b) a further statement has been required but is not submitted within the specified period,
the Secretary of State may make a final decision without further investigation as to the matters to which the objection relates.

(5) Subject to sub-paragraphs (3) and (4), the Secretary of State, before making a final decision, shall afford to the objector an opportunity of appearing before, and being heard by, a person appointed for the purpose by the Secretary of State; and if the objector avails himself of that opportunity, the Secretary of State shall afford an opportunity of appearing and being heard on the same occasion—
    (a) to the Agency; and
    (b) to any other persons to whom it appears to the Secretary of State to be expedient to afford such an opportunity.

(6) Notwithstanding anything in the preceding provisions of this paragraph, if it appears to the Secretary of State that the matters to which the objection relates are such as to require investigation by public local inquiry before he makes a final decision, he shall cause such an inquiry to be held; and where he determines to cause such an inquiry to be held, any of the requirements of those provisions to which effect has not been given at the time of that determination shall be dispensed with.

Telegraphic lines

11—(1) Where an order under paragraph 9 extinguishing a public right of way is made and at the time of the publication of the notice required by sub-paragraph (2) of that paragraph any telecommunication apparatus was kept installed for the purposes of a telecommunications code system under, in, on, over, along or across the land over which the right of way subsisted—
    (a) the power of the operator of the system to remove the apparatus shall, notwithstanding the making of the order, be exercisable at any time not later than the end of the period of three months from the date on which the right of way is extinguished and shall be exercisable in respect of the whole or any part of the apparatus after the end of that period if before the end of that period the operator of the system has given notice to the Agency of his intention to remove the apparatus or that part of it, as the case may be;
    (b) the operator of the system may by notice given in that behalf to the Agency not later than the end of the said period of three months abandon the telecommunication apparatus or any part of it;
    (c) subject to paragraph (b), the operator of the system shall be deemed at the end of that period to have abandoned any part of the apparatus which he has then neither removed not given notice of his intention to remove;
    (d) the operator of the system shall be entitled to recover from the Agency the expense of providing, in substitution for the apparatus and any other telecommunication apparatus connected with it which is rendered useless in consequence of the removal or abandonment of the first-mentioned

apparatus, any telecommunication apparatus in such other place as the operator may require; and

(e) where under the preceding provisions of this sub-paragraph the operator of the system has abandoned the whole or any part of any telecommunication apparatus, that apparatus or that part of it shall vest in the Agency and shall be deemed, with its abandonment, to cease to be kept installed for the purposes of a telecommunications code system.

(2) As soon as practicable after the making of an order under paragraph 9 extinguishing a public right of way in circumstances in which sub-paragraph (1) applies in relation to the operator of any telecommunications code system, the Secretary of State shall give notice to the operator of the making of the order.

Statutory undertakers

12—(1) Where any land has been vested in or acquired by the Agency under this Part of this Act and—

(a) there subsists over that land a right vested in or belonging to statutory undertakers for the purpose of the carrying on of their undertaking, being a right of way or a right of laying down, erecting, continuing or maintaining apparatus on, under or over the land, or

(b) there is on, under or over land apparatus vested in or belonging to statutory undertakers for the purpose of the carrying on of their undertaking,

the Agency may serve on the statutory undertakers a notice stating that, at the end of the period of 28 days from the date of service of the notice or such longer period as may be specified therein, the right will be extinguished or requiring that, before the end of that period, the apparatus shall be removed.

(2) The statutory undertakers on whom a notice is served under sub-paragraph (1) may, before the end of the period of 28 days from the service of the notice, serve a counter-notice on the Agency stating that they object to all or any provisions of the notice and specifying the grounds of their objection.

(3) If no counter-notice is served under sub-paragraph (2)—

(a) any right to which the notice relates shall be extinguished at the end of the period specified in that behalf in the notice; and

(b) if, at the end of the period so specified in relation to any apparatus, any requirement of the notice as to the removal of the apparatus has not been complied with, the Agency may remove the apparatus and dispose of it in any way it may think fit.

(4) If a counter-notice is served under sub-paragraph (2) on the Agency, it may either withdraw the notice (without prejudice to the service of a further notice) or apply to the Secretary of State and the appropriate Minister for an order under this paragraph embodying the provisions of the notice with or without modification.

(5) Where by virtue of this paragraph any right vested in or belonging to statutory undertakers is extinguished, or any requirement is imposed on statutory undertakers, those undertakers shall be entitled to compensation from the Agency.

(6) Sections 280 and 282 of the Town and Country Planning Act 1990 (measure of compensation to statutory undertakers) shall apply to compensation under sub-paragraph (5) as they apply to compensation under section 279(4) of that Act.

(7) Except in a case where paragraph 11 applies—

(a) the reference in paragraph (a) of sub-paragraph (1) to a right vested in or belonging to statutory undertakers for the purpose of the carrying on of their undertaking shall include a reference to a right conferred by or in accordance with the telecommunications code on the operator of a tele-communications code system; and

    (b)   the reference in paragraph (b) of that sub-paragraph to apparatus vested in or belonging to statutory undertakers for the purpose of the carrying on of their undertaking shall include a reference to telecommunication apparatus kept installed for the purposes of any such system.

(8) Where paragraph (a) or (b) of sub-paragraph (1) has effect as mentioned in sub-paragraph (7), in the rest of this paragraph and in paragraph 13—

    (a)   any reference to statutory undertakers shall have effect as a reference to the operator of any such system as is referred to in sub-paragraph (7); and

    (b)   any reference to the appropriate Minister shall have effect as a reference to the Secretary of State for Trade and Industry.

13—(1) Before making an order under paragraph 12 the Secretary of State and the appropriate Minister—

    (a)   shall afford to the statutory undertakers on whom notice was served under paragraph 12(1) an opportunity of objecting to the application for the order; and

    (b)   if any objection is made, shall consider the objection and afford to those statutory undertakers and to the Agency an opportunity of appearing before and being heard by a person appointed by the Secretary of State and the appropriate Minister for the purpose;

and the Secretary of State and the appropriate Minister may then, if they think fit, make the order in accordance with the application either with or without modification.

(2) Where an order is made under paragraph 12—

    (a)   any right to which the order relates shall be extinguished at the end of the period specified in that behalf in the order; and

    (b)   if, at the end of the period so specified in relation to any apparatus, any requirement of the order as to the removal of the apparatus has not been complied with, the Agency may remove the apparatus and dispose of it in any way it may think fit.

14—(1) Subject to this paragraph, where any land has been vested in or acquired by the Agency under this Part of this Act and—

    (a)   there is on, under or over the land apparatus vested in or belonging to statutory undertakers, and

    (b)   the undertakers claim that development to be carried out on the land is such as to require, on technical or other grounds connected with the carrying on of their undertaking, the removal or re-siting of the apparatus affected by the development,

the undertakers may serve on the Agency a notice claiming the right to enter on the land and carry out such works for the removal or re-siting of the apparatus or any part of it as may be specified in the notice.

(2) Where, after the land has been vested or acquired as mentioned in sub-paragraph (1), development of the land is begun to be carried out, no notice under this paragraph shall be served later than 21 days after the beginning of the development.

(3) Where a notice is served under this paragraph the Agency may, before the end of the period of 28 days from the date of service, serve on the statutory undertakers a counter-notice stating that it objects to all or any of the provisions of the notice and specifying the grounds of its objection.

(4) If no counter-notice is served under sub-paragraph (3), the statutory undertakers shall, after the end of the said period of 28 days, have the rights claimed in their notice.

(5) If a counter-notice is served under sub-paragraph (3), the statutory undertakers who served the notice under this paragraph may either withdraw it or apply to the Secretary of State and the appropriate Minister for an order under this paragraph conferring on the undertakers—

(a) the rights claimed in the notice; or

(b) such modified rights as the Secretary of State and the appropriate Minister think it expedient to confer on them.

(6) Where by virtue of this paragraph or an order made by the Secretary of State and the appropriate Minister under it, statutory undertakers have the right to execute works for the removal or re-siting of apparatus, they may arrange with the Agency for the works to be carried out by the Agency, under the superintendence of the undertakers, instead of by the undertakers themselves.

(7) Where works are carried out for the removal or re-siting of statutory undertakers' apparatus, being works which the undertakers have the right to carry out by virtue of this paragraph or an order made by the Secretary of State and the appropriate Minister under it, the undertakers shall be entitled to compensation from the Agency.

(8) Sections 280 and 282 of the Town and Country Planning Act 1990 (measure of compensation to statutory undertakers) shall apply to compensation under sub-paragraph (7) as they apply to compensation under section 279(4) of that Act.

(9) In sub-paragraph (1)(a), the reference to apparatus vested in or belonging to statutory undertakers shall include a reference to telecommunication apparatus kept installed for the purposes of a telecommunications code system.

(10) Where sub-paragraph (1)(a) has effect as mentioned in sub-paragraph (9), in the rest of this paragraph—

(a) any reference to statutory undertakers shall have effect as a reference to the operator of any such system as is referred to in sub-paragraph (9); and

(b) any reference to the appropriate Minister shall have effect as a reference to the Secretary of State for Trade and Industry.

15—(1) The powers conferred by this paragraph shall be exercisable where, on a representation made by statutory undertakers, it appears to the Secretary of State and the appropriate Minister to be expedient that the powers and duties of those undertakers should be extended or modified, in order—

(a) to secure the provision of services which would not otherwise be provided, or which would not otherwise be satisfactorily provided, in relation to relevant land; or

(b) to facilitate an adjustment of the carrying on of the undertaking necessitated by any of the acts and events mentioned in sub-paragraph (2).

(2) The said acts and events are—

(a) the vesting in or acquisition by the Agency under this Part of this Act of any land in which an interest was held, or which was used, for the purpose of the carrying on of the undertaking of the statutory undertakers in question; and

(b)   the extinguishment of a right or the imposition of any requirement by virtue of paragraph 12.

(3) The powers conferred by this paragraph shall also be exercisable where, on a representation made by the Agency, it appears to the Secretary of State and the appropriate Minister to be expedient that the powers and duties of statutory undertakers should be extended or modified, in order to secure the provision of new services, or the extension of existing services, in relation to relevant land.

(4) Where the powers conferred by this paragraph are exercisable, the Secretary of State and the appropriate Minister may, if they think fit, by order provide for such extension or modification of the powers and duties of the statutory undertakers as appears to them to be requisite in order to secure—

(a)   the provision of the services in question, as mentioned in sub-paragraph (1)(a) or sub-paragraph (3); or

(b)   the adjustment in question, as mentioned in sub-paragraph (1)(b), as the case may be.

(5) Without prejudice to the generality of sub-paragraph (4), an order under this paragraph may make provision—

(a)   for empowering the statutory undertakers to acquire (whether compulsorily or by agreement) any land specified in the order, and to erect or construct any buildings or works so specified;

(b)   for applying, in relation to the acquisition of any such land or the construction of any such works, enactments relating to the acquisition of land and the construction of works;

(c)   where it has been represented that the making of the order is expedient for the purposes mentioned in sub-paragraph (1)(a) or (3), for giving effect to such financial arrangements between the Agency and the statutory undertakers as they may agree, or as, in default of agreement, may be determined to be equitable in such manner and by such tribunal as may be specified in the order; and

(d)   for such incidental and supplemental matters as appear to the Secretary of State and the appropriate Minister to be expedient for the purposes of the order.

(6) In this paragraph 'relevant land' means land in respect of which any of the functions of the Agency under this Part of this Act are being or have been exercised.

16—(1) As soon as may be after making such a representation as is mentioned in sub-paragraph (1) or (3) of paragraph 15—

(a)   the statutory undertakers, in a case falling within sub-paragraph (1), or

(b)   the Agency, in a case falling within sub-paragraph (3),

shall publish, in such form and manner as may be directed by the Secretary of State and the appropriate Minister, a notice giving such particulars as may be so directed of the matters to which the representation relates, and specifying the time within which, and the manner in which, objections to the making of an order on the representation may be made, and shall also, if it is so directed by the Secretary of State and the appropriate Minister, serve a like notice on such persons, or persons of such classes, as may be so directed.

(2) Orders under paragraph 15 shall be subject to special parliamentary procedure.

17—(1) Where, on a representation made by statutory undertakers, the appropriate Minister is satisfied that the fulfilment of any obligations incurred by those undertakers in connection with the carrying on of their undertaking has been rendered impracticable by an act or event to which this sub-paragraph applies, the appropriate Minister may, if he thinks fit, by order direct that the statutory undertakers shall be relieved of the fulfilment of that obligation, either absolutely or to such extent as may be specified in the order.

(2) Sub-paragraph (1) applies to the following acts and events—

    (a)   the vesting in or acquisition by the Agency under this Part of this Act of any land in which an interest was held, or which was used, for the purpose of the carrying on of the undertaking of the statutory undertakers; and

    (b)   the extinguishment of a right or the imposition of any requirement by virtue of paragraph 12.

(3) As soon as may be after making a representation to the appropriate Minister under sub-paragraph (1), the statutory undertakers shall, as may be directed by the appropriate Minister, do either or both of the following, that is to say—

    (a)   publish (in such form and manner as may be so directed) a notice—

        (i)   giving such particulars as may be so directed of the matters to which the representation relates; and

        (ii) specifying the time within which, and the manner in which, objections to the making of an order on the representation may be made; and

    (b)   serve a like notice on such persons, or persons of such classes, as may be so directed.

(4) If any objection to the making of an order under this paragraph is duly made and is not withdrawn before the order is made, the order shall be subject to special parliamentary procedure.

(5) Immediately after an order is made under this paragraph by the appropriate Minister, he shall publish a notice stating that the order has been made and naming a place where a copy of it may be seen at all reasonable hours, and shall serve a like notice—

    (a)   on any person who duly made an objection to the order and has sent to the appropriate Minister a request in writing to serve him with the notice required by this sub-paragraph, specifying an address for service; and

    (b)   on such other persons (if any) as the appropriate Minister thinks fit.

(6) Subject to the following provisions of this paragraph, an order under this paragraph shall become operative on the date on which the notice required by sub-paragraph (5) is first published.

(7) Where in accordance with sub-paragraph (4) the order is subject to special parliamentary procedure, sub-paragraph (6) shall not apply.

(8) If any person aggrieved by an order under this paragraph wishes to question the validity of the order on the ground—

    (a)   that it is not within the powers conferred by this paragraph, or

    (b)   that any requirement of this paragraph has not been complied with in relation to the order,

he may, within six weeks from the date on which the notice required by sub-paragraph (5) is first published, make an application to the High Court under this paragraph.

(9) On any application under sub-paragraph (8) the High Court—
- (a) may by interim order wholly or in part suspend the operation of the order, either generally or in so far as it affects any property of the applicant, until the final determination of the proceedings; and
- (b) if satisfied—
  - (i) that the order is wholly or to any extent outside the powers conferred by this paragraph; or
  - (ii) that the interests of the applicant have been substantially prejudiced by the failure to comply with any requirement of this paragraph,

  may wholly or in part quash the order, either generally or in so far as it affects any property of the applicant.

(10) Subject to sub-paragraph (8), the validity of an order under this paragraph shall not be questioned in any legal proceedings whatsoever, either before or after the order has been made.

18—(1) For the purposes of paragraphs 15 and 17, an objection to the making of an order thereunder shall not be treated as duly made unless—
- (a) the objection is made within the time and in the manner specified in the notice required by paragraph 16 or 17 (as the case may be); and
- (b) a statement in writing of the grounds of the objection is comprised in or submitted with the objection.

(2) Where an objection to the making of such an order is duly made in accordance with sub-paragraph (1) and is not withdrawn, the following provisions of this paragraph shall have effect in relation thereto; but, in the application of those provisions to an order under paragraph 15, any reference to the appropriate Minister shall be construed as a reference to the Secretary of State and the appropriate Minister.

(3) Unless the appropriate Minister decides apart from the objection not to make the order, or decides to make a modification which is agreed to by the objector as meeting the objection, the appropriate Minister, before making a final decision—
- (a) shall consider the grounds of the objection as set out in the statement; and
- (b) may, if he thinks fit, require the objector to submit within a specified period, a further statement in writing as to any of the matters to which the objection relates.

(4) In so far as the appropriate Minister after considering the grounds of the objection as set out in the original statement and in any such further statement, is satisfied that the objection relates to a matter which can be dealt with in the assessment of compensation, the appropriate Minister may treat the objection as irrelevant for the purpose of making a final decision.

(5) In any case where—
- (a) after considering the grounds of the objection as set out in the original statement and in any such further statement, the appropriate Minister is satisfied that, for the purpose of making a final decision, he is sufficiently informed as to the matters to which the objection relates; or
- (b) a further statement has been required but is not submitted within the specified period,

the appropriate Minister may make a final decision without further investigation as to the matters to which the objection relates.

(6) Subject to sub-paragraphs (4) and (5), the appropriate Minister, before making a final decision, shall afford to the objector an opportunity of appearing before, and being heard by, a person appointed for the purpose by the appropriate Minister; and if the objector avails himself of that opportunity, the appropriate Minister shall afford an opportunity of appearing and being heard on the same occasion—

    (a)   to the person (being the Agency or the statutory undertakers) on whose representation the order is proposed to be made; and

    (b)   to any other persons to whom it appears to the appropriate Minister to be expedient to afford such an opportunity.

(7) Notwithstanding anything in the preceding provisions of this paragraph, if it appears to the appropriate Minister that the matters to which the objection relates are such as to require investigation by public local inquiry before he makes a final decision, he shall cause such an inquiry to be held; and where he determines to cause such an inquiry to be held, any of the requirements of those provisions to which effect has not been given at the time of that determination shall be dispensed with.

(8) In this paragraph any reference to making a final decision, in relation to an order, is a reference to deciding whether to make the order or what modification (if any) ought to be made.

Interpretation

19—(1) Any expression used in this Part of this Schedule to which a meaning is assigned by paragraph 1 of Schedule 4 to the Telecommunications Act 1984 has that meaning in this Part.

(2) In this Part of this Schedule 'statutory undertakers' means persons who are or are deemed to be statutory undertakers for the purposes of any provision of Part XI of the Town and Country Planning Act 1990; and 'statutory undertaking' shall be construed in accordance with section 262 of that Act (meaning of 'statutory undertaker').

(3) In this Part of this Schedule 'the appropriate Minister' shall be construed as if contained in Part XI the Town and Country Planning Act 1990; and any reference to the Secretary of State and the appropriate Minister shall be similarly construed.

PART III

ACQUISITION OF RIGHTS

20—(1) The Compulsory Purchase Act 1965 (in this Part of this Schedule referred to as "the 1965 Act") shall have effect with the modifications necessary to make it apply to the compulsory acquisition of rights by virtue of section 162(2) of this Act as it applies to the compulsory purchase of land so that, in appropriate contexts, references in the 1965 Act to land are read as referring, or as including references, to the rights or to land over which the rights are or are to be exercisable, according to the requirements of the particular context.

(2) Without prejudice to the generality of sub-paragraph (1), in relation to the acquisition of rights by virtue of section 162(2) of this Act—

    (a)   Part I of the 1965 Act (which relates to compulsory purchases under the

Acquisition of Land Act 1981) shall have effect with the modifications specified in paragraphs 21 to 23; and

(b) the enactments relating to compensation for the compulsory purchase of land shall apply with the necessary modifications as they apply to such compensation.

21 For section 7 of the 1965 Act (which relates to compensation) there shall be substituted the following section—

'7.—(1) In assessing the compensation to be paid by the acquiring authority under this Act regard shall be had not only to the extent, if any, to which the value of the land over which the right is purchased is depreciated by the purchase but also to the damage, if any, to be sustained by the owner of the land by reason of injurious affection of other land of the owner by the exercise of the right.

(2) The modifications subject to which subsection (1) of section 44 of the Land Compensation Act 1973 (compensation for injurious affection) is to have effect, as applied by subsection (2) of that section to compensation for injurious affection under this section, are that for the words "land is acquired or taken" there shall be substituted the words "a right over land is acquired" and for the words "acquired or taken from him" there shall be substituted the words "over which the right is exercisable".'

22 For section 8 of the 1965 Act (which relates to cases in which a vendor cannot be required to sell part only of a building or garden) there shall be substituted the following section—

'8—(1) Where in consequence of the service on a person in pursuance of section 5 of this Act of a notice to treat in respect of a right over land consisting of a house, building or manufactory or of a park or garden belonging to a house ('the relevant land')—

(a) a question of disputed compensation in respect of the purchase of the right would apart from this section fall to be determined by the Lands Tribunal ('the Tribunal'); and

(b) before the Tribunal has determined that question the person satisfies the Tribunal that he has an interest which he is able and willing to sell in the whole of the relevant land and—

(i) where that land consists of a house, building or manufactory, that the right cannot be purchased without material detriment to that land, or

(ii) where that land consists of such a park or garden, that the right cannot be purchased without seriously affecting the amenity or convenience of the house to which that land belongs,

the compulsory purchase order to which the notice to treat relates shall, in relation to that person, cease to authorise the purchase of the right and be deemed to authorise the purchase of that person's interest in the whole of the relevant land including, where the land consists of such a park or garden, the house to which it belongs, and the notice shall be deemed to have been served in respect of that interest on such date as the Tribunal directs.

(2) Any question as to the extent of the land in which a compulsory purchase order is deemed to authorise the purchase of an interest by virtue of the preceding subsection shall be determined by the Tribunal.

(3) Where in consequence of a determination of the Tribunal that it is satisfied as mentioned in subsection (1) of this section a compulsory purchase order is deemed by virtue of that subsection to authorise the purchase of an interest in land, the acquiring authority may, at any time within the period of six weeks beginning with the date of the determination, withdraw the notice to treat in consequence of which the determination was made; but nothing in this subsection prejudices any other power of the authority to withdraw the notice.

(4) The modifications subject to which subsection (1) of section 58 of the Land Compensation Act 1973 (determination of material detriment) is to have effect, as applied by subsection (2) of that section to the duty of the Tribunal in determining whether it is satisfied as mentioned in subsection (1) of this section, are that—

(a) at the beginning of paragraphs (a) and (b) there shall be inserted the words 'a right over';

(b) for the word 'severance' there shall be substituted the words 'right on the whole of the house, building or manufactory or of the house and the park or garden'; and

(c) for the words 'part proposed' and 'part is' there shall be substituted respectively the words 'right proposed' and 'right is'."

23—(1) The following provisions of the 1965 Act (which state the effect of a deed poll executed in various circumstances where there is no conveyance by persons with interests in the land), namely—

(a) section 9(4) (failure of owners to convey);

(b) paragraph 10(3) of Schedule 1 (owners under incapacity);

(c) paragraph 2(3) of Schedule 2 (absent and untraced owners); and

(d) paragraphs 2(3) and 7(2) of Schedule 4 (common land),

shall be so modified as to secure that, as against persons with interests in the land which are expressed to be overridden by the deed, the right which is to be acquired compulsorily is vested absolutely in the acquiring authority.

(2) Section 11 of the 1965 Act (powers of entry) shall be so modified as to secure that, as from the date on which the acquiring authority has served notice to treat in respect of any right, it has power, exercisable in the like circumstances and subject to the like conditions, to enter for the purpose of exercising that right (which shall be deemed for this purpose to have been created on the date of service of the notice); and sections 12 (penalty for unauthorised entry) and 13 (entry on sheriff's warrant in the event of obstruction) of the 1965 Act shall be modified correspondingly.

(3) Section 20 of the 1965 Act (compensation for short-term tenants) shall apply with the modifications necessary to secure that persons with such interests as are mentioned in that section are compensated in a manner corresponding to that in which they would be compensated on a compulsory purchase of the interests but taking into account only the extent (if any) of such interference with such interests as is actually caused, or likely to be caused, by the exercise of the right in question.

(4) Section 22 of the 1965 Act (protection of acquiring authority's possession of land where by inadvertence an interest in the land has not been purchased) shall be so modified as to enable the acquiring authority, in circumstances corresponding to those referred to in that section, to continue to be entitled to exercise the right in question, subject to compliance with that section as respects compensation.

Bibliography

Albert, D (1990), 'Notes on the Financing and Structure of Joint Ventures'.

Albert, D & Watson, J (1990), 1(2), *Journal of Property Finance* 189, 'An Approach to Property Joint Ventures'.

Alexander, R (3 June 1988), 947, *Estates Times* 13, 'Side by side leases'.

Allen, C, Harris, D, O'Brien, M & Hart, G (26 January 1989), *Tax Journal* 20, 'What does "Joint Venture" mean?'

Allen, J & Evamy, M (2 November 1989), 352(5742), *Contract Journal* 12, 'Joint Venture Report'.

Anderson, J & Keenan, D (February 1990), 105(1158), *Accountancy* 100, 'The Companies Act 1989: Accounting Aspects'.

Anon (27 March 1992) [Conference], 'Convertible and Participating Mortgages'.

Anon (November 1991), *The Practical Lawyer* 26, 'Development—release of covenant'.

Anon (October 1991), *The Practical Lawyer* 25, 'Development—release of covenant'.

Anon (September 1990), *Property Finance* 90, 'Financing property development'.

Anon (September 1989), 409, *Property Confidential* 4, 'How to go it alone or share the risk'.

Anon (July/August 1989), 1(7), *Property Finance* 53, 'Collective Investment Schemes'.

Anon (April 1987), 55(2), *Appraisal Journal* 245, 'Discounting Equity Cash Flow Subject to Conventional Participating Debt'.

Anon (June 1985), 54(4), *Valuer* (ISVA) 142, 'Limited Liability'.

Arnheim, C (December 1989), *Management Today* 115, 'Wedded Bliss or Bitter Woe'.

Bailey, A (June 1979), *Director* Supplement 6, 'Partnership is the theme'.

Baring, Housten & Saunders (February 1988), 10, Property Finance Report.

Barnard, C & Livingston, D (February 1990), 9(2), *International Financial Law Review* 17, 'Impact of new UK Companies Act on Financial Markets'.

Barrett, J, Brown, L & Ewart, J (1988), 2(4), Real Estate Accounting and Taxation 85, 'The Impact of Mandatory Allocations on the New Generation of Partnerships and Joint Ventures—Part 2'.

Barrett, J, Brown, L & Ewart, J (1987), 2(3), Real Estate Accounting and Taxation 71, 'The Impact of Mandatory Allocations on the New Generation of Partnerships and Joint Ventures'.

Barter, SL (ed) (1988), 'Real Estate Finance'.

Baybut, BH 'Joint Venture Development Finance'.

Beer, C (6 March 1992), Part II Henry Stewart Conference Pack 389, 'Joint Ventures in Property—Tax Implications'.

Beer, C (6 March 1992), Part II Henry Stewart Conference Pack 419, 'VAT on Joint Ventures—Planning and Pitfalls'.

Bell, R (Winter 1991), 5(4), *Real Estate Accounting and Taxation* 5, 'The Real Estate Joint Venture and the Foreign Investor'.

Boff, J (1990), *Estates Times*, 'Learning to take the best approach to joint ventures'.

Boff, J (August 1988), *Estates Times*, 'A Partnership or a Company for your Joint Venture?'

Bramson, D (27 March 1992) [Conference], 142, 'Joint Ventures and Partnership Funds Today'.

Bramson, D (1990), 1(2), *Journal of Property Finance* 293, 'The Importance of the Letting Provisions in a Forward Funding Agreement'.

Bramson, D 'Negotiating Joint Venture Finance: The Legal Aspects'.

Brett, M (17 August 1991), 9132, *Estates Gazette* 28, 'Property and Money: Mortgages which convert into property'.

Brett, M (13 January 1990), 9002, *Estates Gazette* 13, 'Property and Money: Loans with profit share'.

Brett, M (21 October 1989), 8942, *Estates Gazette* 15, 'Property and Money: Leasebacks old and new'.

Brett, M (29 April 1989), 8918, *Estates Gazette* 12, 'On and off balance sheet'.

Bright, S (1989), *Conveyancer* 99, 'Estate Rent Charges and the Enforcement of Positive Covenants'.

Broadhurst, RS & Finch, RG (7 March 1979), 76(9), *Law Society's Gazette* 234, 'Co-ownership Schemes for Commercial Property Investment'.

Brown, L, Barrett, J & Ewart, J (1988), 2(4), Real Estate Accounting and Taxation 85, 'The Impact of Mandatory Allocations on the New Generation of Partnerships and Joint Ventures—Part 2'.

Brown, L, Barrett, J & Ewart, J (1987), 2(3), Real Estate Accounting and Taxation 71, 'The Impact of Mandatory Allocations on the New Generation of Partnerships and Joint Ventures'.

Bruce-Radcliffe, G (March 1992), *Property Finance* 33, 'Is Institutional Funding Dead? Would you do business with a SPIV?'

Bruce Taylor, D (February 1978), 5(2) *Public Finance and Accountancy* 80, 'Practical Lease/Leaseback Financing'.

Brueggeman, WB & Currie, PR (Winter 1990), 5(3) *Real Estate Finance Journal* 8, 'Financing Strategies in Changing Economic Environments'.

Burkitt, M (June 1990), *World Property* 49, 'Equity and debt in a creative package'.

Carty, P (April 1990), 1160, *Accountancy* 119, 'Slow start for new corporate vehicle'.

Casey, WJ & Norcross, KJ (Winter 1989), *Real Estate Review* 36, 'Equity Leases—An Opportunity for Tenants'.

Catalano, A (16 March 1991), 9110, *Estates Gazette* 79, 'Leasing Canary Wharf'.

Chartres, M (1990), 1(1), *Journal of Property Finance* 26, 'Off Balance Sheet Finance'.

Clark, P, Hall, S & Webber, R (November 1986), *Estates Times*, 'When is a partnership the best option?'

Clark, P, Hall, S & Webber, R (10 October 1986), 865, *Estates Times* 10, 'Joint venture looks the best option'.

Clarke, RJ (1990), 1(3), *Journal of Property Finance* 435, 'Refinancing'.

Clifford Chance Memorandum (March 1991), 'Joint Ventures'.

Cohen, P (31 August 1989), 28(8), *Chartered Surveyor Weekly* 32, 'Plotting your way through the maze: creative financing'.

Corgel, JB & Smith, HC (1987), 'Real Estate Perspectives', pp 101, 510–512, 675, 750.

Crichton, J (August 1990), 106(1164), *Accountancy* 32, 'A new approach to Consolidated Accounts'.

Crump, V (13 February 1992) *Contract Journal* 14, 'Joint Ventures: Venturing into a Tangled Web'.

Cummings, J (1987), 'Real Estate Financing: A Guide to Money-Making', pp 312-316.

Currie, PR & Brueggeman, WB (Winter 1990), 5(3), *Real Estate Finance Journal* 8, 'Financing Strategies in Changing Economic Environments'.

Darlow, C (ed) (1988, 2nd edn), Estates Gazette Books, 'Valuation and development Appraisal'.

Darrow, JE & Fisher, MI (Fall 1989), 5(2), *Real Estate Finance Journal* 20, 'Joint Ventures using Wyoming Limited Liability Companies'.

David, J & Dennis, Z (Spring 1990), 5(4), *Real Estate Finance Journal* 17, 'Debt versus Equity Characterisation of Participating Mortgages'.

Davidson, S (12 December 1991), *Taxation* 290, 'Joint Ventures—II'.

Davidson, S (5 December 1991), *Taxation* 242, 'Joint Ventures—I'.

Davidson, S (16 May 1991), *Taxation* 164, 'Reaching Deadlock'.

Davis, JC (November 1988), 30(12), *National Real Estate Investor* 110, 'Entrepreneurial approach yields to joint ventures as developers and investors make the marriage work'.

Day, MJ & Finch, RG (27 October 1977), 244, *Estates Gazette* 280, 'Co- Ownership Schemes for Commercial Property Investment'.

Dennis, Z & David, J (Spring 1990), 5(4), *Real Estate Finance Journal* 17, 'Debt versus Equity Characterisation of Participating Mortgages'.

Dore, M (28 September 1991), 9138, *Estates Gazette* 210, 'Overage payments on development land'.

Drake, C (1983, 3rd edn), 'Law of Partnership'.

Dye, JA (Summer 1990), 9(3), *Commercial Investment Real Estate Journal* 20, 'Sale/Leasebacks: The Choice is Clear, Or is It?'

Eadie, C (24 July 1993), 9329, *Estates Gazette* 90, 'Joint Venture Finance'.

Ellington, PR (1989), Law and Business Forum Conference on 'Profiting from Synergy' D1, 'Dealing with Co-Owners' Interests'.

Evamy, M (9 February 1989), 347(5704), *Contract Journal* 20, 'Underneath the Arches with Laing'.

Evamy, M & Allen, J (2 November 1989), 352(5742), *Contract Journal* 12, 'Joint Venture Report'.

Ewart, J, Barrett, J & Brown, L (1988), 2(4), Real Estate Accounting and Taxation 85, 'The Impact of Mandatory Allocations on the New Generation of Partnerships and Joint Ventures—Part 2'.

Ewart, J, Barrett, J & Brown, L (1987), 2(3), Real Estate Accounting and Taxation 71, 'The Impact of Mandatory Allocations on the New Generation of Partnerships and Joint Ventures'.

Fafenrodt, AA & Feldsted, JF (April 1990), 44(4), Taxation for Accountants, 'How Best to Design Real Estate Joint Ventures to Provide Investors with Maximum Tax Benefits'.

Fairchild, RW (1990), 1(1), *Journal of Property Finance* 50, 'Limited and Non-Recourse Property Loans: The Current Market'.

Fazakerley, CC (March 1988), 40(3), *Association Management* 79, 'Joint Venture Ownership: The Attractive Alternative'.

Feldsted, JF & Fafenrodt, JF (April 1990), 44(4), Taxation for Accountants, 'How Best to Design Real Estate Joint Ventures to Provide Investors with Maximum Tax Benefits'.

Finch, RG & Wood, D (23 July 1983), 267, *Estates Gazette* 328, 'Side-by-Side Leases—II'.

Finch, RG & Wood, D (16 July 1983), 267, *Estates Gazette* 229, 'Side-by-Side Leases—I'.

Finch, RG & Wood, D (1 June 1983), 80(21) *Law Society's Gazette* 1405, 'Side-by-Side Leases'.

Finch, RG & Broadhurst, RS (7 March 1979), 76(9), *Law Society's Gazette* 234, 'Co-Ownership Schemes for Commercial Property Investment'.

Finch, RG & Day, MJ (27 October 1977), 244, *Estates Gazette* 280, 'Co-Ownership Schemes for Commercial Property Investment'.

Fisher, MI & Darrow, JE (Fall 1989), 5(2), *Real Estate Finance Journal* 20, 'Joint Ventures using Wyoming Limited Liability Companies'.

Fraser, WD (1984), 'Principles of Property Investment', Chapter 19.

Fraser, WD (9 May 1981), 258, *Estates Gazette* 521, 'Lease buy and leaseback decisions'.

Freeman, DJ (1992), Legal Briefing, 'Convertible Mortgages: a USA-UK Comparison'.

Freeman, DJ (November 1991), 3(10), *Property Finance* 120, 'Property Joint Ventures'.

Freeman, DJ (December 1990), Legal Briefing, 'Property Joint Ventures'.

Freeman, DJ (December 1989), Legal Briefing, 'The Companies Act 1989'.

Fruchom, P (September 1989), 25(9), 'How to Negotiate Real Estate Joint Ventures'.

Garcia, D (1989), Law and Business Forum on 'Profiting from Synergy' G1, 'VAT, Construction and Joint Ventures'.

Gates, J (February 1983), 42(2), *House Builder* 46, 'Joint Venture—short-term palliative or here to stay?'

Gray, K (1987), 'Elements of Land Law'.

Gray, R (May 1990), 68(5), *Management Accounting* 10, 'The Act Commences... '.

Green, T (31 January 1992), *Estates Times*, 'Revamping land mortgages: Law Commission Proposals'.

Hall, S, Clark, P & Webber, R (November 1986), *Estates Times*, 'When is a partnership the best option?'

Hall, S, Clark, P & Webber, R (10 October 1986), 865, *Estates Times* 10, 'Joint venture looks the best option'.

Harper, A (1991), *Conveyancer* 193, 'Land Taxation: Reservation of Entitlement to Potential Development Gains'.

Harris, D, Allen, C, O'Brien, M & Hart, G (26 January 1989), *Tax Journal* 20, 'What does 'Joint Venture' mean?'

Hart, C & Sheard, M (29 June 1991), *Accountancy Age* 14, 'Taxing times for property'.

Hart, G, Harris, D, Allen, C & O'Brien, M (26 January 1989), *Tax Journal* 20, 'What does 'Joint Venture' mean?'

Hazell, T (Winter 1988), 11, *Property Director* 46, 'Sell it now and pay for it later—sale and leaseback'.

Henry Stewart Conference Pack (6 March 1992), 'Structuring and Documenting Joint Ventures in Property: Problems and Solutions'.

Herbert-Smith, T (14 September 1991), *Estates Gazette* 86, 'Property and the 1989 Act'.

Hersom, S (1989), Law and Business Forum Conference on 'Profiting from Synergy' E1, 'Financing the Property Joint Venture'.

Johnson, B (February 1992), *Accountancy* 75, 'Accounting for Limited Partnerships'.

Johnston, S & Miller, S (1990), 1(1), *Journal of Property Finance* 117, 'Joint Venture: Breaking the Deadlock'.

Keenan, D (1986, 6th edn), 'Company Law'.

Keenan, D & Anderson, J (February 1990), 105(1158), *Accountancy* 100, 'The Companies Act 1989: Accounting Aspects'.

Kelley, PC (September 1988), 17(1), *Real Estate Review* 54, 'Advantages of Participating Mortgages'.

Kelley, SM (September 1988), 22(11), *Institutional Investor* 36, 'Is the Thrill Gone?'

Kidby, R (1992), Part II Henry Stewart Conference Pack 434, 'Provisions for Avoiding Dispute'.

Koehne, S (3 October 1986), 864, *Estates Times* 10, 'Whose block is it anyway?'

Lanch, D (27 November 1980), 183(5520), *Accountant* 850, 'Forming a partnership—advantages and disadvantages'.

Laughton, H & Vann, AB (August 1989), 17(4), *Australian Business Law Review* 231, 'The structuring of project participation arrangements in property developments'.

Lee, G (27 April 1989), 16, *Tax Journal* 14, 'Property I: Investment or Trading?'

Lee, P (January 1989), *Euromoney* Supplement 27, 'Good management, high value'.

Levin, MA (Winter 1990), 17(2), *Journal of Real Estate Taxation* 186, 'A contingent interest in profits as debt'.

Lewis, D (2 April 1988), 8813, *Estates Gazette* 22, 'Investing in US real estate: how to structure a joint venture'.

Lindley & Banks (1990, 16th edn), 'On Partnership'.

Ling, DC & Peiser, R (Summer 1987), 17(2), *Real Estate Review* 39, 'Choosing among alternative financing structures: the developer's dilemma'.

Livingston, D & Barnard, C (February 1990), 9(2), *International Financial Law Review* 17, 'Impact on few UK Companies Act on financial markets'.

Lo, H (1989), 1(2), *Managerial Finance* 5, 'History and development of leasing in the UK'.

Maas, RM (2 May 1979), 76(6), *Law Society's Gazette* 441, 'Taxation aspects of property funding'.

McCarthy, P (25 November 1989), 8947, *Estates Gazette* 30, 'Partnerships and joint venture developments'.

Magnus, AM (1992), Part II Henry Stewart Conference Pack 252, 'Possible Structures: Company and Partnership'.

Mainly for Students (6 February 1988), 8805, *Estates Gazette* 72, 'Development funding'.

Mainly for Students (2 October 1982), 264, *Estates Gazette* 63, 'Development finance and sale and leaseback'.

Miller, S (1990), 1(1), *Journal of Property Finance* 601, 'Joint venture: breaking the deadlock'.

Miller, S & Johnston, S (1990), 1(1), *Journal of Property Finance* 117, 'Joint venture: breaking the deadlock'.

Miller, S & Nicholson, D (1991), 2(1), *Journal of Property Finance* 87, 'Profit sharing mortgages'.

Milman, D (1984), 5(1), *Company Lawyer* 10, 'Partnerships 3: Problems and Dissolution'.

Milman, D (1983), 4(5), *Company Lawyer* 199, 'Partnerships 1: Problems with Identification'.

Moore, P (May 1989), *Euromoney* Supplement 20, 'Funding adapts itself to the UK'.

Morpeth, I, 'Institutional Property Funding'.

Mueller, WA (October 1988), 60(10), *American Agent and Broker* 78, 'Joint ventures'.

Murdoch, S (21 September 1991), 9137, *Estates Gazette* 153, 'Exercising an option'.

Murdoch, S (12 January 1991), 9101, *Estates Gazette* 117, 'Options and the 1989 Act'.

Murdoch, S (12 August 1989), 8932, *Estates Gazette* 53, 'Options to purchase land—price fixing'.

Nabarro Nathanson Note (May 1991), Practical Law for Companies 55, 'Failure of joint ventures: ways to exit'.

Nicholson, D & Miller, S (1991), 2(1), *Journal of Property Finance* 87, 'Profit sharing mortgages'.

Norcross, KJ & Casey, WJ (Winter 1989), 18(4), *Real Estate Review* 36, 'Equity leases—an opportunity for tenants'.

Oates, D (October 1989), 43(3), *Director* 169, 'How to make idle assets work'.

O'Brien, M, Harris, D, Allen, C & Hart, G (26 January 1989), *Tax Journal* 20, 'What does 'Joint Venture' mean?'

Owen, N (10 May 1991), 1095, *Estates Times* 11, 'Escalating activity in sale and leasebacks'.

Peiser, R & Ling, DC (Summer 1987), 17(2), *Real Estate Review* 39, 'Choosing among alternative financing structures: the developer's dilemma'.

Perry, A (14 September 1990), 1064, *Estates Times* 16, 'Fresh approach to property financing'.

Perry, D (23 November 1989), 11, *New Builder* 13, 'Venturing on forethought'.

Pimm, D (June 1990), 105(1162), *Accountancy* 88, 'Off balance sheet vehicles survive redefinition'.

Price, RS (1989), Law and Business Forum Conference on 'Profiting from Synergy' C1, 'Property Joint Venture Agreements'.

Rayney, P (August 1991), 108(1176), *Accountancy* 60, 'Property disposals 2: UK development deals'.

Rayney, P. (July 1991), *Accountancy* 86, 'Property disposals 1: trading or investment'.

Reeves, DE (5 December 1979), 76(43), *Law Society's Gazette* 1218, 'Partnership developments—net income on equity sharing agreements'.

Reuben, R & Simpson, B (1 June 1991), 9121, *Estates Gazette* 98, 'The life cycle of an option agreement'.

Ross, N (1 July 1988), 951, *Estates Times* 14, 'Property investment: so is it really a crime?'

Ross, S (Spring 1987), 17(1), *Real Estate Review* 28, 'Real estate master limited partnerships: why investors like them'.

Ryland, D (January 1992), 'Notes: Joint Ventures—Associated Issues'.

Ryland, D (29 November 1991), 1122, *Estates Times* 13, 'New way of borrowing: participating and convertible mortgages'.

Ryland, D (9 November 1991), 9144, *Estates Gazette* 163, 'Authorised property unit trusts'.

Ryland, D (1 August 1991), 36(6), *Chartered Surveyor Weekly* 16, 'Authorised to buy property: unit trusts let off the leash'.

Ryland, D (12 April 1991), 135, *Solicitors' Journal* 435, 'Participating mortgages'.

Ryland, D (3 August 1990), 134(35), *Solicitors' Journal* 966, 'Corporate or property acquisition?'

Ryland, D (19 May 1990), 9020, *Estates Gazette* 20, 'Property development: joint venture vehicles'.

Sayer, ST (1986), 7(3), *Company Lawyer* 91, 'International technology joint ventures: a UK perspective'.

Sheard, M & Hart, C (29 June 1991), *Accountancy Age* 14, 'Taxing times for property'.

Simpson, B & Reuben, R (1 June 1991), 9121, *Estates Gazette* 98, 'The life cycle of an option agreement'.

Smith, HC & Corgel, JB (1987), 'Real Estate Perspectives', pp 101, 510-512, 675, 750.

Smith, T (18 June 1981), 184(5547), *Accountant* 663, 'Sale and leaseback of property assets'.

Soares, PC (October 1984), 5(5), *Property Law Bulletin* 38, 'Is there a property development partnership?'

Solomon, D (9 January 1987), *Estates Times*, 'Balancing risk with reward—the advantages and pitfalls of joint ventures'.

Southern, M (17 July 1991), 27, *Law Society's Gazette* 25, 'A capital loan to the builders'.

Sproul, D (16 November 1990), 1073, *Estates Times* 24, 'Creative financing: APUTs'.

Sproul, D (1990), 1(2), *Journal of Property Finance* 307, 'Convertible mortgages'.

Sproul, D (1989), Law and Business Forum Conference on 'Profiting from Synergy', 'Taxation of Property Joint Ventures'.

Steiner, P (13 July 1991), 9127, *Estates Gazette* 70, 'Options and conditional contracts'.

Steley, P (1 August 1991), 36(6), *Chartered Surveyor Weekly* 29, 'Flexibility means the freedom to choose'.

Sterling, M (2 February 1990), 1032, *Estates Times* 21, 'Taking account of new Act: Companies Act 1989'.

Sutcliffe, RJ (1989), Law and Business Forum Conference on 'Profiting from Synergy' A1, 'Structuring Property Joint Ventures'.

Taylor, R (1992), Part I Henry Stewart Conference 4, 'Desirability and Relevance of Joint Ventures in Today's Market'.

Temple, P (May 1989), 103(1149), *Accountancy* 133, 'Brewers loosen old school tie'.

Tillett, D (1990), 1(1), *Journal of Property Finance* 31, 'The companies axe falls'.

Tillett, D (February 1990), *Certified Accountant* 42, 'Accounting changes for subsidiaries'.

Tillett, D (11 March 1989), 8910, *Estates Gazette* 26, 'Gearing up with the Companies Bill?'

Van des Bos, J (May 1991), *Europroperty* 22, 'Big blue looks for partners'.

Vann, AB & Laughton, H (August 1989), 17(4), *Australian Business Law Review* 231, 'The structuring of project participation arrangements in property developments'.

Watson, J & Albert, D (1990), 1(2), *Journal of Property Finance* 189, 'An Approach to Property Joint Ventures'.

Webber, R, Clark, P & Hall, S (welcome datacompNovember 1986), *Estates Times*, 'When is a partnership the best option?'

Webber, R, Clark, P & Hall, S (10 October 1986), 865, *Estates Times* 10, 'Joint venture looks the best option'.

Wood, D & Finch, RG (23 July 1983), 267, *Estates Gazette* 328, 'Side-by-Side Leases—II'.

Wood, D & Finch, RG (16 July 1983), 267, *Estates Gazette* 229, 'Side-by-Side Leases—I'.

Wood, D & Finch, RG (1 June 1983), 80(21) *Law Society's Gazette* 1405, 'Side-by-Side Leases'.

Young, N (1991), 1104, *Estates Times* 10, 'Long live the 25 year lease'.

Index